XERISCAPE
COLORADO
THE COMPLETE GUIDE

by **Connie Lockhart Ellefson**
and **David Winger**

XERISCAPE

WESTCLIFFE PUBLISHERS
westcliffepublishers.com

2

INTERNATIONAL STANDARD BOOK NUMBER: 1-56579-495-8

TEXT COPYRIGHT: Connie Lockhart Ellefson and David Winger, 2004.
All rights reserved.

PHOTOGRAPHY COPYRIGHT: David Winger, 2004. All rights reserved.

ILLUSTRATIONS COPYRIGHT: Connie Lockhart Ellefson, 2004. All rights reserved.

ADDITIONAL PHOTOGRAPHY: Bonnie Arnold, Ken Ball, Don Buma, and Connie Ellefson

EDITORS: Michelle Dally and Jenna Samelson Browning

DESIGNER: Rebecca Finkel, F + P Graphic Design, Inc., Fort Collins, CO

PRODUCTION MANAGER: Craig Keyzer

PUBLISHED BY: Westcliffe Publishers, Inc.
P.O. Box 1261
Englewood, CO 80150
www.westcliffepublishers.com

PRINTED IN CHINA BY: H & Y Printing Ltd.

LIBRARY OF CONGRESS
CATALOGING-IN-PUBLICATION DATA: Ellefson, Connie Lockhart, 1954-
Xeriscape Colorado : the complete guide / text by
Connie Lockhart Ellefson and David Winger.
p. cm.
Includes bibliographical references and index.
ISBN 1-56579-495-8
1. Xeriscaping--Colorado. 2. Drought-tolerant plants--
Colorado. I. Winger, David. II. Title.
SB439.8.E58 2004
635.9'525'09788--dc22
2003064549

*For more information about other fine books and calendars from Westcliffe Publishers,
please contact your local bookstore, call us at 1-800-523-3692, write for our free
color catalog, or visit us on the Web at* WWW.WESTCLIFFEPUBLISHERS.COM.

Xeriscape™ is a registered trademark of Denver Water, Denver, CO,
and is used here with permission.

PLEASE NOTE: The authors, editors, and publisher disclaim any liability for injury
or other damage caused by performing any activity described in this book.

OPPOSITE: *A late-summer garden.*

To Mom and Dad,
who always told me I could do
anything I put my mind to.
And to Peg Bracken, whose irreverent
1960s books (still selling) about hating to
cook and keep house taught me early on
that a lot of life's mundane tasks could be
pretty funny if you kept your sense of humor.

—CONNIE LOCKHART ELLEFSON

ACKNOWLEDGMENTS

Thanks to Ken Ball and Jim Borland for keeping us straight on the Xeriscape and horticultural facts (and throwing in a few good one-liners to boot), and Robbie Zephirin for keeping a sharp eye out for adequate humor. Thanks to all the other people mentioned in the book along the way, and the others who helped out, too. You know who you are, and you are appreciated!

David Winger wrote the chapters covering irrigation and maintenance and supplied the lion's share of the photographs. Connie Ellefson wrote the remaining chapters and created the illustrations in the design chapter.

Small water features, as in Tim LaPan's garden, are appropriate for Xeriscape landscapes.

CONTENTS

TOP LEFT: *Sunrose* (Helianthemum nummularium) *blooms in early summer.*
TOP RIGHT: *Groundcovers provide color through many seasons.*
Creeping phlox (Phlox subulata) *is one that brightens in early spring.*
OPPOSITE: *At the Colorado Springs Xeriscape Demonstration Garden,*
Xeriscape is right at home in Colorado.

PREFACE

A SECOND CHANCE

Twelve years ago I wrote a book called *Xeriscape Gardening* with the hope of showing readers how Xeriscape™ could be both lush and beautiful, fun and exciting. The book was published by Macmillan Publishing, the longtime producer of school textbooks. I'm eternally grateful to Macmillan for having the courage to publish a book about a topic so new and unfamiliar that the first half of the book was devoted to convincing the reader of the importance of the subject matter.

Because of editorial constraints, however, the book ended up covering the whole country, not just the Rocky Mountains, as I'd first intended. The text got longer and longer, and the pictures got smaller and smaller. The result was, well, basically a textbook, with little or no opportunity to *show* rather than just tell how beautiful Xeriscape can be.

After that, the drought essentially dried up, so to speak. In Colorado it kept raining and snowing and so forth, without a break. And even though the Xeriscape movement kept bravely on, most people dismissed it as unnecessary, the province of the earnest, nay-saying granola-heads, like me. I have to admit, I wondered myself.

Then the Colorado drought of 2002 hit. And what few people really believed would ever happen, did: The snow stopped coming for a time, the reservoirs became empty, and our lush gardens dried up. We had to buck up and quit lavishing the drinking water on our yards just like everyone else who lives in a dry climate.

So now I get a second chance to write the book I wanted to write in the first place, one focused on Xeriscape in the Rockies. An informative book, good-natured, inspiring (I hope), and most of all, full of pictures that can do justice to the true beauty and potential of water-thrifty landscaping.

LEFT: *Xeriscapes are meant to be lush and colorful.*
BELOW: *Colorado's booming population growth is one reason why Xeriscape becomes more important each year.*
OPPOSITE: *A well-planned Xeriscape, such as Kelly Grummons' garden, benefits the eye as well as the bottom line. "If it isn't beautiful, it isn't Xeriscape!"*

A "ROCKY" WATER PICTURE

Colorado was unprepared for a drought for two main reasons. First, most of our domestic water supply reservoirs were built between 1960 and 1985 and had projected planning ranges of about 40 years. Since '85, plans to build new large reservoirs have been met by a protesting public and quickly abandoned. So supply was bound to get stretched pretty thin.

At the same time the water supply has remained stagnant, demand has skyrocketed. The population of the Denver region has doubled in the last 20 years. For a while the strain didn't show because the region enjoyed unusually wet weather. Normally Coloradoans see an 11-year cycle of dry to wet years, but we missed the last drought cycle. It was only a matter of time until climatic reality struck.

The year 2002 brought the worst drought in Colorado in 300 years. (In case you're wondering who was keeping weather records back then, it was the trees and their rings.) More drought was predicted for 2003, but we got some breathing room in the form of heavy spring snows and early summer rains. But we can't afford to be fooled by this. The need for water conservation isn't going to go away.

ABOVE: *Colorado's modern system of water collection is more sophisticated than this windmill, but water is just as precious now as it was in pioneer days.*
RIGHT: *Installing low-water-using plants such as lemon thyme almost always means lower maintenance, and alternatives abound with Xeriscape.*

This drought-tolerant planting featuring coreopsis and bachelor buttons needs just one good yearly trimming.

FACING CLIMATIC REALITY

Denver's metro population is expected to grow by another million—that's a 50 percent increase—in the next 10 to 20 years. Experts (and increasingly the public) realize that the wet spring of 2003 was just a respite, and we've got to start preparing now for the crunch ahead. Water planners are already thinking in terms of adding smaller reservoirs in the mountains along the foothills and enlarging already existing ones to avoid a severe environmental impact. But this will take years to accomplish.

Few who went through The Big Dry of '02 will forget the pain of watching ill-adapted landscapes shrivel up and die. So, for now, and for the future, one way our water picture can get better is through Xeriscape, and dedicated people like you who are willing to do what it takes to get a landscape designed to weather all our weather!

— CONNIE L. ELLEFSON
Aurora, Colorado

INTRODUCTION

WHAT IS XERISCAPE ANYWAY?

Xeriscape is a fancy, trademarked word for purposefully creating a beautiful, restful outdoor environment without consuming thousands of gallons of expensively purified water in the process. And we're not talking gravel and cacti here (unless you love the particular exotic Southwest look). Xeriscape can easily be beautiful, lush, and adaptable to most any landscape style, just as it was always intended to be.

But xeriscaping is not *only* about saving water; it's about saving effort, too. It's a comprehensive way of thinking, from planning to maintenance and back again. In fact, planning landscapes

around water usage has multiple benefits, largely because, as a general rule of thumb: *Plantings that take the most water also require the most maintenance.*

Thirsty plantings might be cheap to put in, but in the long run they cost more money and take more effort than water-thrifty plants. For instance, developers love Kentucky bluegrass because it's inexpensive to install (a mere $1.50 per 50 square feet). But they're not the ones who have to maintain it. This common grass requires up to 3 vertical feet (or 36 inches) of water a year to remain constantly green. Colorado gets an average of 15 inches of precipitation a year. The rest of the water needed to sustain this kind of lawn generally comes from supplies of purified drinking-quality water. Aside from the watering,

this grass also requires constant, labor-intensive mowing, trimming, and fertilization. Certainly not a way to simplify your life.

But be careful here! Xeriscaping isn't some anti-grass conspiracy (see the following section, "What Xeriscape Isn't"). If you like grass, you can still have it. Xeriscaping means you just work with it intelligently. You don't water it in the middle of the day, when water is lost to evaporation. You consider carefully where you plant it and how much you plant.

This intelligence is what xeriscaping is all about. Once, we set the sprinkler schedule in the spring and never touched it again all summer; now we know to adjust it regularly based on weather changes, or even to just run it when the soil is dry. It's about paying attention to soil nutrition, soil moisture, and cultural practices.

OPPOSITE, TOP: *Xeriscape can be as simple as a collection of native wildflowers.*
LEFT: *Xeriscape adapts to many landscape styles, from formal to rustic, as is Arun Das' garden.*
BELOW: *Water waste is what the seven interconnected Xeriscape principles —from planning to maintenance and back again—aim to prevent.*

ABOVE: *A creative approach to landscape, such as Xeriscape, inspires the home landscaper to combine different forms, textures, and colors.*
LEFT: *Plants matched to their environment, such as these evening primrose and lavender, allow more time for enjoyment and require less time for watering and maintenance.*

Xeriscaping is also about thinking positively (what would I like my landscape to look like) rather than negatively (what can't I have). And it's about balance. I love to try out new plants and see how they grow. This means I have to reserve space for all my experiments. I also like to have a landscape that doesn't look like everyone else's. For these reasons I try to have as little lawn in my yard as possible.

There are positive sides of turfgrasses, as well: the prevention of soil erosion, the moderation of temperature around the house, and the production of oxygen. I also like how they provide contrast to, and give the eye a rest from, the busier aspects of a landscape. The point with the "new Xeriscape" is not that we just remove all the turf we can, and think that will do the trick. The idea is to have a balance of low-water-using groundcoverings, including whatever we want from a mix of turf, of ornamental plants, hard-scape, mulch, and so on.

If you love lawn, want lawn, or need lawn, then have it. But just using lawn because you can't think of anything else is less than water-bright. As well, there are some alternatives to Kentucky bluegrass that require less water to stay green throughout the summer. So, you can have your lawn and not water it, too. It just takes a little planning and thinking.

In this way, Xeriscape gives you the oppor-tunity to infuse your landscape with color and texture by deciding just how much lawn you really need (practical turf areas) and changing out the rest into lavish and practical vignettes of shrubs, trees, flowers, ornamental grasses, vines, groundcovers, and more!

There are seven basic principles in Xeriscape, and this book is designed to explore each one of them. The first principle is *planning and design,* and Chapters 1 and 2 cover this area. The second principle is *soil analysis and improvement,* and Chapters 3 and 4 address this concept. The third principle is to have *practical turf areas,* and Chapters 5 and 6 show you exactly how to do this. The fourth principle is *informed plant choice,* and Chapters 7–9 cover flowers to trees and everything in between. Chapter 10 delves into efficient *irrigation,* which is the fifth principle. Chapter 11 covers the basics of *mulching,* which is the sixth principle. And Chapter 12 makes sure things keep looking good by giving you tips for appropriate *maintenance,* which of course is the seventh and final principle. Each chapter in this book is color-coded so you can easily see where each of these seven principles is discussed.

It's all right here: everything you need to jump into the exciting world of xeriscaping. But before we go any further, let's talk about what xeriscaping ISN'T.

WHAT XERISCAPE ISN'T

A number of myths have grown up around xeriscaping in the past dozen years or so, leaving many potential xeriscapers with both false impressions and little motivation. So, before I go any further, let me explain, once and for all, what Xeriscape is NOT.

First, Xeriscape is not vast seas of gravel and concrete. It is not a few forlorn cacti surrounded by rocks. Nor is it more brown than green, or all dry and dusty. And it is certainly not, and never was, "zero-scape." If you've seen yards

covered in two or three coordinating colors of gravel laid in an interesting design around a couple of parched, pathetic trees, you've seen zero-scape. And that's not what this is.

We like to say, "If it isn't beautiful, it isn't Xeriscape!" Cute and simplistic, I know, but it does rather sum things up. A well-planned Xeriscape always pleases the eye, as well as benefiting the bottom line. If it doesn't, it's probably zero-scape.

Let's bust some of the myths about Xeriscape right now, going principle by principle.

- First, in terms of planning and design: Xeriscape doesn't have to look ugly, wild, or reedy. In fact, Xeriscape is adaptable to any type of landscape, from the most rustic wildflower meadow or rock garden to a formal groomed lawn with accent plants.

   And, while significant grass lawn buffers are soothing and important in larger-scale private and public areas, plantings of trees, shrubs, evergreens, and flowers are far more eye-catching, not to mention stress-relieving, for you and your property than the same old turf-and-tree routine. Landscapes of our natural surroundings are, in fact, very lovely.

Drought-Tolerance, Drought-Avoidance, Drought-Resistance

You might have come across these terms in reading about water-conserving plants and thought they mean the same thing, but they don't. For the record, I'd like to acknowledge that, in the interest of strict scientific accuracy, the terms are not interchangeable.

- Drought tolerance = plant's ability to withstand drought without dying (might look like heck, but it doesn't die)
- Drought avoidance = its ability to endure drought, but still look good (unstressed)
- Drought resistance = similar to drought avoidance

Kentucky bluegrass, for instance, starts to look brown and pathetic shortly after being stressed, but takes a very long time to die (low drought-avoidance, high drought-tolerance). Turf-type tall fescue stays green long into drought (high d-avoidance), but dies quickly after showing signs of stress (low d-tolerance).

Unfortunately, there's still not a lot of information on individual plants and where they fit in this com-parison scale, so for the sake of simplicity, in this book, "drought-tolerant" means "survives drought after establishment and still looks reasonably attractive."

ABOVE: *A well-maintained formal-style Xeriscape.*
BELOW: *A dead lawn creates a clean slate for Xeriscape.*
BOTTOM: *It is* striking, *but it's definitely zero-scape!*
Photo by Connie Ellefson.

- Second, when it comes to soil, there's no such thing as "bad soil" and "good soil." There's just soil that works as is, or doesn't work, depending on what you want to plant. Paying attention to soil nutrients and adding the right amount of organic matter in the soil is one of the most cost-effective ways to ensure the long-term success and low-water use of diverse plantings. It becomes increasingly important when using more traditional (e.g., what we're "used to," like Kentucky bluegrass) plants in your landscape.

  In the case of a more native planting, it might be important not to amend soil. At both ends of the spectrum, paying attention to this detail will do much to ensure the beauty of your landscape.

- Third, when it comes to turf areas, there's no single "right" grass. Fescue, buffalograss, and even Kentucky bluegrass all have their strengths and weaknesses. Fescue is a bunch-grass, so it can get sparse under excessive wear, though it is a beautiful green color. Native buffalograss, which truly can virtually survive on normal rainfall, is great where a natural landscape is desired. Being a warm-season grass, it is buff or tan from late September to late May, or about four months longer than most cool-season grasses. Certain varieties have been developed to improve the "greenness" of its blue-green color, and the length of time it stays green.

  For beauty, toughness, and resilience as a playing surface, few grasses do better than Kentucky bluegrass. But because we're basically keeping this grass in a very immature and vulnerable state by mowing the top off every week or two, Kentucky bluegrass is quite needy. It requires extra water in order to stay in its suspended "young" condition. (Like those high-maintenance movie stars we're always hearing about.) Fertilizing and mowing and trimming are also required. So unless you need a soccer field or otherwise heavily traveled lawn, you might want to consider a different turf option.

  Turf alternatives abound and are one of the most studied subjects of horticultural research. Good planning can reduce lawn maintenance expense, water expense, and —last, but not least—the resulting noise and air pollution from mowers and blowers.

• The fourth principle of Xeriscape focuses on appropriate plant choice, and, unfortunately, some mistakenly believe that this means only native plants. Nothing could be further from the truth.

It turns out the Colorado climate is quite beneficial for growing perennial flowers, with its normally cold winters and bright, sunny summers. Many native and non-native wildflowers also do astonishingly well despite the severest drought. Evergreens and many deciduous shrubs also thrive in Colorado, especially when their soil and water needs are met. There are many natives that are "thirsty," needing ample water.

The key is to group plants with similar water needs together so they can be watered or not watered accordingly. The variety of plants available for Xeriscape allows for much exciting year-round interest.

• Irrigation in xeriscaping is often subject to myths on either end of the spectrum. On one hand many believe that Xeriscape needs no water; others think that watering daily, or watering all plants on the same schedule, is just fine. Neither of these beliefs is true.

A few years ago a test was done at Colorado State University on plots of

ABOVE: *This landscape shows several alternative treatments for an area where turf is neither practical nor useful.*
BELOW: *Colorado's climate is surprisingly beneficial for growing perennial flowers, whether they are native or non-native species.*

Kentucky bluegrass. Only half the recommended watering was applied, and all the plots survived. The surprising finding of the test was that the grass continued to look pretty good, even when stressed. In truth, with continued short rations of water, bluegrass will eventually decline in quality, but many, many tests and situations arise that point out we're often overwatering this highly prevalent plant. Checking soil moisture before watering would forestall a lot of waste.

Daily watering encourages shallow root growth, which makes plants more susceptible to drought stress. Using different types of irrigation for different plants and changing watering schedules once a month can lead to significant water savings.

While ALL plants, whether "Xeriscape" or not, need regular watering at least through the first year to get them established, the more dry-adapted plants will need less applied water each year.

• Mulching, the sixth principle of Xeriscape, is often subject to derisive comment such as, "It just blows away anyway." But mulching is an easy way to save both water and effort. Mulching saves water by cutting down evaporation, keeping plant roots cool, and sharply reducing weed growth, which competes for nutrients and water. It saves effort by minimizing weeds, which of itself should be reason enough to use it.

And there are simple steps you can take to keep mulch from blowing away. Experience has taught that shredded wood — sometimes known as cedar mulch—knits together and resists blowing away very well. The use of plastic may lead to "skidding away." On slopes or windy areas, landscape fabric with a fuzzy nap will help hold the mulch in place. On flatter (calm) areas, smoother landscape fabrics can be used for plants that don't need open ground to spread.

• The seventh principle of Xeriscape—appropriate maintenance—often has skeptics frowning at the thought of extra work. And yet, it means just the opposite.

Maintenance is really where the payoff is in a well-designed Xeriscape. Areas that can be turned over to planting beds rather than lawngrass usually need attention only a few times a year once established. Lawngrass, on the other hand, requires weekly attention from April to October. In addition, the diversity of plants found in the best Xeriscapes attracts a variety of birds and wildlife that, in turn, keep insects and other pests in balance.

I like to think of Xeriscape as a good way to show personal flair. Over the years it can save you time, water, and money. But more importantly, a good Xeriscape can also set you off as progressive and creative, stating this fact in no uncertain terms by its compelling beauty.

A well-designed Xeriscape has eye-appeal all year long.

An X-Rated Sense of Humor

Americans have a pretty good sense of humor, once they stop whining and see it's seriously time to adapt. Garden Centers of Colorado is now adapting an amusing idea first introduced in 1982 when the Denver Water Department Xeriscape demonstration garden was dedicated with an "X-rated" party. That's "X" for Xeriscape.

In the garden centers, now many water-thrifty plants sport a new classification based on how drought-tolerant they are, so you can get your X-rated, your XX-rated, and your XXX-rated plants! This campaign shows how a potentially disastrous situation — big-time drought — can be turned into an entertaining opportunity.

It's also fun to really pay attention to what we're doing and do it right. For too long we've all thought water conservation was "cool" and the "right thing to do." Now we can actually do it!

The most fun of all is the realization that by using these techniques we'll end up with landscapes that are even more colorful, varied, attractive to wildlife, and functional for outdoor enjoyment than they are now!

CHAPTER 1
PLANNING

The first principle of Xeriscape is planning and design. So we'll start at the beginning, with planning.

ABOVE: *Proper planning turned this sloping, narrow strip into a colorful, low-water showcase.*
OPPOSITE: *Color and rhythm are two basics for planning in any type of landscape.*

MAPPING OUT THE BASICS

There are three good reasons to make a plan.

- First, you can save stacks of water and maintenance by thinking hard about the lay of your land, what challenges it might give you, and what you really want to use the landscape for—a place to look at, a place to putter or slave in, or a place to relax in?

- Second, you, or some contractor, will be better able to figure out how much the materials are going to cost you, without a lot of icky surprises.

- Third, and best of all, with the plan down on paper where you can look at it and think about it, your Xeriscape will come into being way quicker than if you just keep it in your head.

So what exactly does a Xeriscape plan look like? It's just a little (or large) scale drawing of your yard on graph paper. I know, I know—

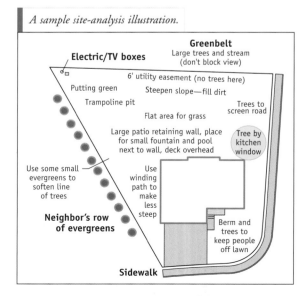

A sample site-analysis illustration.

Greenbelt
Electric/TV boxes Large trees and stream (don't block view)

6' utility easement (no trees here)
Putting green Steepen slope—fill dirt
Trampoline pit
Trees to screen road
Flat area for grass
Large patio retaining wall, place for small fountain and pool next to wall, deck overhead
Tree by kitchen window
Use some small evergreens to soften line of trees
Use winding path to make less steep
Neighbor's row of evergreens
Berm and trees to keep people off lawn
Sidewalk

the words "graph paper" and "drawn to scale" make a lot of people panic at this point. Don't let it scare you. Even the intuitive person who prefers to gaze at dozens of garden catalogs and wander around the botanic garden getting ideas rather than sitting down with a straight-edge and calculator can create a beautiful Xeriscape. You're going to get into it when you see it's just like putting together a giant painting!

Though it sounds boring, good planning is absolutely essential to landscaping, any kind of landscaping. What you're doing is making a sketch of the land you have, with all of its particular quirks. That way you've got it all in front of you when you start to design.

Be sure to include existing plants you want to keep and utilities that will affect your landscape design, such as overhead wires, and gas, electric, and cable TV lines. For most of this stuff, you can call just one number and get all the information you need, specific to your yard. In Colorado, the Utility Notification Center is 1-800-922-1987. Do not skip this step! Consequences range from interrupting service for your whole neighborhood to getting blown up if you hit a gas line.

Making a scale drawing means that your picture is proportionate to your yard. Because

During the planning stage, analyze all your yard's potential uses, such as play space, entertainment areas, or specialty gardens.

you don't want to have a piece of paper as big as your yard, you just use a smaller scale on the paper. For instance, if you make ⅛ of an inch equal to 1 foot, or 1 inch equal to 10 feet, you'll generally get a drawing that fits an 11-by-17-inch piece of paper. If you have a small yard, you can use a scale of ¼ inch equals 1 foot and still fit the drawing on an 8½-by-11-inch standard piece of paper. If you just can't be bothered with rulers or complicated measuring tools, just use the squares on a piece of graph paper. You can count four of those ¼-inch squares as equaling a foot.

With larger scale, such as a ¼ inch equals a foot, you can get more detailed, and the detail is easier to see. However, plan sheets bigger than 11 by 17 inches can be unwieldy and downright annoying if you're not used to handling them. Whatever you decide, make a bunch of copies of your drawing for trying out different ideas. If all else fails and you can't cope with making a

to-scale drawing of your yard "as is," bribe one of your friends who seems genetically programmed to do something like this.

USE, CIRCULATION, AND SITE ANALYSIS

The basics of planning are not much different for Xeriscape than for any other kind of landscape. Once you get down what your yard looks like on graph paper, then you take a good look at it from a few different points of view. Analysis is the "showy" word for looking at something from all directions.

USE

How you want to use your yard should make a big difference in what you plan to plant. For instance, if you want to run around and play hard in your yard, you'll probably want turf. (Think kids, volleyball, putting greens.)

If you're more into entertaining, outdoor eating, and relaxing hobbies, spacious areas devoted to these pastimes usually mean less water use if they feature hardscape surface. If the cost of hardscape makes you wince, just think: With our pleasant evenings in Colorado, a patio is almost as good as an extra room in your house at a fraction of the cost! Ken Ball, one of the founders of the Xeriscape concept, pointed out to me that you could build a teeny-tiny 3-by-5-foot deck to enjoy every night at home for the same price as one night at a Broncos game with good seats, dinner, parking, and the accompanying perks. Three more games and you could have a 12-by-20-foot deck!

You might use your yard for pets, which can pose a problem in any landscape design. Generally, you have to keep dogs off the yard most of the time if you want a landscape. You could divide the territory and let your dog(s) have the perimeter while you claim the center for yourself and entertaining.

A more elegant version of the dreary old dog run involves constructing a rather nice fence along the dog area. Consider something like a cedar fence, the sparse wood fence with chicken wire, a wrought-iron fence, or even chain link covered in vines—all tied up with a tasteful gate. You can plant shrubs and flowers along the front of the fence so your guests can kid themselves that that's the end of your property. (Make sure to check out the Mulching and Maintenance chapters for more hints on coexisting with dogs.)

And, of course, there are those who use their yard for tool, trash, or junk storage. No point pretending this doesn't happen. Some people can't live without their piles of "useful" tires, and repairable lawnmowers. Just take it in hand

Well-defined pathways make circulation of garden admirers and workers, with their equipment, a breeze.

and screen it with 6-foot fences. I've seen this done successfully, and no one would ever know it was there.

Or you might be a diehard gardener, whether it be vegetables, flowers for cutting, roses, chartreuse foliage, you name it. Or you might even have your eye on some future construction project, like a bigger garage, a tennis court, or even a heliport. Now is the time to note it down and plan accordingly.

CIRCULATION

The next thing you have to look at is what kind of stuff you're going to have to carry, push, pull, or otherwise bring through your yard: lawnmowers, wheelbarrows, trash cans, garden slaves carrying tools, tricycles, golf carts, ATVs, pedestrians, even garden admirers. Just make a little note to yourself and then keep on going.

SITE

Now take a look at what's going on in your yard. What are its natural strengths? Does it

A brick staircase can take you from one level to the next with elegance.

have hospitable areas protected from wind and too much sun or shade? Are there places just downstream of downspouts, which will naturally get more water? Are there useful slopes facing the house that could be turned into beautiful terrace gardens? Existing trees in good locations? You get the picture.

On the other hand, where are your yard's natural weaknesses? Where are the areas too open, windy, hot, dry, shady, rocky, poorly drained, or sloping the wrong way? Tailings ponds should be included here.

While you're doing this, don't forget to take a moment to look through your windows and off the porch and deck. Figure out what lovely views, such as greenbelts or neighbors' mature trees, you want to preserve by not blocking them, or enhance by framing them with plants.

Now look at the other side of the coin. What yucky views and noisy aspects would you be happy to block out? Make another "note to self." You've just completed the "site analysis."

OTHER PLANNING CONSIDERATIONS

WILDLIFE

Believe it or not, you might actually *want* to attract wildlife to your yard. Hawks, squirrels,

salamanders, and butterflies are just a few of the creatures that can make a garden that much more interesting and attractive. Though not specifically a water-saving issue, this topic is often of interest to xeriscapers. Increasing the variety of plants in our landscapes goes hand in hand with providing habitat for a wider variety of wildlife. You might as well go full bore and plan for it on purpose!

A diverse palette of plants attracts varied wildlife, from a painted lady butterfly on a butterfly bush to a fox.

Also, if you put in a little water supply for birds and other wildlife, such as a birdbath or tiny pond, you can go a long way toward invoking that oasis feeling in a landscape otherwise designed to be very water-sparse.

Basically, it boils down to providing food, water, and shelter on an ongoing basis for whatever wildlife you're interested in attracting. There are many sources of information on this fascinating topic—books, magazine articles, and, of course, Colorado State University's Cooperative Extension Service (CSU CES) publications. It's worth studying up on to make the best plant choices.

For instance, you might guess that birds would like an eastern redbud, as it does provide shelter and, one assumes, fruit, because it blooms beautifully in the spring. But further research would reveal that it's only of limited value to birds (the fruit is a pod), and a flowering dogwood is much more useful.

The National Wildlife Federation has a great website (www.nwf.org/backyardwildlifehabitat) for information on attracting certain types of wildlife, such as butterflies, frogs, and pollinating insects, and repelling other less popular garden animals, as well as a program to certify your landscape as a "Backyard Wildlife Habitat."

You also might want to check out *The Xeriscape Flower Gardener: A Waterwise Guide for the Rocky Mountain Region* (Johnson Books, 1991) by Boulder landscape architect and writer Jim Knopf. The book includes a chapter and an appendix on landscaping for critters.

ZONING AND OASIS

"Zoning," a key Xeriscape concept, refers to the practice of grouping plants with similar water needs together, so they can be watered or not watered accordingly. This makes it easier on you, saves much water, and is better for the plants' health.

If you don't zone, you're going to get tired of rescuing the one or two plants that always seem to be gasping for water, while the rest around them are doing fine with the water they're getting. Or some of your flowers might become all leggy and tacky because you have to keep the adjacent favorites soaked to keep them alive. Common sense comes in. "I didn't zone!" you'll cry.

Fitting nicely with zoning is the main contribution of desert landscaping to Xeriscape: the "oasis" concept. The highest-water-using plants are grouped close to the house, perhaps around a patio, where they are easiest to water and most visible. In the desert, the areas most distant from the house might be bare ground or rock mulch with native plants that rarely require watering.

In this Southwestern-style garden, the plants have been zoned, or grouped according to their water use. Photo by Connie Ellefson.

winter-interesting plants so you won't just have season-long color; it will be year-round!

Winter interest is generated by:

- Evergreen trees and shrubs, both coniferous and broadleaf.
- Ornamental grasses, which are left through the winter and trimmed back to the ground mid-spring.
- Groundcovers and perennials that have evergreen foliage, or interesting seed or spent flower heads.
- Deciduous trees and shrubs that feature persistent fruit, or unusual bark texture or color.

In the mountain West, this might be translated into close-in flowerbeds, or cool-season grass lawn, with the areas farther out planted in shrub and mulch beds—one of the lowest water AND maintenance types of plantings—or a lower-water/native grass area.

Using both of these strategies will help you make the most of your time and your water.

COLOR

Color is important in any landscape design, but especially in successful xeriscaping. You'll need to put in some evergreens or other extremely

Ornamental grasses and desert plants provide winter interest.

In the oasis concept, dense plantings are kept closer to the house for high visibility and ease of watering.

Ten not to Miss

Here are 10 general planning and design concepts to keep in mind. Not unique to xeriscaping, these points are useful in all landscaping endeavors:

1. Unity. Or more specifically, unity of landscape with architecture. Things like the walkway having the same texture and color as the house, or at least a complementary look. Just don't overdo it. It's been said that

one thing that sets off a professional-looking design from an amateur one is a limited number of different hardscape materials used in the landscape. It just looks more pulled-together when you refrain from using brick, stone, wood, stucco, patterned concrete, and corrugated metal roof panels all in the same yard!

2. Privacy. Have some areas open to the public view? How much privacy do you want, vs. how willing are you to share your landscaping efforts with the neighbors? Do you want an open landscape or an enclosed one, as below?

3. Entrance emphasis. Using a pathway, plantings, or other attention-getters, make sure the entrance is obvious and inviting. Nothing is more disconcerting to the new guest, mail carrier, or Tiffany's delivery person than to be standing about scratching his or her head, trying to figure out where the front door is. One way of framing the entrance is found in an old favorite landscape design method of planting large trees on the outskirts of the front yard, with gradually smaller trees or shrubs funneling down toward the door.

4. Screening. Take a look at your views, good and bad; pathways; corridors; existing features such as large trees; windows in the house. Most important are the views through windows from inside your house, and the "windows" from the "outdoor rooms" called for by every landscape designer ever. You know what you love when you look out of all these rooms, and what jars.

One key concept in screening is that the closer you put the screening plant to where you're looking at the icky view, the smaller the plant can be. For example, a vine on a trellis next to the patio will block the view as well as a 50-foot tree at the end of the yard, and it only takes one to two seasons to grow, instead of 20 years.

Also, if you're into the public's view of your house, pace around quite a bit, from both directions in front of your house, all the while imagining how your plan will look to the envious neighbors. (You might have to squint a little.)

5. Variation. The form and texture and height of plants need to be varied and coordinated. Whether round, erect, flat, coarse, or smooth, plants add to each other's beauty, so mix it up! Variety is the key, whether purposeful or random. The effect of a landscape on human stress has actually been studied scientifically, and it was found that a more varied, complex landscape soothes the weary soul more effectively than a boring, limited plant palette. Balancing the height of plants on each side—not necessarily strict symmetry—or using a single element as a focal point can do wonders for your mood.

8. Seating. It can be there to allow you to enjoy the view or just to rest. First, make sure you'll actually use the seating, or it will just end up being quaint, but ineffectual (and FORLORN). I tend to be puttering around the garden when I'm outside, and rarely lounging around in it, so I'd give the marble bench or Adirondack chair a miss, but you might be different.

6. Traffic patterns. How are people (including dogs and the letter carrier) going to approach your home? After several years as a Denver Water design clinic consultant, it always warms my heart at how many times I've been told earnestly that "the letter carrier always comes this way, and we don't want to block that off." (Gardeners are such nice people, I tell you.)

7. Budget. Time and money, that is. The amount of money available for installation and the realities of scheduling can make a big difference. Professional landscape installation can run from $2 to $20 per square foot or more (lawn to hardscape), depending on how elaborate the design. Landscapes often seem to take the back seat financially, especially if you're still reeling from the cost of building a house.

If you're considering "doing it yourself," just remember: Oh, man, is it ever hard work! Choose what you are going to do intelligently. You might thank yourself for contracting out at least some of the work to the people who have skid-loaders and whatnot. Soil preparation, retaining wall construction, water features, lighting, and irrigation are some items to consider leaving to the pros.

Scheduling can take place over several years to ease the strain on backs and/or pocketbooks. One piece of advice I never forget is to "plant the trees first." They normally take the longest to grow, and nothing can give your landscape that beloved, homey look more than a nicely matured tree.

9. Structures. To add form or just a little extra interest, think structures, including sculpture. That bench or Adirondack chair I didn't think I'd be using for seating might fill in as sculpture, to set scale or add a human touch. Trellises, arches, fences, and gazebos can fill in some vertical interest while you wait for the puny little trees and shrubs to soldier up to their mature height. Any of these items with a fast-growing vine planted by it will add vertical plus instant green. If you're a minimalist who does not like or want to be bothered with figuring out some striking flowerbed, a compelling sculpture such as an urn, obelisk, or column surrounded by groundcover is the ultimate in elegance. Scarecrows and animal statues serve the same purpose on the rustic side.

10. Future construction. One of my neighbors built a beautiful family room addition to the back of his house. He shortened the room in one direction to allow a huge beloved cottonwood tree (a limb of which stopped him from falling off the roof during construction and probably saved his life!) to remain. Unfortunately, the construction cut off so much of the tree's root system that it died. Not only is my neighbor's heart broken, but the estimate he got to remove the dead tree was $3,000.

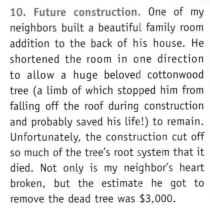

MICROCLIMATES

Water-related planning and design considerations have a lot to do with working with what you have. Now's the time to make some choices about how you want to impact the environment. We're not talking only about water use here, but also about what other chemical inputs such as herbicides, fertilizer, fungicides, insecticides, and other potentially hazardous materials you could eliminate.

Microclimates—small portions of your yard that are affected differently by the various elements of sun, shade, and prevailing winds—are especially important here. These three elements can have a profound effect on soil moisture, and differing soil moisture content can give you a range of plant choices.

But microclimates aren't a static concept. They often change with the seasons. For people moving into houses with existing landscapes, it has even been recommended to wait a whole growing season before doing any planting. This allows you to keep an eye peeled for areas that get full sun, partial sun, full shade, constant calm, constant wind, or snow drifting or storage. This gives you a very good excuse to take a breather.

As you guessed, windy areas dry out faster, sunny spots can be dry to baking (depending on if they're in morning or afternoon sun), and shade can be either dry or moist. Studying these patterns gives you an easy way to organize your plant zones.

For instance, my "new" 25-year-old house faces north, and it has a small front yard with a huge Austrian pine covering about half of it. The back is big and almost completely open with only a couple of smallish trees hanging out. Everything else is dead from the drought. In my renovation scheme, I decided to forgo lawn in the front, as the area isn't big enough to be effective.

Part of the front yard will be planted with a shade-tolerant groundcover; another section will be part-sun, part-shade groundcover and a few flowers; and the protected area just north of the house will be my fussy, higher-water, part-shade perennials. This section is amped up to the max with organic amendments, hydro-gels, weed-barrier fabric, and mulch—in short, everything I could think of to save me from having to water.

Wind isn't much of a problem at my house, but if it were, I'd probably be planting something to screen and break the wind A.S.A.P. to get that

mitigation going! Still, the back yard is primarily in the baking category, so I've planned a small oval drought-tolerant grass area (probably 'Ephraim' crested wheatgrass—see Practical Turf Areas I chapter, p. 94), a wee prairie garden, a vegetable garden also loaded with amendments, a couple of trees for future shade, and lots of mulch beds in which to try out drought-tolerant shrubs.

For me, it's easy now with this planned out. Every time I come across a new plant I want to try, I pretty much know instantly where it will go, according to which microclimate it likes.

Microclimates give you a chance to try some plants that might be marginally cold-hardy or

ABOVE: *Extra water from a downspout makes this spot a hospitable microclimate for lush plantings.*
BELOW: *Stunning variegated irises adapt to microclimates ranging from harsh to protected.*

drought-tolerant in one part of your yard, but could find just the right home in another. I hear about "cold troughs" sometimes occurring at the bottom of slopes, which doesn't make much sense to me, but I think it has to do with cold air falling down and making the plants even colder in winter than in the rest of the area. Cold troughs are also sites of longer-term snow storage, so there's more moisture in the soil. It's conceivable that between your "cold trough" and your protected south-facing little cozy nook, you could have a difference of one whole cold-hardiness level.

The drainage provided by this slope is beneficial for the foundation as well as the root systems of plants growing there.

DRAINAGE

The first rule of drainage is this: You *always* have to have the ground sloping away from your house, for at least 5 feet at a slope of 5 percent, to ensure against some fiercely disastrous problems with expansive clay soils next to your home's foundation or water getting into the basement.

Beyond that, the ground usually slopes to the street, side, or back lot line at 2 percent or more. This is a minimum, usually required of the builders to establish initially, which will theoretically prevent standing water on your land. Until recently, all the engineers have been striving to meet this requirement in order to make sure that storm-water runoff gets into the streets and storm sewers as quickly as possible, in effort to avoid flooding and wet spots.

Now these same engineers are saying, "Not so fast," because the hot issue in drainage currently is improving water quality—removing pollutants such as fertilizer—before sending the water back to the river. This means slowing the water down, running it across grass buffers, and hoping some of it will soak into the ground where the plants and soil will do an excellent job of cleansing it.

In an effort to slow your water down, you can flatten the slope a little, or, more easily in an established landscape, build some little dams along the flow path to capture part of the runoff for your plants' use. Just make sure there's still a way for the water to get out before it gets too high, or you might end up with that flooded basement after all.

Other more extreme slopes give you an excellent opportunity to eliminate some very hard-to-care-for turf and throw in something else. If the ground slopes away from your house out of sight, you can build a retaining wall to increase the usable flattish area, and just mulch the area down below and forget it, or create some magical secret garden arrived at by stairway or rope ladder. (OK, OK. I get carried away, I know.)

If the ground slopes toward the house, you can make an interesting terrace garden, as explained in the "Dry, Hot, South-Facing Slope" example in the next chapter (see p. 49).

The place where the roof drain downspouts out into the yard gives you another good chance to do some low-tech water harvesting by planting the higher-water plants downstream. You

Eliminate hard-to-care-for turf on a slope like this by substituting colorful flowers.

might even want to extend the end of the down-spout to get the water to outlet into a more beneficial spot. This can be a source of a tremendous amount of water, and it comes out pretty fast sometimes, so make sure you protect the ground around the end and break up the energy of the rushing water with a concrete splash block or some decorative rock dissipater.

PLANT COMMUNITIES

Consider what the dominant plant type is in your area. The closer you adapt to that, the less water you will probably use. Most of us live in grassland, for example, so having lots of trees and flowers will generally require more water. This isn't just ecologically correct; it's also common sense and can make your life a lot simpler.

Plants grow together in communities based on topography, orientation toward the sun, micro-climate, and soil. The dominant plant in a community is the one that takes best advantage of the conditions.

In Eastern forests, for example, the high rainfall rate is favorable to extremely large deciduous trees (some as tall as 150 feet). When not interfered with by humans, the trees are the

ABOVE: *Shrubs provide great fall color on a slope.*
BELOW: *A stucco wall retains the slope and makes a strong architectural statement.*

dominant plant. They tower over the forest floor, creating shade and intercepting some of the rainfall, which, in turn, affects the development of the understory, or subdominant layer, also known as shrubs and smaller trees.

In the Midwest and Great Plains, rainfall isn't high enough to support massive trees, so the prairie grasses dominate these dry, sunny regions. Crossover happens in both extremes. A south-facing slope in the forest will have open patches of meadow where the trees have lost the fight for dominance because too much moisture evaporates from that side of the hill. In the grassland, a north-facing hill will not lose as much moisture in the shade, thus giving shrubs and trees a foothold.

After thinking about plant communities a bit, it begins to dawn on us where the plants we want in our landscape should be located. We see that it doesn't make sense to plant grass under a very shady tree because we know that grasses are most successful where they don't have to contend with shade. By the same token, plunking a tree down in the middle of the lawn could hold the tree back if it has to compete with the grass for water and nutrients.

Trees and shrubs tolerant of blazing sun and other extremes of weather can provide protection for some of the more tender perennials and shrubs underneath them. Sections of your house, fences, and walls can all provide microclimates. A south-facing flowerbed protected by an L-shaped house might still have petunias blooming at Thanksgiving, even in cold, wind-battered Wyoming (mine did once).

Plants grow together in communities based on soil and climactic conditions. Tailoring your plantings according to the existing environmental conditions increases the plants' chances for success.

GETTING PROFESSIONAL HELP

You might be able to observe the commonsense aspects of what would work best for your Xeriscape, yet lack the aesthetic ability to put it all together in a beautiful way, or the time and desire to learn all you need to learn to make intelligent plant choices. If so, do not hesitate to hire a landscape architect or designer to prepare a master plan. The money spent will be well worth it in terms of direction, information gained about costs and phasing of improvements, and other considerations of which you might not be aware.

In addition, for those who want to make their own master plan, some designers will consult with you for an hourly fee. You will be surprised at how much useful advice you can get in a short session.

Most of us have a lot of good ideas about our landscape. We just need a little expert help in pulling it all together, and a cohesive plan from an experienced professional will help us create a landscape that will look better every step of the way. Having ponied up for a professional plan, do then *follow* the plan, so you haven't wasted the time and money.

ABOVE: *A professional landscape architect or designer has creative ideas to perk up the most mundane spot. Don't hesitate to consult with one if you need help.* Photo by Bonnie Arnold.

BELOW: *This protected side yard provides a haven for delicate plants. Photo by Connie Ellefson.*

CHAPTER 2
DESIGN

You've done all the planning;

now it's time to design...

ABOVE: *Delicate purple coneflowers are a colorful counterpoint to the strong lines of the boulder.*
OPPOSITE: *Whether naturalistic or formal, a well-designed Xeriscape is colorful year-round.*

...which means you'll be making decisions and writing on your carefully graphed and analyzed portrait of the lay of the land. This chapter is in three parts. First, you'll find a general, step-by-step guide to plotting your design so you're not doing a lot of erasing. Second, there's a brief rundown of some commonly found Xeriscape situations in Colorado and what to do about them. Before-and-after scenarios and landscape plan drawings illustrate some of the concepts in this section. Last, you'll find a section called "Special Goals," which will help you get exactly the look and type of landscape you're aiming for.

FIRST THINGS FIRST

TURF

Whether you're dealing with a brand-new or existing landscape, a good first step is to define exactly how much, if any, turf area you need and where it will be.

We don't need to kick lawns out of our lives; just think carefully about how much lawn you really need for sports, play, entertainment, showing off, and whatever other activities you indulge in. Lawns are great for playing on, unifying the landscape, and providing a backdrop for more textural and colorful Xeriscape plantings, but it's rarely necessary to have lawn blanketing the scene from fence to fence. Exclude lawngrass from every area where it will be hard to water or mow efficiently, or where it doesn't really serve any of the before-mentioned functions. Consider using some of the more drought-tolerant turfgrasses for part of the area where you'd still like the smooth, unbroken line of a grass. (See the chapters on Practical Turf Areas for the rest of this extensive story.)

I saw one of my favorite uses for lawngrass at the home of a woman in Virginia whose passion was experimenting with growing perennials. She used grass as a 4-foot-wide path for access to her huge flowerbeds! You could do the same here, featuring our great xeric perennials.

HARDSCAPE

Any inanimate, non-plant, non-furniture element you include in a landscape design is called "hardscape." It can include masonry work (from stone walls to brick patios), woodwork (decks, planters), and tile (paths, ponds).

Hardscape does a lot to establish the style of your landscape. The formal look is enhanced by bricks set in square patterns, for example, and an informal landscape might feature irregular stone pavers with groundcovers between stones, or wooden decking.

There are even porous hardscape materials available now that allow some of the precipitation reaching them to be retained onsite. The recent explosion of patterned and colored concrete products has made many, many of these same hardscape looks available at a lower cost. So you can have your bricks and not spend a fortune

on them, nor have to set them a foot apart to make the budget!

Hardscape may be something for the future, too, as the finances allow, but keep in mind one important thing. You can't go changing the air/soil/roots ratio under an existing mature tree very dramatically or you'll end up like my neighbor: all "patio-ed up" with no tree to shade you. Plant those trees and nearby hardscape at the same time!

STORAGE, ACCESS, AND BASIC PLANTS

Map out any utilitarian areas such as storage for garbage cans or other outdoor equipment and straightforward access from one area to another. These usually fall into place fairly easily as there will only be a limited number of logical places for them. Then locate whatever other planting areas or specialty gardens you want. (See Appropriate Plant Choice chapters for further considerations on different types of plants you might want to include.)

I keep a folder called "My Garden" in the most frequently used section of my filing system. I throw in lists of plants I've heard about that I want to try, a couple of key catalogs I use, and whatever sketches I make in passing. This helps me visualize my plan. One good use for the zillions of garden catalogs that start magically appearing in your mailbox when you so much as start thinking about plants is to cut out pictures of favorites to try in combination.

WINTER INTEREST

Double-check and make sure you've included in your design something that will stay green or add color throughout the year. Spread your "winter interest" areas, described in the "Color" section of the last chapter (see p. 25), throughout the plan, or at least where they'll be visible to someone driving by, or to a cabin fever victim gazing out on the winter landscape with a baleful eye. Now you're ready to fill in the rest of the plan, using the information from the Appropriate Plant Choice chapters and the troubleshooting situations that follow.

TOP: *Hardscape is a low-water alternative to turf in this front yard.*
LEFT: *Decks lend a friendly, informal air to the landscape.*
OPPOSITE: *With berries, leaves, or interesting bark, even deciduous shrubs can lend winter interest.*

TYPICAL XERISCAPE PROBLEMS —AND THEIR SOLUTIONS

DENVER SQUARE/BUNGALOW

SLOPED FRONT YARD

Hundreds of homes were built in central Denver around the turn of the last century with front yards that slope down to the sidewalk. These houses were built on little plateaus created by piling up the soil in a sharply sloped shelf (often as steep as 3 to 1) just behind the sidewalk for 2 to 3 vertical feet. The front yard then flattens to a level area where the house sits and continues clear on through to the house on the adjoining street, where the same steep slope occurs back down to the sidewalk.

There were two reasons for this, neither landscape-oriented. One was to balance

before

after

The plantings in the "hell strip" (see p. 40) and right next to the house will be most colorful in the late spring and early summer, as shown in this scene. Later in the summer, color emphasis will shift to the wall area. Grouping your plants this way gives them maximum impact, as opposed to mixing plants of all seasons.
Photo by Connie Ellefson.

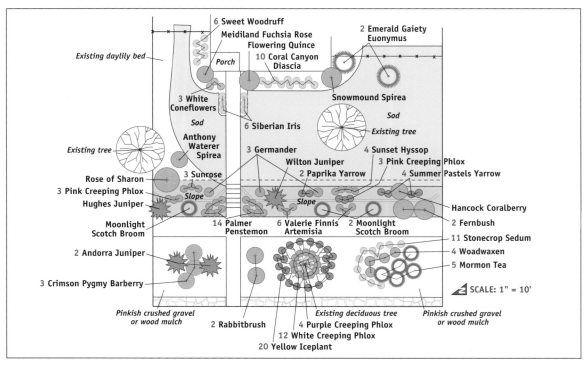

Existing daylily bed

6 Sweet Woodruff
Meidiland Fuchsia Rose
Flowering Quince
10 Coral Canyon Diascia
Porch

2 Emerald Gaiety Euonymus

3 White Coneflowers
Sod
Anthony Waterer Spirea

6 Siberian Iris

Snowmound Spirea
Sod
Existing tree

Existing tree

Rose of Sharon
3 Pink Creeping Phlox
Hughes Juniper
Moonlight Scotch Broom

3 Sunrose
Slope

3 Germander
Wilton Juniper
2 Paprika Yarrow

4 Sunset Hyssop
3 Pink Creeping Phlox
4 Summer Pastels Yarrow
Slope

Hancock Coralberry

14 Palmer Penstemon
6 Valerie Finnis Artemisia
2 Moonlight Scotch Broom

2 Fernbush
11 Stonecrop Sedum
4 Woadwaxen
5 Mormon Tea

2 Andorra Juniper

3 Crimson Pygmy Barberry

SCALE: 1" = 10'

Pinkish crushed gravel or wood mulch

2 Rabbitbrush

Existing deciduous tree
4 Purple Creeping Phlox
12 White Creeping Phlox
20 Yellow Iceplant

Pinkish crushed gravel or wood mulch

the cut and fill grading on each lot so no dirt had to be hauled in or out. This also cut basement excavation in half because the house was sitting up higher. The other reason was for status. A house sitting up 3 to 4 feet above the sidewalk looked much grander.

Meanwhile, Denver homeowners are stuck with a perpetual challenge: watering *and* mowing a slope that neither holds water nor provides a level surface. Ken Ball, one of the people who founded the Xeriscape concept, came across a woman trying to mow one of these steep slopes and took a picture just as she slipped and fell. Luckily, she wasn't injured. This classic photo (above) appeared in many early Xeriscape slide shows and is a good cautionary tale warning of the dangers of high-water landscaping!

Covering or leaving this slope in bluegrass is the worst choice you can make for that strip. You have several alternatives, depending on how much installation work you're up for.

Option one would be to remove the grass and replace it with evergreen groundcover, such as blue-chip or Wilton juniper. Make sure you use a good weed-barrier fabric and cedar mulch to ensure weeds are kept under control. Use the fuzzy weed-barrier fabric to help prevent that mulch from sliding down the hill. With junipers and any other groundcover that spreads out above the ground rather than below it, it's even possible to simply kill the grass with glyphosate, wait the required interval, and then install plants, fabric, and mulch over the dead grass. This helps prevent erosion as the grass' fibrous root system is still in place.

Groundcovers that spread by underground rhizomes and roots can also be used, but then you have to forgo the weed-barrier fabric so the plants can spread and fill in. There will be more weeding, and a little more mulch sliding down the slope. (Black poly netting can be used to hold the chips in place until the plants grow in.) Industrial-strength edging or some other barrier on the uphill side of your slope will slow the grass from your lawn retaking the slope. For these plants, it's better to remove the grass.

Your second option would be to remove the grass and plant a more colorful groundcover, such as daylilies or a drought-tolerant turfgrass, or a mixture of perennials, ornamental grasses, and small evergreen shrubs. A few good-sized rocks could be added here if you're into it, but make sure they're not puny, as small rocks don't make a very effective landscape statement. (This is the West, you know; we don't pussyfoot around out here!)

A third option would be to remove all grass and rebuild the

TOP: *One of the dangers of high-water landscaping. Photo by Ken Ball.*
MIDDLE: *Although it's not the preferred option, this is one way to treat a slope.*
BELOW: *A selection of low-water perennials, groundcovers, and shrubs makes a good substitute for turf on this slope.*

slope with one or two layers of terracing material (short retaining walls), such as stone or landscape timbers. In the City and County of Denver, you must make sure the first layer of the wall is set back at least 18 inches behind the sidewalk, as it's illegal to build a permanent structure in the public part of the street between your property line and the curb. Fill in the terraces with whatever riot or subdued explosion of plants you want in order to provide a focal point of color and interest. You can be a little wilder about it because the walls already provide a restful boundary.

THE HELL STRIP

Another treat for central Denver homeowners is the now-famous "hell strip," that area between the sidewalk and the street that you are required to maintain even though it's not yours (see the before-and-after scenario on p. 38). The "hell strip" nomenclature was made famous by Lauren Springer in her delightful book, *The Undaunted Garden: Planting for Weather-Resilient Beauty.* Here are some possibilities for handling hell strips, in order from easiest-to-install to most labor-intensive.

A strip of stone pavers hugging the curb allows visitors parking alongside it easy access to your home without trampling the plants inhabiting the hell strip.

First and easiest, you could plant a couple of shrubs (36 inches tall or less, for driver visibility), or maybe a deciduous tree (if your original gigantic street tree has long since left this world). After that, just roll out the weed-barrier fabric and mulch of your choice, and you're done.

Or you could always install a strip of nice brick or stone pavers along the curb 12 to 18 inches wide for the comfort of your visitors alighting from their motorcars. The pavers then feed into a central path to ease their way across the remaining 3 to 5 feet of hell strip to the sidewalk. (This is the most *genteel* solution, should you require it.) Fill in the rest with a selection of well-behaved groundcovers, or the first option. Just make sure the shrubs/trees are

Western sandcherry and junipers brighten this xeriscaped hell strip with little need for upkeep.

of small mature girth so your guests won't need to bring along a machete as well.

A third option is to continue the colorful plantings found in the slope above, or play it simple with just a carpet of iceplant for your hell strip. The purple ones *(Delosperma cooperi)* have gorgeous flowers all summer, though their winter foliage is a little dreary. And the yellow ones *(D. nubigenum)* have equally bright, but briefly blooming, flowers, and striking reddish foliage in the winter. They both put up with the heat and drought of the hell strip like nobody's business.

Design word to the wise: If you've chosen the riot of color and texture for both the hell strip and the slope, you'll probably want to keep the rest of the yard pretty simple, just the lawn or lawn substitute and a few subdued shrubs (maybe spring-blooming, as much of your flower garden will probably bloom later) to dress up the foundation. Otherwise, it will just get *too* busy-looking.

before

after

*Two design concepts draw attention to the front door in this front **yard** (just in case you couldn't find it!). First, placing the tallest plants at the yard's outer edge, then gradually lowering the plant height as you approach the door, helps to frame the house. Second, the brightest plants are placed closest to the door.* Photo by Connie Ellefson.

NEW SUBURBAN HOME ON A SMALL LOT

Here I'm talking about the new- or newer-construction homes with the typical lawn and tree in the middle and the barren rectangular back yard.

First consider just how small that back yard is, and whether you have tiny tots who will be using it. Beth Chatto, author of *The Dry Garden,* made the no-nonsense statement that, "If your yard is less than 1,000 square feet, grass is a waste of time." Better, she said, to fill it with a nice hardscape for patio living and a jungle of plants around the edge.

Most parents of small children want a grass area in the back so they can keep the little ones corralled and under the parental eye. Similarly, a small dog may have the run of a lawn area without ripping it to shreds.

However, if your back yard is too small to play any games other than badminton on, your dog is anything but small, or your kids are big enough that they're now normally playing in the street, you might be ready for the bold step of a no-grass back yard! Look around to see if there are any appalling current or future views you might want to screen, and think about where the best place might be to put a hobby area, such as a rose or vegetable garden. Plan for those; then have a big time filling about half the rest of the back yard with your choice of hardscape.

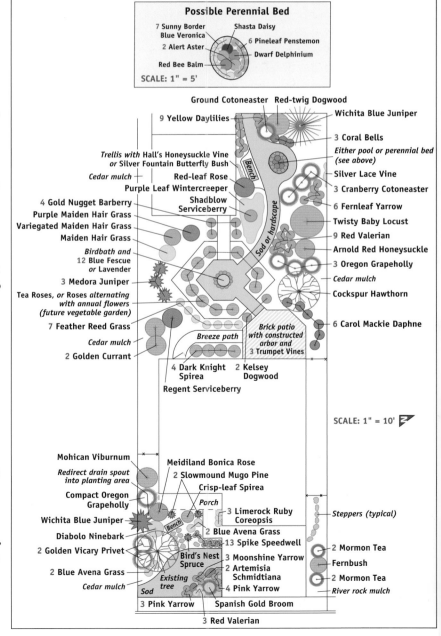

Possible Perennial Bed

7 Sunny Border Blue Veronica
Shasta Daisy
2 Alert Aster
6 Pineleaf Penstemon
Dwarf Delphinium
Red Bee Balm
SCALE: 1" = 5'

Ground Cotoneaster Red-twig Dogwood
Wichita Blue Juniper
9 Yellow Daylilies
3 Coral Bells
Either pool or perennial bed (see above)
Trellis with Hall's Honeysuckle Vine or Silver Fountain Butterfly Bush
Silver Lace Vine
Cedar mulch
Red-leaf Rose
3 Cranberry Cotoneaster
Purple Leaf Wintercreeper
6 Fernleaf Yarrow
Shadblow Serviceberry
Twisty Baby Locust
4 Gold Nugget Barberry
9 Red Valerian
Purple Maiden Hair Grass
Arnold Red Honeysuckle
Variegated Maiden Hair Grass
3 Oregon Grapeholly
Maiden Hair Grass
Cedar mulch
Birdbath and
12 Blue Fescue or Lavender
Cockspur Hawthorn
3 Medora Juniper
Tea Roses, or Roses *alternating with annual flowers (future vegetable garden)*
6 Carol Mackie Daphne
7 Feather Reed Grass
Breeze path
Brick patio with constructed arbor and 3 Trumpet Vines
Cedar mulch
2 Golden Currant
4 Dark Knight Spirea
2 Kelsey Dogwood
Regent Serviceberry

SCALE: 1" = 10'

Mohican Viburnum
Meidiland Bonica Rose
Redirect drain spout into planting area
2 Slowmound Mugo Pine
Crisp-leaf Spirea
Compact Oregon Grapeholly
Porch
Steppers (typical)
3 Limerock Ruby Coreopsis
Wichita Blue Juniper
2 Blue Avena Grass
Diabolo Ninebark
13 Spike Speedwell
2 Mormon Tea
2 Golden Vicary Privet
Bird's Nest Spruce
3 Moonshine Yarrow
Fernbush
2 Blue Avena Grass
2 Artemisia Schmidtiana
2 Mormon Tea
Existing tree
4 Pink Yarrow
River rock mulch
Cedar mulch
Sod
3 Pink Yarrow
Spanish Gold Broom
3 Red Valerian

Design a pleasing boundary for the hardscape on paper first, then go out into the territory and actually lay it out on the ground with garden hoses, thin rope, or what-have-you. You might come up with a slightly different arrangement on the ground that is more appealing to your eye. Trust your eye in this instance because it definitely knows what it's doing. The brain works rather mysteriously in these cases, and if you stubbornly stick with the paper design, you might always find yourself mildly annoyed with the result.

Also, though it's not cast in stone from a design standpoint, small areas are better adapted to squared-off lines, which could be expressed in a basic square or rectangle, or a series of interconnected shapes. Small yards just don't have enough room visually to accommodate big sweeping, naturalist curves. (But, like I said, feel free to abandon any "design aesthetic" you care to if your eye likes something else.)

If you decide to do a concrete patio, think about adding some containers to break up the

The center area of this small back yard could be either a grass pathway or hardscape, for a more formal look.
Photo by Connie Ellefson.

heat and expanse. Surround the hardscape outline with shrubs, trees, flowers, and/or groundcovers—plus mulch—and you'll have a chic and enjoyable backyard retreat! Naturally, benches, patio furniture, and barbecue grills are right at home here.

What you do with the front yard depends on whether you want to conform to the neighborhood landscape norm and/or adhere to homeowner association covenants, or be fiercely independent. Some developers will install sod, a tree, and a couple of shrubs for you. Perhaps you want to leave that for the time being to focus on the back, contenting yourself with adding a few colorful shrub roses, vines, or additional trees in the front while you think about it.

As mentioned before, one good piece of advice —if you have little or no money to landscape early on—is to get those trees in first, even if you start with small ones. They take the longest to grow and ultimately have the most impact on both the beauty of your landscape and cool summer temperatures inside your house.

Pay close attention to the ultimate size of the trees you select, making sure they won't overwhelm your house or lot size—or your neighbor's —in a few years. Also, don't get too carried away with trying to fill in the landscape in two years with multitudes of plants. Friends of mine bought a six-year-old house with so many shrubs planted they could easily have started their own nursery. Remember, these things mature and get bigger. You don't want to require a chainsaw to get through parts of your yard.

Butterfly bushes and tall ornamental grasses such as maiden hair grass are great for filling in a landscape quickly while slower-growing plants mature.

One trick to enhance the curb appeal of your landscape is to plant the tallest trees near the outside edges of your front yard, and create a visual focal point at the door of your house by planting gradually shorter trees or shrubs as you approach the door from both sides. Just don't wall yourself in with plants if you favor the open look.

New Suburban Home on a Corner Lot

OK, now we're talking about the house on that irregularly shaped, barren piece of land that every kid in the neighborhood wants to cut across. There are two schools of thought about the grass and planting border scheme most people end up with in these kinds of front yards. One way to go is to put the grass out front, so you blend in better with the neighbors—but this makes for heavy maintenance and doesn't discourage those shortcutters in the least.

A second way to go would be to make the planting area next to your house as big as you think the traffic will bear. Put a planting bed next to the sidewalk, thereby eliminating hundreds of hours of edging maintenance, with the grass area closer to the house, and another planting area next to the house. Make sure the planting bed(s) are at least 4 feet wide, otherwise they'll look cramped and puny. Of course, 8- to 10-foot widths are better, and the width can always vary along the length of the bed for interest and variety.

You should keep all plantings 3 to 5 feet away from the foundation. Everyone's heard at least one cracked foundation horror story, and, in fact, many cities and counties require

before

A little berming and a shield of shrubs helps to discourage foot traffic across a corner lot. This landscape is especially colorful in the fall, but will also be effective year-round, as several of the shrubs are evergreen. Photo by Connie Ellefson.

after

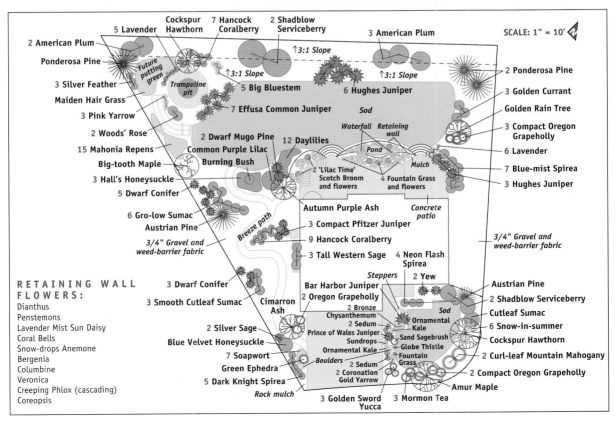

SCALE: 1" = 10'

5 Lavender
Cockspur Hawthorn
7 Hancock Coralberry
2 Shadblow Serviceberry
3 American Plum
2 American Plum
Ponderosa Pine
↑3:1 Slope
↑3:1 Slope
↑3:1 Slope
2 Ponderosa Pine
Future putting green
3 Silver Feather
Maiden Hair Grass
Trampoline pit
5 Big Bluestem
6 Hughes Juniper
3 Golden Currant
Golden Rain Tree
3 Pink Yarrow
7 Effusa Common Juniper
Sod
3 Compact Oregon Grapeholly
2 Woods' Rose
Waterfall   Retaining wall
6 Lavender
15 Mahonia Repens
2 Dwarf Mugo Pine
Common Purple Lilac
12 Daylilies
Pond
7 Blue-mist Spirea
Big-tooth Maple
Burning Bush
Mulch
3 Hughes Juniper
3 Hall's Honeysuckle
2 'Lilac Time' Scotch Broom and flowers
4 Fountain Grass and flowers
5 Dwarf Conifer
6 Gro-low Sumac
Austrian Pine
Autumn Purple Ash
Concrete patio
3/4" Gravel and weed-barrier fabric
3 Compact Pfitzer Juniper
Breeze path
9 Hancock Coralberry
3/4" Gravel and weed-barrier fabric
3 Tall Western Sage
4 Neon Flash Spirea
Steppers
2 Yew
Austrian Pine
3 Dwarf Conifer
Bar Harbor Juniper
2 Oregon Grapeholly
2 Shadblow Serviceberry
3 Smooth Cutleaf Sumac
Cimarron Ash
2 Bronze Chysanthemum
Sod
Cutleaf Sumac
2 Sedum
Ornamental Kale
6 Snow-in-summer
2 Silver Sage
Prince of Wales Juniper
Sand Sagebrush
Cockspur Hawthorn
Blue Velvet Honeysuckle
Sundrops
Globe Thistle
2 Curl-leaf Mountain Mahogany
7 Soapwort
Ornamental Kale
Fountain Grass
2 Compact Oregon Grapeholly
Green Ephedra
Boulders
2 Sedum
5 Dark Knight Spirea
2 Coronation Gold Yarrow
Amur Maple
Rock mulch
3 Golden Sword Yucca
3 Mormon Tea

RETAINING WALL FLOWERS:
Dianthus
Penstemons
Lavender Mist Sun Daisy
Coral Bells
Snow-drops Anemone
Bergenia
Columbine
Veronica
Creeping Phlox (cascading)
Coreopsis

before

This back yard was not only large, it had a steep slope to contend with. Thanks to many, many truckloads of dirt, plus a retaining wall, it was transformed into a flat, grassy area, which allows space for hobbies (putting green and trampoline) on different levels. Photo by Connie Ellefson.

after

areas and can also serve to discourage foot traffic. Keep these berms short though, or they can look contrived. Cemeterylike burial mounds in your landscape are not ideal!

Berms are the place for the most drought-adapted plants, as the water drains off quickly from a berm. Slow it down with little wells around each plant and mulch. If the plants are not the type that spread by underground rhizomes, or reseeding, the nappy landscape fabric will help to keep whatever mulch you choose in place.

If you ended up with an obscenely long, narrow back yard, and don't really desire to put in a football field, orchard, or vegetable garden big enough to start a roadside stand, don't be afraid to fence or screen some of it off and just ignore it. If water is plentiful some year, you can put in some native grass seed and let nature take its course. Just keep the weeds mowed occasionally so you don't add to your neighbors' problems, or risk repeat visits from the zoning control officers (ZCOs). Even yours truly has gotten a visit from the ZCOs. While I was working on this book, I was also struggling to get a couple of groundcovers going instead of grass. I had to leave town for a week, and the weeds got ahead of me. I was issued a weed citation while I was absent, and was warned against becoming a repeat offender, or I'd have to go to court! I called up the officer, explained what I was trying to do, and she said, "That's OK. We just don't know all the plants yet."

If you do want to use the whole space, the water needs of a big back yard can be curtailed by breaking out a bluegrass area close to the house, creating some sort of transition with a mulched area or other boundary, and then planting a drought-tolerant grass area farther back. If you really need the whole grassed area to be bluegrass, pay close attention to the Soil Improvement, Irrigation, and Maintenance chapters.

a minimal distance from the house for all but carefully hand-watered xeric plants.

If you do have the corner lot where folks are just naturally inclined to cut across the front of your yard, this second option might be the one to adopt, along with a decorative two-rail fence, boulders, iron spikes, or land mines. If your builder left you with "tasteful" gravel margins in these locations, you can keep it if you like the color, adding more as needed, or move it to cover up some of the huge expanse in the back yard.

A little bit of berming adds greatly to the interest generated by these frontline planting

EXISTING MATURE LANDSCAPE, HEAVILY SHADED

You might be itching to cut down some of those trees, especially those that shade your house year-round, blocking light and winter warmth. I don't blame you. Just do take some time to analyze each tree to see whether it is serving some useful as well as aesthetic purpose. The existing trees and shrubs are accustomed to the current amount of air, light, and water they're getting, so it's usually better to make the changes slowly, giving them time to adapt.

The services of a professional arborist could come in very handy here, helping you to assess the health of your mature trees. Some trees might need to go just on the basis of health and safety. Trees weakened by disease or drought or those very close to the house can pose a danger to both life and property if the right storm comes along.

My own mom and stepdad had no idea that a 60-foot, scrawny pine tree located about 5 feet from their vacation cabin was rotted out from the inside. A windstorm came along while they were away, blew it over, and broke the thing right off. The tree crashed down exactly parallel to the house. Ninety degrees to the left, and it would have taken out the whole house and I shudder to think what else!

Always try to retain the deciduous tree(s) on the south and west sides of your landscape. It's easy to become so used to how much cooler these trees keep your house in the summer; take the wrong ones out and you could be absolutely staggered by the scorching difference their removal makes.

Before you cut a tree down, ask yourself: Is this a healthy tree, providing food or shelter for wildlife? The National Arbor Day Foundation even asks us to consider leaving an old or dead tree alone, if it's in a little-used or less visible part of your

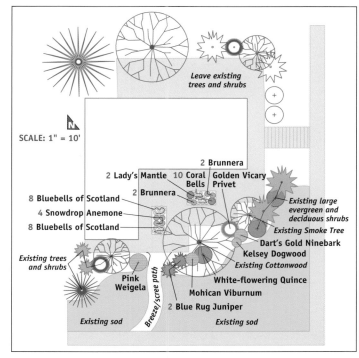

SCALE: 1" = 10'

Leave existing trees and shrubs

2 Brunnera
2 Lady's Mantle 10 Coral Bells Golden Vicary Privet
2 Brunnera
8 Bluebells of Scotland
4 Snowdrop Anemone
8 Bluebells of Scotland

Existing large evergreen and deciduous shrubs
Existing Smoke Tree
Dart's Gold Ninebark
Kelsey Dogwood
Existing Cottonwood
White-flowering Quince
Mohican Viburnum

Existing trees and shrubs

Pink Weigela

Breeze/scree path

2 Blue Rug Juniper

Existing sod   Existing sod

It's hard to believe, but there's actually a beautiful house behind this wall of trees and shrubs. Open up the whole scene with selective deletions and add plants adapted to dappled shade, instead of intense gloom.
Photo by Connie Ellefson.

before

after

Deciduous American plum trees shade this house in the summer and allow light to enter in the winter. Keep large evergreens to the north side of your house to prevent perpetual gloom.

landscape. The dead trees are the only nesting sites for certain birds, owls, and tree frogs. The insects working on breaking down these trees also provide birdfeed. Of course, if you're in a highly urban area, you'll want to think carefully about whether such a tree could be a liability for you.

Light is always a consideration where trees are involved. That huge evergreen on the south side of your house could be adding year-round gloom and blocking out warming winter sun. I, personally, am addicted to light and sunny spaces, so I wouldn't think twice about deep-sixing an extraneous overgrown evergreen on the south side of the house. The same tree on the north or east side might be providing a windbreak. It also might be overshading your neighbor's living area, so give it some thought.

If you can't bear to trash a mature, healthy evergreen, contact your local parks department or golf course, and donate or sell the thing. They'll be happy to receive a tree worth several hundreds of dollars. Some tree-moving contractors are willing to remove the tree with a tree spade with the intent of storing it, and they'll resell it to recoup their own costs. In the phone book, look for someone willing to buy or trade trees, and who has access to a huge tree spade!

Sometimes all it takes to lighten up a mature, overgrown landscape is a concerted effort at thinning out the underbrush. Take out some of the leggy shrubs, and you'll feel better already.

Have you been pouring water on the grass, only to watch it thin more and more over the years because of shade? Switch to a shade-tolerant grass, such as fine fescue, or reduce that lawn area to take advantage of the sunny places. Just be aware that the trees have been using that water you thought you were wasting on the grass, so keep a close eye on them after you remove a big grass area, ensuring that the trees aren't getting drought-stressed. Wean them slowly.

EXISTING BLAH, BARREN YARD

This is actually one of the most enjoyable situations to be faced with: what amounts to a blank slate (or blank clay, as the case may be), so there are no guilty feelings about whether or not to keep a bunch of existing plants you may or may not like. You also have the advantage of being able to assess how plants are doing in their locations in order to spot possible trouble areas that might better be turned over to non-plant material.

Chances are you'll either be switching out your existing lawngrass for a more xeric one, or removing part of your yard from lawn production to other groundcoverings. A common technique for removing part of the lawn is to lay out the new lawn edge with a garden hose and mark the edge with powdered chalk or marker (not spray!) paint, or flour, if you're quite low-tech. Then use an edging spade to cut a division between the two, and spray the future non-grass side with glyphosate or remove the grass with a sod-

cutter. The slice is important when glyphosate is on the agenda, as there's always a little cross-over of roots between the two areas, and this way the chemical won't affect the grass you want to keep.

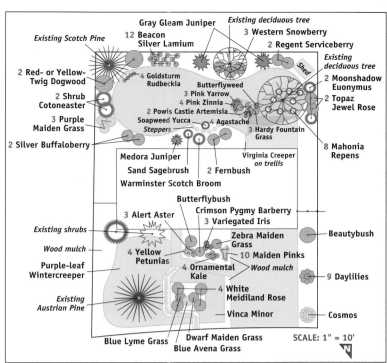

Labels in diagram:
Gray Gleam Juniper · Existing deciduous tree · 3 Western Snowberry · 2 Regent Serviceberry · Existing Scotch Pine · 12 Beacon Silver Lamium · Existing deciduous tree · 2 Red- or Yellow-Twig Dogwood · 4 Goldsturm Rudbeckia · 2 Moonshadow Euonymus · Butterflyweed · 2 Topaz Jewel Rose · 2 Shrub Cotoneaster · 3 Pink Yarrow · 4 Pink Zinnia · 2 Powis Castle Artemisia · 3 Purple Maiden Grass · Soapweed Yucca · 4 Agastache · 8 Mahonia Repens · Steppers · 2 Hardy Fountain Grass · 2 Silver Buffaloberry · Virginia Creeper on trellis · Medora Juniper · Sand Sagebrush · 2 Fernbush · Warminster Scotch Broom · Butterflybush · Crimson Pygmy Barberry · Beautybush · 3 Alert Aster · 3 Variegated Iris · Existing shrubs · Zebra Maiden Grass · Wood mulch · 4 Yellow Petunias · 10 Maiden Pinks · Purple-leaf Wintercreeper · Wood mulch · 9 Daylilies · 4 Ornamental Kale · Existing Austrian Pine · 4 White Meidland Rose · Cosmos · Vinca Minor · Blue Lyme Grass · Dwarf Maiden Grass · Blue Avena Grass · SCALE: 1" = 10'

before

The south-facing back yard features desert plants next to the baking-hot brick house, and colorful flowers out away from the house. A large existing tree near the patio provides shade for people and evergreen groundcover (Mahonia repens). Photos by Connie Ellefson.

before

Groundcovers and grasses keep the yard green and lively year-round without mowing. The protected, partly shady area near the house is the "oasis zone." Thirsty plants here can be raised with less water, thanks to the shade. The soil is sandy at this site, and watering near the house hasn't caused any structural problems in 25 years.

after

after

Large boulders add a rustic tone to this slope.

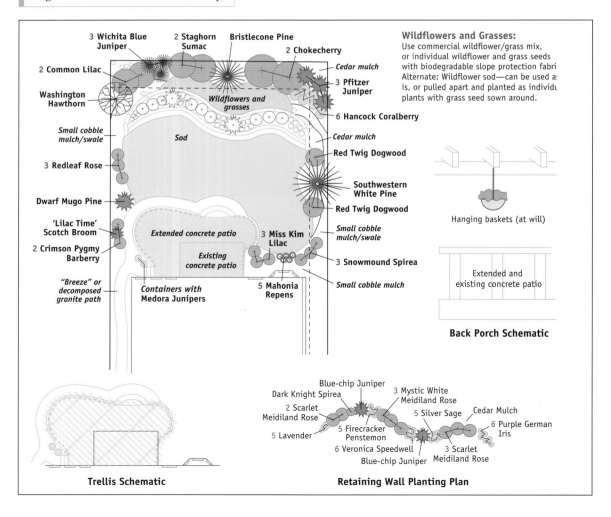

3 Wichita Blue Juniper

2 Staghorn Sumac

Bristlecone Pine

2 Chokecherry

2 Common Lilac

Cedar mulch

3 Pfitzer Juniper

Washington Hawthorn

Wildflowers and grasses

Wildflowers and Grasses:
Use commercial wildflower/grass mix, or individual wildflower and grass seeds with biodegradable slope protection fabri Alternate: Wildflower sod—can be used a: is, or pulled apart and planted as individu plants with grass seed sown around.

Small cobble mulch/swale

Sod

6 Hancock Coralberry

3 Redleaf Rose

Cedar mulch

Red Twig Dogwood

Dwarf Mugo Pine

Southwestern White Pine

Red Twig Dogwood

'Lilac Time' Scotch Broom

Extended concrete patio

3 Miss Kim Lilac

Small cobble mulch/swale

Hanging baskets (at will)

2 Crimson Pygmy Barberry

Existing concrete patio

3 Snowmound Spirea

Small cobble mulch

"Breeze" or decomposed granite path

Containers with Medora Junipers

5 Mahonia Repens

Extended and existing concrete patio

Back Porch Schematic

Trellis Schematic

Blue-chip Juniper

Dark Knight Spirea

3 Mystic White Meidiland Rose

2 Scarlet Meidiland Rose

5 Silver Sage

Cedar Mulch

5 Lavender

5 Firecracker Penstemon

6 Purple German Iris

6 Veronica Speedwell

Blue-chip Juniper

3 Scarlet Meidiland Rose

Retaining Wall Planting Plan

DRY, HOT, SOUTH-FACING SLOPE

This is one situation where bluegrass definitely doesn't belong, but you can get away with buffalograss if you really want turf. Blue grama grass is equally efficient in water use, but it grows taller when unmowed, which adds to your work.

This situation offers you a good chance to showcase the colorful plants available for Xeriscape. Stick to the most dry-adapted plants for this scenario. The height on the top tier, together with some tall plants, makes an excellent screen. Photo by Connie Ellefson.

before

after

The Denver Botanic Gardens has an interesting idea for a plant-based slope treatment. The "crabapple walk" features a variety of species of crabapple trees fairly uniformly spaced with different examples of groundcovers planted in between. It's staggeringly beautiful in the spring during blossom time. A lot of the "crabapple walk" slope is shaded from the south, but a more drought-tolerant version could be devised. Be sure to build little water-catching basins around the trees when you plant them, to help them get established.

A south-facing slope is usually more expansive than the Denver Square slope, so you can get a little more dramatic in scale, if you like. Instead of a small retaining wall, you can bring in some good-sized boulders to retain the ground. This is a good place for a rock garden, as it looks much more natural than the constructed berm some rock garden enthusiasts must resort to.

Whatever material you use for the walls, make sure it harmonizes with the material of your house. As mentioned in the earlier planning section on slopes, the hill may be located at the back of your lot, and slope away from the house, out of sight. In this case, you might get away with a low-cost retaining wall with mulch at the bottom (no plants) to save a lot of water and hassle. Or, depending on the eyesore potential, you could even put a fence at the top and let nature vegetate and maintain the slope. This option is for special situations only, as nature is usually not too tidy or organized about the work it does.

If you're into dry streambeds, a slope is a good place to slip one in. I know I might get lynched for making this statement, but God's truth is

that I think dry streambeds are silly, especially big ones. Little ones with a few artfully fallen autumn leaves aren't so bad. But, in general, dry streambeds don't give me the feeling of "ephemeral water." They give me the feeling of "bone-dry"—more depressing than if they weren't there at all. "The Emperor's New Clothes" comes to mind.

A terrace garden can be built with any number of plant options on the terraces. The easiest to maintain would be drip-irrigated shrub beds with mulch. Cascading rock garden type plants look outstanding in this setting, and some people even use these terraces for vegetable or other specialty gardens, as there is a lot of sun. Just make sure to improve the soil and utilize as much mulch as possible or you'll end up with more water trouble than you would have had with grass.

The most drought-tolerant desert plants make a good choice for specialty gardens. Many of them will thrive in this setting. And, as in the first example in this section, be sure to balance the high-intensity visual impact of a varied terrace wall installation with some smooth, unbroken lines in the rest of the yard.

MOUNTAIN PROPERTY

A Xeriscape in the mountains offers some interesting possibilities and constraints. The bad news is, some of the traditionally available landscape plants used on the plains might not grow at higher elevations, thanks to the shorter growing season. You also might have more shade to deal with than you're used to. The good news is, you probably have more snow and rainfall, cooler temperatures, and, occasionally, a slightly more acid soil than "down below," so there are other plants you can grow without additional irrigation.

A lot of mountain dwellers simply let nature do the landscaping and add a few containers and hanging baskets for bright color accents. For a more extensive flower or vegetable garden, you will probably need to bring in some good-quality soil, as most mountain soils are gravelly or non-existent.

On a cheerier note, the cooler temperatures allow certain flowers such as delphiniums, columbines, and Iceland poppies to fare much better in the mountains than they do on the plains. You can get good ideas for what plants thrive simply by observing eye-catching mature gardens in your area. Chances are their owners have tried a lot of different things, and the plants that make it are truly up to living in the special conditions of the mountains! The Evergreen Garden Club and Metropolitan District (303-674-4759) maintains a Xeriscape Demonstration Garden and several other gardens designed to help mountain dwellers.

The owners of this mountain home were ready for a complete update of their landscape and house, and they opted for more fire-resistant stucco. They removed shrubs and trees too close to the house, added a front hardscape area near the door, and brought in colorful flowers and easily contained shrubs. This had the multiple effects of providing entertainment space, reducing fire risk around the home, and opening up the hillside view of the mountains. And, yes, aspens are ideal here—as opposed to the plains, where they struggle—because this is their native environment. Photo by Connie Ellefson.

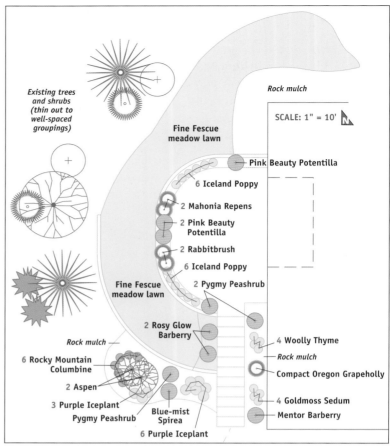

Existing trees and shrubs (thin out to well-spaced groupings)

Rock mulch

SCALE: 1" = 10'

Fine Fescue meadow lawn

Pink Beauty Potentilla

6 Iceland Poppy

2 Mahonia Repens

2 Pink Beauty Potentilla

2 Rabbitbrush

6 Iceland Poppy

2 Pygmy Peashrub

Fine Fescue meadow lawn

2 Rosy Glow Barberry

4 Woolly Thyme

Rock mulch

Rock mulch

Compact Oregon Grapeholly

6 Rocky Mountain Columbine

4 Goldmoss Sedum

2 Aspen

Mentor Barberry

3 Purple Iceplant

Pygmy Peashrub

Blue-mist Spirea

6 Purple Iceplant

before

after

In this mountain landscape, aspens and a rocky berm are a natural transition from the lawn to the surrounding native area. Photo by Connie Ellefson.

Many mountain gardeners are frustrated by the damage that wildlife causes to their landscapes. Unfortunately, when deer and elk are hungry, there is almost nothing they won't eat, so fencing is the only foolproof way to keep them out. Hardcore gardeners have been known to surround ornamental or vegetable gardens with 8-foot-high "elk fencing." Some install these fences around their whole property.

While birds are always welcome, deer, elk, raccoons, and even squirrels, moles, and voles are discouraged by carefully selected plants from a palette that these animals dislike. A thorough brochure on deer-resistance strategies, including a plant list, is the CSU CES Fact Sheet #6.520, "Preventing Deer Damage," available at www.cerc.colostate.edu/factsheet.html. You can access this and other related publications on this website by clicking the "Natural Resources" and then "Wildlife" links.

Reducing Fire Risk

Protecting your mountain home from fire—as well as the surrounding forest from a fire started at your house—has become a high priority in Colorado. An extremely green landscape is actually a good defense against these hazards, but it may or may not be possible depending on your water source. It's illegal to irrigate with most well permits, and a house without drinking water is about as valuable as one that has burned to the ground!

You might have moved to the mountains to get away from all that yard work, but most of the recommended steps for reducing fire risk are of the maintenance, rather than the planting, variety. Remember, a quarter of Colorado's population lives within the "red zone"—6 million acres of forestland at highest risk for wildfire—so you're not alone in this. Here are some maintenance tips for increasing your home's fire resistance:

- Make sure you have a non-flammable or Class A roof—forget the rustic cedar shake shingles.
- Clean out gutters on the roof regularly.
- Move flammables (such as woodpiles!) away from the house. Some sources say this distance should be 15 feet, others say 30 feet, and still others say 100 feet. So, no matter how far, just get that thing away from the house! Some houses have reportedly burned down just from the adjacent woodpile being ignited by a passing fire.
- Remove leaves, needles, and dead branches from underneath shrubs and trees near the house.
- Prune branches that are too close to or overhanging the house, and up to 10–12 feet on conifers.
- Cut brush and shrubs that might be too close to the house and from under the canopy of trees.
- Some nearby trees can be left if there is a distance of at least 10–12 feet between the crowns. Conifers are best kept away from the house, as they tend to contribute plant debris regularly, and all are extremely flammable.

The best defense against fire is to not live in a wildfire area. The second best is to keep the landscape around your house green or sparse. You might feel that removing all trees and shrubs from around your mountain home takes away too much of the enjoyment of it. That's a choice you'll have to make.

Substantial additional information on "defensible space" (buffer zones with increasingly more clear area as you approach the house) is available online or in CSU CES Fact Sheets #6.302, 6.303, and 6.304 (www.cerc.colostate.edu/fact sheet.html). The spaces are extended if your home is on a slope, as fire tends to rush uphill, with the flame front efficiently preheating adjacent vegetation.

If you want to be more proactive about your mountain landscape with respect to fire protection, those brochures cover the subject very well. Some preventative steps include:

- Start with a 3-to-5-foot rock mulch layer directly around the outside of the house/deck. Don't plant anything here except fire-resistant shrubs, which are kept away from windows or ventilation pipes, and are pruned to keep their growth low and compact.
- Any excuse for non-wood hardscape—doing double duty to both create outdoor living space and provide fire protection—or a wider zone of fire-retardant mulch near the house should be taken advantage of.
- Courtyard walls and terrace walls also create fire buffers.
- Plant a "meadow lawn" of fine fescue grass farther out. Keep it mowed regularly, especially as you get closer to the house.
- Make sure your shrubs are well-spaced, or have space around groups of shrubs or small trees.
- Groundcovers with fleshy leaves such as iceplant, vinca minor, and woolly thyme can help slow the spread of fire, especially if they are watered.
- Removing all vegetation also can lead to soil erosion. Better to remove selected plants and do some reseeding to balance fire protection and soil conservation.

In any case, you can at least give your home some protection against fire by keeping all dead materials cleared out of the surrounding area and your close-in plants, whether natural or planted by you, watered in very dry weather if you can.

Xeriscape is right at home in the Colorado mountains.

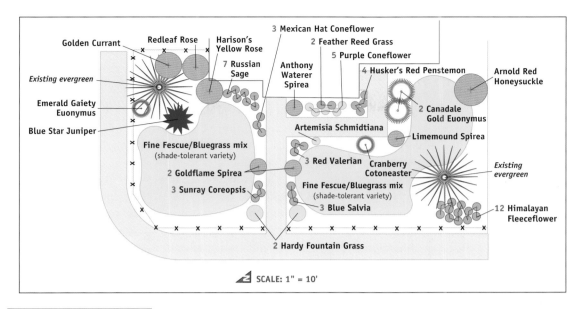

Golden Currant
Redleaf Rose
Harison's Yellow Rose
7 Russian Sage
Anthony Waterer Spirea
3 Mexican Hat Coneflower
2 Feather Reed Grass
5 Purple Coneflower
4 Husker's Red Penstemon
Arnold Red Honeysuckle
Existing evergreen
Emerald Gaiety Euonymus
Blue Star Juniper
2 Canadale Gold Euonymus
Artemisia Schmidtiana
Limemound Spirea
Fine Fescue/Bluegrass mix (shade-tolerant variety)
2 Goldflame Spirea
3 Sunray Coreopsis
3 Red Valerian
Cranberry Cotoneaster
Fine Fescue/Bluegrass mix (shade-tolerant variety)
Existing evergreen
3 Blue Salvia
12 Himalayan Fleeceflower
2 Hardy Fountain Grass
SCALE: 1" = 10'

SPECIAL GOALS

Now that we've covered special "problem" situations, let's talk about some specific goals you might have, like having the most carefree landscape possible, or planting your yard as close to nature as you can get.

LOW-MAINTENANCE XERISCAPE

By now you know that high water demand for landscape plants usually means high maintenance. Xeriscape is a natural for a low-maintenance landscape, as it works to take the issue on squarely.

Do you want grass at all? The lowest-maintenance choice for grass is using a species like buffalograss, which is low enough to remain unmowed and still be considered a "turf." Even if you like it shorter, you'd only need to mow buffalograss about once a month in the summer.

Watering is on a similar frequency, with a little extra needed if you do choose to mow.

Maximizing the use of hardscape usually results in lower maintenance, too. And, if there's no turf in your yard, it might be the only way you and your guests can easily access the landscape.

One key way to reduce maintenance is to make sure all plants have enough room for their maximum size so you don't have to prune them to keep your landscape passable. Unfortunately,

before

after

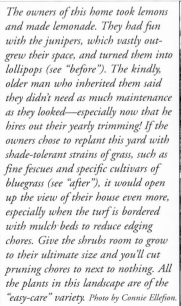

The owners of this home took lemons and made lemonade. They had fun with the junipers, which vastly out-grew their space, and turned them into lollipops (see "before"). The kindly, older man who inherited them said they didn't need as much maintenance as they looked—especially now that he hires out their yearly trimming! If the owners chose to replant this yard with shade-tolerant strains of grass, such as fine fescues and specific cultivars of bluegrass (see "after"), it would open up the view of their house even more, especially when the turf is bordered with mulch beds to reduce edging chores. Give the shrubs room to grow to their ultimate size and you'll cut pruning chores to next to nothing. All the plants in this landscape are of the "easy-care" variety. Photo by Connie Ellefson.

this is going to make things look a little austere for the first couple of years, so steel yourself, or include a few fast-growing temporary plants to fill in for a while.

Numerous books feature lists of plants that require little maintenance, and these make good references when you're making your plan. Shrubs are a safe bet—and this is why you see them almost exclusively on low-maintenance commercial landscapes. It's worth some time to look around at these landscapes, noticing which plants seem to be faring well. I can almost guarantee they are getting little or no maintenance, so if that's your goal, these tough guys are a good choice. I went out on such a mission to a light industrial/office complex area in my town and saw that one of my previously less-favorite plants, Russian sage (see opposite), was at the head of the pack for looking good in neglect-land. Crimson pygmy barberry wasn't far behind.

On the other hand, the home landscaper often has a wider variety of plants to choose from, and if you care to, you can create a design that's much more colorful than the average commercial landscape. Start talking with the owners of garden centers over the winter when they're less busy, and you're likely to get lots of helpful input. These people really love plants and love to talk about them when they're not overwhelmed with business.

When choosing flowers, avoid ones that need staking or deadheading to keep looking their best. Some flowering groundcovers can be neatened up and encouraged to bloom again with just one judiciously executed weed-whacking a year.

ABOVE: *Tulips take care of themselves on this highway planting.*
BELOW: *Naturalized daylilies make an excellent groundcover with a minimum of attention.*

Often, a lower-maintenance plant can be found to use in place of one that you have a fondness for, and the research time you spend now will pay off later! If all else fails, don't begrudge the time your plants ask you to spend on them. Tasks that take you out to the garden help you keep your link with nature.

RIGHT: *Russian sage, one of the most dependable plants for dry, hot locations, survives with little care.*
BELOW: *Basket-of-gold and creeping phlox blanket this slope in the spring and require little or no maintenance, except for an occasional dandelion digging.*

Jim and Dorothy Borland's all-native front yard brightens the neighborhood.

GOING NATIVE

There are a lot of good things to be said for native plant Xeriscapes. They increase the type of habitat needed for native wildlife, they are generally adapted to our extremes of weather, and they help us keep tuned in to the beauty of our specific corner of the world.

The plains wilderness might be just beyond your door, or you might just wish it was. This is a good place to transition quickly to the wild area by using a native turfgrass that you mow close to your house and let grow farther out.

For a truly "natural" look, you've got to be aware of what the West naturally looks like. Joan Woodward, author of *Waterstained Landscapes: Seeing and Shaping Regionally Distinctive Places* (Johns Hopkins University Press, 2000), points out that green growth naturally occurs in the West only in certain areas, such as north-facing slopes, stream corridors, and water-fed edges that catch the runoff from bordering rock surfaces. Woodward, a professor of landscape architecture at California State Polytechnic, suggests we can emulate the way water has touched the landscape in Western history with certain "signatures." She recommends planting evergreens along the north side of the property or planting a "homestead" shade tree at the southwest corner of a home. Other signatures include adding beauty spots of

dry-adapted perennials around the mailbox and fruit-bearing shrubs at the base of some of our fence posts. In the Wild West, these would have been planted by the birds that perched there, Woodward says, so leave one or more posts blank for the future! Native grass and sparse dots of shrubs with boulders (water storage underneath) on south-facing slopes, along with denser plantings on north slopes, also add to the Western theme.

Put these ideas together with the "oasis" concept of Xeriscape—perhaps planting some bright flowers, native roses, or a small kitchen garden near the house just as determined, early Western gardeners did—and you'll have a landscape that not only echoes natural history, but human history.

The biggest thing to be aware of is that native plants will also suffer when our extremes are exceeded, as they were (big time!) in 2002. Using native plants doesn't mean you won't have to give them some TLC, just as you would with a non-native, assuming you want them to live.

Remember, native doesn't necessarily mean only "native to Colorado," considering that nature doesn't really care about state lines. Some of the plants you might like to use are at the northern end of their range in Colorado, and others are at the southern end. I just discovered recently, while looking at a list of wildflowers recommended for Colorado, that the pasqueflower grows as far north as the Arctic Circle, while the Mexican evening primrose is at the north end of its range in this state.

The Internet has made plant research for this book a hundred times easier and more enjoyable than it was a decade ago, as there are multiple entries for virtually any plant you might be thinking about using in your native plant palette. The City of Boulder open space website at www.ci.boulder.co.us/openspace/ has a great section on native plants (along with photos of many species). And the CSU CES website at www.cerc.colostate.edu/factsheet.html is a wealth of information on size, shape, and attributes of native trees, flowers, and shrubs for Colorado.

The University of Colorado Museum of Natural History also has a website at http://cumuseum.colorado.edu that includes a searchable list of native plants by county in Colorado. It's not an exhaustive list, of course; it just includes the plant sitings that have been sent in, but is instructive on which plants are native and grow together right in your

very own region. You could also try the Colorado Native Plant Society website at http://carbon.cudenver.edu/~shill/conps.html.

before

after

The owners of this home treasured their wide-open view of the plains and just wanted to frame it up a little with some cozy color, smoothing the transition from house to plains. All the plants in this landscape are native to Colorado, with the exception of the 'Wichita Blue' juniper, which is itself a cultivar of a native plant. It's not essential to have all native plants, but it is fun to research the topic. And, as you can see, natives can be very colorful.

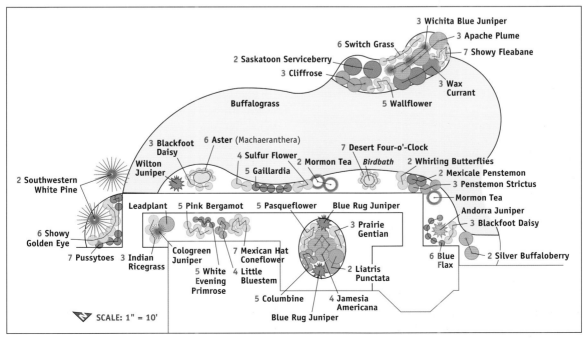

3 Wichita Blue Juniper
3 Apache Plume
6 Switch Grass
7 Showy Fleabane
2 Saskatoon Serviceberry
3 Cliffrose
3 Wax Currant
5 Wallflower
Buffalograss

3 Blackfoot Daisy
6 Aster (Machaeranthera)
7 Desert Four-o'-Clock
Wilton Juniper
4 Sulfur Flower
2 Mormon Tea   *Birdbath*
2 Whirling Butterflies
2 Mexicale Penstemon
5 Gaillardia
3 Penstemon Strictus
2 Southwestern White Pine
Mormon Tea
Andorra Juniper
Leadplant   5 Pink Bergamot   5 Pasqueflower   Blue Rug Juniper
3 Blackfoot Daisy
3 Prairie Gentian
6 Showy Golden Eye
7 Pussytoes   3 Indian Ricegrass
Cologreen Juniper
7 Mexican Hat Coneflower
6 Blue Flax
2 Silver Buffaloberry
5 White Evening Primrose
4 Little Bluestem
2 Liatris Punctata
5 Columbine
4 Jamesia Americana
Blue Rug Juniper

SCALE: 1" = 10'

CHAPTER 3

SOIL ANALYSIS

The second basic principle
of Xeriscape is soil analysis
and improvement.

ABOVE: *Simplify your Xeriscape by using plants adapted to the existing soil.*
OPPOSITE: *Matching the plant species to the soil encourages the plants to flourish.*

Many people just pour fertilizer and other chemicals on a landscape without figuring out whether they're the right additive or even whether they're needed. In xeriscaping, when water conservation is the objective, this sort of willy-nilly chemical assault is counterproductive because most of those chemicals have to be well watered in. To be water-wise, figure out what soil you have and need BEFORE you plant. Appropriate soil can help plants stay healthy so they can fight off the weeds—and it cuts down on watering, as the soil then makes more stored moisture available to them.

Soil analysis means figuring out what sort of soil you have (so you're not planting something that loves sandy silt in a back yard full of clay), and then adding material, if needed, to it to make the most of it. It's absolutely vital to pay attention to your soil because, although many

Runoff from the rocks makes the soil moisture slightly higher next to large boulders.

plants are extremely adaptable to different soil types, they aren't all that way. The type of soil you have affects which plants will grow well without a lot of input, and which will be about impossible, no matter what you do.

There are two schools of thought about how far to go to change the existing soil. If you match the plants with the existing soil, you don't have to amend at all. (That's Plan A.) Or you can plant anything you want as long as you're willing to alter the soil content as much as needed. (Plan B.)

For instance, it is better not to amend the soil (Plan A):

- For native flowers and shrubs. Many are adapted to our native soil and actually languish if given too rich a soil. Desert plants such as penstemons and rabbitbrush are especially susceptible: They get all leggy and floppy and, with penstemons, they live fast and die young.

The tallgrass prairie, an example of which thrives at the Denver Botanic Gardens, flourished in the Midwest, where rainfall is higher and soil is richer. Photo by Connie Ellefson.

- For buffalograss and blue grama grass lawns. Ditto. You can add amendments, but it's usually not necessary, and it just gives the weeds a leg up, too.
- When you want to have a prairie garden, and you live on the prairie.
- When you want to grow aspens and Scotch pine, for example, and you live in the mountains. Both these trees do well in the mountains because they're adapted to the gravelly soil often found there.
- For individual trees and shrubs. See "Trees, Shrubs, and the Limits of Organic Amendments" in the next chapter.

You're seeing the pattern by now.

Examples of when amending is necessary (Plan B) are if:

- You want to grow Kentucky bluegrass, traditional flowers and vegetables, or non-native trees and shrubs.
- You have excessively salty soil, soil with too high a pH, or intractable hardpan. Sometimes raised beds are the only way to garden.
- You want to grow a garden of woodland wildflowers, for instance, and you have the heaviest clay soil imaginable.

THINGS I KNOW ABOUT SOIL

Knowing a little about soil can make it a lot easier to understand how plants grow (or why they're not growing). First and foremost, plant growth is limited by whichever of these factors is the least available: light, root space, heat, air, water, and nutrients. And of these six factors, *soil supplies, in part or completely, all but the light.*

STRUCTURE

Soil is said to have a good structure if individual soil particles group together into granules or crumbs ("aggregates") with air spaces in between ("pores"). It's the structure that allows water and air to penetrate to the roots. Those roots grow through the spaces between the granules, not through the soil itself, and the better the soil is structured, the faster and deeper roots can grow in it.

ELEMENTS

Soil usually contains the following elements in these proportions: water, 25 percent; air, 20–25 percent; organic matter, 5 percent; minerals, 45–55 percent. Minerals are whatever combination of sand, silt, and clay your soil has. The mineral solids of unimproved soil govern the "behavior" of the soil, and the percentage of clay influences the properties of the soil far more than sand and silt. Plants need about the same amount of air as water to thrive. Organic matter is the partially or wholly decayed matter from vegetables or animals that both feeds the plant and increases the ability of the soil to retain water. This is the "good stuff" that everyone wants. In some soils the percentage of organic matter may be near zero.

PLANT INFLUENCE

Not only does soil affect which plants grow on it, but the plants that grow in an area also affect the soil. Trees shed an annual layer of leaf mulch, but don't have a very fibrous root system. As a result, the ground under heavily forested areas has rich organic soil just below the surface, but sometimes-poor soil farther down. This is why when rainforests are cleared for crops, the farming is not always successful—the rich soil layer may be very thin.

Prairie grasses in the Midwest have amazingly fibrous root systems that can reach down 6 feet or more, even for short grasses. As the years pass, the roots die and are replaced, leaving a legacy of humus (organic matter). This makes prairie soil some of the richest in the world. As you move farther west into semiarid and arid lands, vegetative cover gets progressively thinner, and the soil gets correspondingly poorer. Pine needles, which are acidic, drop under a pine tree for many years and gradually turn the soil more acidic—even more hospitable to pines.

TYPES OF SOIL

There are four main types of soil: sand, clay, silt, and loam. Most soil is a mixture of two or three of these elements.

SANDY SOIL is "structure-less" because the particles can't clump together in nice little crumbs of nutritious soil. Sandy soil has too much air space, and the particles are basically tiny, rounded rocks that don't stick together and don't feed

plants. Water goes straight down through it, rapidly taking whatever nutrients dissolved in it down, too, sometimes beyond the reach of the plant roots.

CLAY SOIL is at the opposite end of the spectrum, with flat microscopic particles that stack themselves up like thin dishes wedged together. The "plates" are covered with negatively charged ions that attract and hold water—the reason certain clay soils swell and expand—as well as positively charged ions such as calcium, potassium, and ammonium. It's clay that serves as a reservoir for nutrients, holding them for the plant's use.

Clay soil has very tiny pores. And, because of the high surface tension between the water and the thin plates, as well as the small pore size, it's hard for air and water to move through the soil. As a result, plant roots may variously be denied moisture, suffer oxygen starvation, or even drown! Clay soil can hold up to 4 inches of water in the top foot, but only 2 inches may be available to the plants, as water is held more tightly in the soil than the plant can withdraw it. Water spreads out sideways through clayey soil, not always reaching far enough down into the root system.

SILTY SOIL, a mixture of clay and sand, might sound like it would be just perfect, but it's really just an unsatisfactory hybrid, being either broken-down sand particles or clay-in-the-making (coming from the same parent material as clay, but not yet as chemically or physically weathered). It behaves more like sand, and it is not too thrilling as a soil material unless balanced with sand and clay.

LOAM is what some garden primers talk about when they mention "ideal soil." It has roughly equal portions of sand, silt, and clay. Loam balances the disadvantages of the more extreme soils. It drains well but doesn't dry out too fast. It holds plenty of plant-available water and has enough airspace for healthy plant growth. Turf-grasses and most fleshy plants will have a deeper root system in loam than in clay.

But, alas, ideal soil is very rare. Who in Colorado has ideal soil? Even if it did start out that way, most housing construction strips away the nutritive topsoil. Whatever is left has been compacted, and probably wasn't that good to begin with because it had too much sand or clay!

All this talk about "ideal soil" is pretty silly anyway, as it assumes we all want to grow the same thing. If you want to grow jewel-like alpine flowers, the "ideal soil" is gravelly and low in

Dragon's blood sedum (S. spurium 'Dragon's Blood') *and woolly thyme* (Thymus pseudolanuginosus) *make great rock garden plants, as they fare well in poor soil.*

nutrients—poor soil. If you want to grow back-East perennials, then you need well-drained, humus-rich soil. If you want a cactus garden, your plants will blossom in dry, alkaline soil. You get the picture.

FIGURING OUT WHAT YOU'VE GOT

Do it Yourself

You can make a rough guess about whether you've got clay or sandy soil by rolling a little ball of the soil, moistened slightly, in your hand. If it falls apart quickly when you let go, it's probably *sandy soil,* the structureless one.

The heavy *clay soil* won't move a muscle when you let go; it will just remain motionless in whatever shape you molded it into. Oddly enough, wet compacted clay soil is also structure-less, but for the opposite reason: too much soil and not enough air. This is why the wise gardener doesn't mess with clay soil when it's wet; it just makes things worse.

If your glob of soil behaves somewhere in between those two extremes, it might be *silty soil.* Or, it could also be *loamy soil.*

There's also the question of how much organic matter, or humus, your soil has. Is your soil a dark, rich brown or black color? This is a clue. Humus-y soil is dark, and loose but well-structured. It has loads of nutrients in it, nicely broken down and available, and it causes the birds to sing sweetly in the trees. This is no joke. Rich, humus-y soil means more worms, something birds appreciate! This is what the growers of non-natives live for and sometimes work years to achieve.

Or Use a Pro!

Loam or silt? Humus or not? Don't get a head-ache over this! The pros can tell you what type soil you have—plus a whole lot more—*for a pittance.* It's not just about how much sand, clay, or organic matter your soil has. There are other chemical factors unique to the drought-prone West that can put a snag in your garden plans, such as alkalinity vs. acidity (pH), and salt in the water and soil. It's a real trial to significantly alter the pH, structure, and salinity of the soil in a big way. So, it's better to have the full story before you make your plant decisions.

In Colorado, our industrious and efficient Colorado State University Cooperative Extension Service (CSU CES) makes getting a soil test about as easy as it could be—and very inexpensive, too. For around $18, you can get soil tested for pH, electrical conductivity, organic matter content, salinity, and several elemental nutrients such as nitrogen, potassium, and iron. (Back in 1992 the fee was $15, so inflation doesn't really run rampant at the state's soils lab.)

Not only that, but CSU CES also includes suggested remedies for problem soil. Be sure to spend the extra four bucks for the salinity test; it's worth it! (More about salinity further on in this chapter.) To get a detailed analysis of your soil, contact the university's Soil, Water, and Plant Testing Laboratory at 970-491-5061. You can either call for a sample bag and instructions or look for all the information online at www.colostate.edu. Search for "soil testing lab."

Another thing that you might choose to leave to the pros is dealing with hardpan. Sometimes topsoil has a tough, compacted soil layer a few inches down that is very difficult for plant roots to penetrate and can cause extremely poor drainage. It might be a natural formation, or it might have been caused by heavy equipment compacting the subsoil during construction or by foot traffic on moist clay soil.

I have sandy soil in Aurora and was puzzled to find what seemed to be a hardpan layer about 6–8 inches down. Lise Mahnke, Denver-area landscape lecturer and designer, told me it could be there because when this land was once farmland, that's the depth to which it would have been plowed!

A clayey subsoil that gets wet while exposed can dry to a rocklike hardness. If the hardpan layer is not too thick, you might be able to break it up by having your soil plowed to a depth of 18 inches or more. (When the rototiller bounces off the existing soil, you know you have hardpan and might want to call in professional help.) A landscape contractor will likely scarify the surface first with the ripper teeth of a front-end loader, then do the plowing or tilling.

For a thicker hardpan layer, installing a system of drain tiles will improve the situation, or you can get the entire planting area excavated with heavy equipment to a depth of about 24 inches —as Denver rosarian and lecturer Joan Franson did to grow roses in her heavy clay soil—then have organic matter thoroughly mixed in. Franson lined the bed with gravel for drainage before filling it with rich, purchased soil.

If correcting this problem is looking like more of a hassle and expense than it's worth, use raised

OPPOSITE: *Clay soil doesn't slow daffodils down!*

Clay Soil Lovers

Flowers and Groundcovers

BOTANICAL NAME	COMMON NAME
Ajuga reptans	Carpet bugle
Alchemilla mollis	Lady's mantle
Aster spp.	Aster
Bergenia spp.	Pigsqueak
Buchloe dactyloides	Buffalograss
Festuca arundinacea	Tall fescue
Helenium spp.	Sneezeweed
Lamium spp.	Dead nettle
Mahonia repens	Creeping mahonia
Narcissus spp.	Daffodil
Rudbeckia fulgida 'Goldsturm'	Black-eyed Susan
Solidago spp.	Goldenrod

Trees and Shrubs

BOTANICAL NAME	COMMON NAME
Cotoneaster spp.	Cotoneaster
Mahonia spp.	Oregon grapeholly
Quercus bicolor	Swamp white oak
Ribes spp.	Currant
Symphoricarpus spp.	Coralberry

Sandy Soil Lovers

In plant references, those that ask for well-drained soil for your plant are usually referring to sandy soil. Many of the plants listed here will also grow in more clayey soil, but they might not grow as quickly.

Plumbago (Ceratostigma plumbaginoides) *comes up very late in the spring and looks stunning in the fall—definitely worth the wait.*

Flowers and Groundcovers

BOTANICAL NAME	COMMON NAME
Achillea spp.	Yarrow
Alyssum spp.	Alyssum
Antirrhinum spp.	Snapdragon
Armeria spp.	Thrift
Bouteloua gracilis	Blue grama grass
Ceratostigma plumbaginoides	Plumbago
Dianthus spp.	Pinks
Gaillardia spp.	Blanket flower
Gypsophila spp.	Baby's breath
Iris spp.	Iris
Kniphofia uvaria	Red-hot poker
Penstemon spp.	Penstemon
Perovskia atriplicifolia	Russian sage
Salvia spp.	Salvia
Sedum spp.	Sedum
Thymus spp.	Thyme
Tropaeolum spp.	Nasturtium
Tulipa spp.	Tulip, especially species tulips

Trees and Shrubs

BOTANICAL NAME	COMMON NAME
Amelanchier spp.	Serviceberry
Buddleia davidii	Butterfly bush
Caryopteris x clandonensis	Blue-mist spirea
Cercocarpus spp.	Mountain mahogany
Chamaebatiaria millefolium	Fernbush
Chrysothamnus spp.	Rabbitbrush
Cowania mexicana	Cliffrose
Cytisus spp.	Broom
Fallugia paradoxa	Apache plume
Hippophae rhamnoides	Sea buckthorn
Pinus spp.	Pine
Pinus mugo spp.	Mugo pine
Potentilla spp.	Potentilla
Rhus spp.	Sumac
Robinia pseudoacacia	New Mexico locust
Sophora japonica	Japanese pagoda tree

Creeping mahonia (Mahonia repens) *is an excellent groundcover with year-round interest.*

Three-leaf sumac (Rhus trilobata) *is a colorful and adaptable Colorado native.*

Cutleaf sumac (Rhus typhina laciniata) *and rabbitbrush* (Chrysothamnus nauseosus) *make an excellent pair for sandy soil.*

Snow-in-summer (Cerastium tomentosum) *spreads enthusiastically in sunny spots to cover lots of ground in many soil types.*

Adaptable Plants

These are plants that can deal with both sandy and clayey soils.

Flowers and Groundcovers

BOTANICAL NAME	COMMON NAME
Antennaria rosea	Pussytoes
Calamagrostis acutifolia 'Karl Foerster'	Feather reed grass
Campanula rotundifolia	Harebell
Cerastium tomentosum	Snow-in-summer
Delosperma spp.	Iceplant
Gallium odoratum	Sweet woodruff
Linum perenne	Perennial blue flax
Parthenocissus quinquefolia	Virginia creeper
Polygonum spp.	Fleeceflower
Ratibida columnifera	Mexican hat coneflower

Trees and Shrubs

BOTANICAL NAME	COMMON NAME
Acer spp.	Maple
Berberis thunbergii	Red barberry
Catalpa spp.	Catalpa
Celtis spp.	Hackberry
Ceratoides lanata	Winterfat
Crataegus spp.	Hawthorn
Forestiera neomexicana	New Mexico privet
Fraxinus spp.	Ash
Juniperus spp.	Juniper
Koelreuteria paniculata	Golden raintree
Kolkwitzia amabilis	Beautybush
Prunus spp.	Plum
Quercus spp.	Oak
Rhus trilobata	Three-leaf sumac
Rosa glauca	Red-leaf rose
Spiraea spp.	Spirea
Yucca spp.	Yucca

beds for your plantings, filling them with good-quality soil and making sure they are deep enough for plant growth.

MATCHING PLANTS TO SOIL

Once you know what kind of soil you have, you'll be able to see if it's going to limit you too much, or if you'll have enough plant choices to work with. Certain plants will be a "better fit" for your soil than others. So, if you're a Plan A (little or no soil amending) person, those are the ones you'll plant. I've provided a few lists for you (at left), depending on what kind of soil you have. Note the list of adaptable plants, species that grow in a wide range of soils from sandy to clayey.

WHAT'S IN THE SOIL

GOT SALT?

Salt not only wreaks havoc with your blood pressure —it can also spell trouble for your plants! Plant symptoms of high-salt soils include poor germination and growth, scorched and yellow leaves or browned and withered leaf margins (salt burn), and sometimes a dark, bluish green color. Basically salt robs plants of water because it causes water to move out of the roots.

In arid parts of the West, soils may contain high concentrations of salts that have developed from weathering of minerals naturally found in the soils. Add to this the possible addition of salt from irrigation water, inorganic fertilizers, chemical amendments, and manures. Poor drainage is another culprit, either within the soil itself or on the surface.

Strategies to combat this condition include:

- Improving internal drainage in the soil by adding organic amendments.
- Making surface drainage better with drain tile systems.
- Avoiding the use of high-salt amendments.
- Using raised beds. (In extreme cases, you can do all plantings on berms of low-salt soil brought into your site. These raised beds are underlain with a gravel and/or fabric barrier to prevent capillary action from drawing the salt up into the new soil.)

Feel like you're going to war? In terms of real numbers, the high end of low-salt concentrations in soil is listed at roughly 2.0 millimhos (the unit for measuring soil salinity) per centimeter. Above this level, sensitive plants such as roses, most maples, pines, and most viburnums show symptoms of salt burn. Above 3.0 mmhos/cm, raspberries, strawberries, beans, carrots, and onions also begin to burn.

Salt-Tolerant Plants

Here are some of the tough-guy plants that can take higher soil-salinity levels.

Trees with Moderate Salt-Tolerance
(4.0–6.0 mmhos/cm)

BOTANICAL NAME	COMMON NAME
Acer negundo	Boxelder
Betula populifolia	Gray birch
Celtis occidentalis	Hackberry
Fraxinus excelsior	European ash
F. quadrangulata	Blue ash
Juniperus scopulorum	Rocky Mountain juniper
J. virginiana	Eastern redcedar
Koelreuteria paniculata	Golden raintree
Maclura pomifera	Osage orange
Robinia pseudoacacia	Black locust
Sophora japonica	Japanese pagoda tree, Chinese scholar tree
Ulmus pumila	Siberian elm

Trees with High Salt-Tolerance (6.0–8.0 mmhos/cm)

BOTANICAL NAME	COMMON NAME
Amelanchier canadensis	Shadblow serviceberry
Crataegus crus-galli	Cockspur hawthorn
Pinus thunbergii	Japanese black pine
Ptelea trifoliata	Wafer ash
Thuja occidentalis	American arborvitae

Shrubs with Moderate to High Salt-Tolerance
(4.0–8.0 mmhos/cm)

BOTANICAL NAME	COMMON NAME
Caragana arborescens	Siberian pea shrub
Juniperus chinensis 'Pfitzerana'	Pfitzer juniper
J. conferta	Japanese shore juniper
J. horizontalis	Creeping juniper
Lonicera tatarica	Tatarian honeysuckle
Potentilla spp.	Potentilla
Rhamnus frangula	Glossy buckthorn
Spiraea vanhouttei	Vanhoutte spirea

Creeping juniper (Juniperus horizontalis) *and its multiple cultivars cope well with salty soil.*

Shrubs with Very High Salt-Tolerance
(above 8.0 mmhos/cm)

BOTANICAL NAME	COMMON NAME
Atriplex canescens	Four-wing saltbush
Baccharis halimifolia	Groundsel
Cytisus scoparius	Scotch broom
Hippophae rhamnoides	Sea buckthorn
Rhamnus cathartica	Common buckthorn
Rosa rugosa	Rugosa rose
Shepherdia canadensis	Buffaloberry

Grasses with Very High Salt-Tolerance
(ranked from lowest to highest, 8.0–18.0 mmhos/cm)

BOTANICAL NAME	COMMON NAME
Agropyron smithii	Western wheatgrass
A. elongatum	Tall wheatgrass
Distichlis stricta	Saltgrass
Puccinellia distans	Alkaligrass
Pymus canadensis	Canada wildrye
Sporobolus airoides	Alkali sacaton

SOURCE: Dr. James R. Feucht and Jack D. Butler, *Landscape Management: Planting and Maintenance of Trees, Shrubs and Turfgrasses* (Van Nostrand Reinhold Company, 1988).

Golden raintree (Koelreuteria paniculata) *is one of the few summer-blooming trees.*

Bluegrass grows poorly at or above 4.0 mmhos/cm, and most landscape plants will show injury when the reading is between 4.0 and 8.0.

If you're a Plan B person and you want to try to amend for salinity, see "Salinity Solutions" in the next chapter for the dos and don'ts of salinity amending. For Plan A (no amending) people who are willing to live with the salty soil situation, see the above list.

SWEET OR SOUR SOIL OR pH

Don't ask me where this goofy cute-ism came from, but it's supposed to be a fun way to say whether a soil is alkaline (sweet) or acid (sour)— in other words, whether your soil is high or low in pH (percent Hydrogen).

Not too long ago, a rich California couple moved to Montrose, Colorado, and insisted they wanted azaleas and rhododendrons in their landscape. Their landscape advisor tried to steer them clear with the truth about pH, and how the soil was far too alkaline for these beautiful plants. He warned them the shrubs would not live more than a very few seasons in such inhospitable soil. The wife replied, "I don't care if they die every year. I'll just have them replaced!"

Well, for sure, you can outsmart Mother Nature with a lush enough budget if you're determined to. But, let's face it, those plants aren't going to get very big—so who's outsmarted whom?

In xeriscaping, as in any other low-maintenance gardening effort, it's far better to pick plants that can grow in the range of your soil's existing pH than to try to alter it substantially. Soil pH is one of the chemical variables that affects whether you'll be able to grow certain plants. Fortunately, many plants are tolerant of a wide pH range, but there are limits. And, though it's relatively simple to add sufficient amounts of humus to improve the soil's organic matter, *you're fighting an uphill battle in trying to permanently and significantly alter the pH of the soil.* Because you can't control the factors that made the soil the way it is, such as the underlying material, the amount of rainfall, and the pH of your irrigation water, there are no quick fixes here.

Soil pH affects plant growth by influencing the availability of certain essential nutrients. When soil pH is between 6.0 and 7.5, nutrients such as phosphorus, calcium, potassium, and magnesium are most available to plants.

As it drops below that range into an acidic condition, these nutrients become insoluble and less available for uptake by the plant, while iron, trace minerals, and some toxic elements such as aluminum become more available. Phosphorus, iron, and many trace minerals become insoluble and unavailable when the soil alkalinity rises above pH 8.0.

Soil pH also affects nitrogen availability because the nitrogen is actually bound up in organic matter. It must be converted by soil bacteria into forms usable by the plants. When the pH is too high or too low, this bacterial activity decreases dramatically and little nitrogen is made available to the plants.

Remember that pH, like decibels, is a logarithmic scale, so a soil with a pH of 5.0 is 10 times more acidic than one with a pH of 6.0. Turfgrasses prefer neutral soil (6.5–7.5). It doesn't happen much in Colorado, but if you live in an area with acid soil, it's necessary to amend the soil where the grass goes to make it more neutral.

On p. 79 of the next chapter, I include a chart that shows the quantities of chemical soil amendment needed to raise or lower pH to the neutral level. Or, you could save yourself some hassle by picking a turfgrass adapted to your soil's existing pH level. If not, your irrigation water might be acid or alkaline and could hasten the soil's return to its original pH. Then you have to fret about what's wrong with the grass, and eventually do this again.

A NUTRITIOUS SOIL

People need vitamins, amino acids, and minerals to grow. Plants need chemical elements. At least 15 are essential for plant growth:

- Carbon, oxygen, and hydrogen make up about 90–95 percent of the dry weight of the plant and are obtained from the carbon dioxide of the air and the water of the soil. They make up the plant structure.
- Nitrogen, phosphorus, and potassium, obtained from soil, are used in the metabolism of plant structure, especially in forming proteins and chlorophyll. This is why nitrogen availability affects the greenness of plants.
- Calcium and magnesium are usually deficient in acid soils. They increase root hair growth and help in photosynthesis.
- Sulfur is obtained from soil, especially organic matter, irrigation water, and gypsum. It heightens green color in grass, improves cold tolerance, and helps in metabolism.
- Iron, zinc, manganese, copper, boron, and molybdenum are micronutrients. Usually none are needed on acid soil, though iron might be needed on alkaline soils. The function of these elements is not completely understood, but they are thought to be part of enzymes that regulate plant metabolism. Deficiencies usually cause slow growth, but, except for iron, deficiencies in the soil are uncommon.

The soil test results from a lab should note any deficiencies that need correcting and should recommend solutions.

If you plan to amend with wood products such as sawdust or wood chips, you can prevent a temporary nitrogen deficiency in the soil by adding 2 pounds of a complete fertilizer such as 10-6-4, or ¼ pound of ammonium sulfate, for each 100 square feet at planting time. The microbes in the soil that break down these materials tie up some of the nitrogen in the soil for a few months, then let go of it again. This happens most often with sawdust, as it has more surface area.

CHAPTER 4

SOIL IMPROVEMENT

The purpose of soil amendments, other than to provide pure nutrients, is to improve the soil's structure.

ABOVE: *Neither buffalograss nor the spectacular desert candle, or foxtail lily* (Eremurus stenophyllus var. bungei), *requires much soil improvement.*
OPPOSITE: *A little soil improvement gives you a wider selection for your plant palette.*

ORGANIC AMENDMENTS

When I was writing this book's parent, I picked up Beth Chatto's *The Dry Garden,* a book originally published in 1983 in London and updated several times since then, most recently in the late '90s, and adapted for American gardeners. Though it was well-known in Xeriscape circles, I had resisted it because I couldn't imagine what I could learn on the subject from someone who lives in a country that drips constantly—or so I thought!

I was extra happy to find that Chatto lives in an area that receives an annual rainfall of about 20 inches, not much higher than the 15 or so inches a year we have in Colorado. Furthermore, she says, she often gardens through a summer-long drought and on such poor soil that "even the native weeds sometimes curl up and die."

In a recent addition to her series on the Dry Garden, Chatto has a newer book out called *Beth Chatto's Gravel Garden: Drought-Resistant Planting Through the Year* (Frances Lincoln, 2000). In it she further characterizes her gardening environment as "possibly the driest, and most wind-swept soil in England." Sounds like Rocky Flats to me! This book lovingly describes the most drought-tolerant plants of all, those that survive without watering in dry, stony soil.

I was much struck with the simplicity of her statement, "I really don't hold with watering." Even as a more-water-conscious-than-average American, I realized such a straightforward position on how to structure landscape watering had never occurred to me.

Her secret is soil improvement. Every one of the hundreds of plants she has installed in her country gardens gets an ample measure of moisture-retentive organic material mixed into the planting hole.

And, because organic material eventually breaks down, she will rejuvenate a worn-out-looking perennial bed, sometimes after six or seven years, by actually digging everything up, mixing in organic matter again, and dividing and replanting the plants. Tiring, but true.

Plant choice figures in, too. Chatto noted that early in her gardening career she was occasionally given bog-loving plants, which she attempted to raise. But no matter how much organic material she mixed into their planting holes, they would die. Rather than change her determination not to water, she evolved a plant palette more adaptable to the climate and soil.

Organic amendment to all types of soil improves structure, or the soil's water- and air-holding capacity.

A good soil is one that supports healthy plant life and also conserves moisture. *Basically, the purpose of soil amendments, other than to provide the pure nutrients mentioned in the last chapter, is to improve the soil's structure.*

Jim Feucht, Ph.D., retired professor of landscape plants at Colorado State University, used to say that most of the soils sent to his lab for testing contained adequate nutrition; they just needed some help with the structure.

To improve structure in sandy soil, we want to increase its ability to retain both moisture and nutrients for the plant's use. In sandy soil, the humus found in well-decomposed amendments such as compost and aged manures acts as tiny reservoirs for holding water and dissolved nutrients, so the soil stays moist longer.

Improving structure in clay soils means increasing aeration and drainage. The humus provides a base for soil particles to gather onto, forming aggregates that do exactly what we need: increase aeration and drainage. Fibrous materials such as wood chips, peat, bark, or straw are best for this purpose.

In any soil, the breakdown of organic matter is accomplished by microorganisms that produce, in the process, humic acid. This chemical is believed to help bind particles of soil together, further enhancing the structure-building process of the soil.

One of the drawbacks of organic materials is that they break down sooner or later, sometimes

within a few months. Especially in sandy soils, organic matter eventually becomes small enough to be washed away and has to be renewed periodically.

These amendments break down in weeks to months:

- Grass clippings
- Manures
- Composts

These decompose slowly, sometimes over several years:

- Peat
- Hardwood bark
- Wood chips (redwood, cedar)

Including some of both of these types of organic materials in your soil amending can give you fast as well as long-lasting improvement in the soil's structure. Obviously, organic amendments are most successful where the soil will be reworked regularly, such as in gardens and annual flowerbeds. If possible, plan to amend poor soil every year and build up its quality gradually.

Generally, 3 cubic yards per 1,000 square feet (a layer of 1¼–1½ inches) per year is usually the recommended limit, especially on salty soils. However, with turf, building up the soil slowly isn't very practical, unless you care to get out and spread a thin layer of compost or manure on your lawn every year. With turf grasses you really only have the one chance, so a lot of contractors like to beef that up a little, applying 4 to 5 cubic yards per 1,000 square feet.

Many Xeriscape groundcovers do well with little or no soil improvement.

TREES, SHRUBS, AND THE LIMITS OF ORGANIC AMENDMENTS

In some cases, organic amendment is *not* helpful, and might actually stunt plant growth. To be honest, I'm so used to amending everything I plant, it's hard even for me to get my mind around this next bit. But it's hard to argue with science.

Several universities around the country conducted long-term studies on the impact of adding organic soil amendments to the planting holes of trees and shrubs. *It was found at each site that trees and shrubs planted without organic amendments developed more extensive root systems and stronger top-growth than those planted with amendments.* Apparently the struggle the "unamended" trees had to go through to become established led to their increased vigor later on.

Carl Whitcomb, Ph.D., now retired from Oklahoma State University, did one such study. Side-by-side comparisons (see below) showed a substantial increase in the size of trees grown without organic soil amendments compared to those grown with amendments.

If the quality of soil in the planting hole is enriched too much compared to the surrounding soil, or if the artificial medium container-grown plants are raised in is very different from the soil they're planted in, a barrier is created. Roots then have difficulty moving out into the poorer soil, and there is reduced soil volume available for absorbing water and nutrients.

By themselves, the seedlings grown with amendments did not appear to have been hindered, as they looked healthy and well shaped. But compared to the test group, they were about half the size after a few years. Photo by Carl Whitcomb.

Organic amendments can cause other problems in the planting holes of large plants. These amendments may hold too much moisture, which most roots don't tolerate. When the roots begin to grow into the soggy amended soil, they suffocate. Conversely, when the amendments dry out, they can be difficult to rewet, so even though the soil outside the planting hole may be moist, within the hole it could become too dry.

The problem, Dr. Whitcomb explained, comes when we amend *only* the planting hole for a tree or shrub. The plant roots tend to remain in the hole, thus limiting the size of the plant. *If you*

Coral bells (Heuchera sanguinea), *blue avena grass* (Helictotrichon sempervirens), *and catmint* (Nepeta x faasenii) *thrive in the soil of Tim LaPan's garden.*

have the opportunity to amend the entire planting bed for a group of new trees or shrubs, then the plants can benefit from the organic amendments.

I talked to Dr. Whitcomb recently, and he's still sticking with his story. He said several university testers have tried to prove him wrong on this matter, only to end up confirming his results.

Doug Welsh, Ph.D., horticulture professor and extension specialist at Texas A&M University, and former president of the National Xeriscape Council, confirms that this research still stands.

"I wouldn't recommend the use of organic amendments in just the planting holes of trees unless the soil is extremely rocky."

When incorporating organic amendments, always try to spread about one-third of the amendment over the soil, till that in to a depth of 4–6 inches, and then spread the remainder of the amendment and till it in. This way a sharp line of unmixed layers won't form between the existing and improved soil; there will be a more gradual transition.

WORM BEDS

You could do worse than to get some assistance with soil building from your slimy friends in the animal kingdom! According to the U.S. Department of Agriculture's National Resources Conservation Center, worms do all of these for the soil:

- Help increase nutrient availability from organic matter to plant. As they process soil through their stomachs, the "castings" (feces or poop) that emerge have many more microbes in them than what went into the worm. The microbes are what we count on to convert that organic matter into nutrients.
- Increase water infiltration. The burrows worms create while eating their way through the soil allow more water to drain into the soil instead of running off.
- Create channels for root growth. These same burrows, lined with nutrients, allow roots to grow faster through the soil.
- Mix soil and improve its structure. Worms bring soil up to the surface from deeper regions and carry organic matter down. Their castings make nice clumps (or aggregates), which are preferred in a good soil. Worms can turn over the top 6 inches of soil all by themselves in 10 to 20 years.

Worms also bury and shred plant residue when they take it down to their lairs. Which brings me to the more proactive part of this discussion: Worm populations go down when the amount of organic matter goes down, so you can encourage your group of worms by setting aside a small area in your garden for recycling your non-meat, non-dairy food scraps.

You can even create your own worm bin in order to harvest those black gold castings easily. "Denver Recycles"—part of the City and County of Denver Public Works/Solid Waste Management department—explains in a pamphlet that the best worms for such a task are red wiggler worms. These worms recycle fruit and vegetable trimmings, tea bags, coffee grounds and filters, used paper towels, and even worm bin pamphlets!

According to Denver Recycles, almost 11 percent of the waste produced by Denver residents is recyclable food waste. I'll bet it's similar in your community, no matter where you live in Colorado. So here's another chance to be public-spirited and reap some rewards, too. Those castings are hot stuff, from what I hear, containing many more times the nitrogen (and other nutrients) as plain old soil.

INORGANIC SOIL AMENDMENTS

Inorganic amendments are used to improve the structure of clayey or sandy soil. Sand was once recommended for loosening tight clay soil, but experience showed this to be futile. You had to add *tremendous* quantities of sand in order to counter the effect of the clay and get anything but adobe. Forget the sand.

It's better to select another soil amendment to lighten clay soil. Plan B people, those who choose to amend, can remove an amount of soil substantially larger than the root ball from a planting hole and replace it with another soil blend that better suits the plant. Plan A people, non-amenders, would choose to simply use plants that do well in clay soil.

Inorganic amendments used to open up clay soil include perlite (heat-treated limestone), vermiculite (heat-treated mica), and cross-linked polyacrylamide (CLP). Compared to organic amendments, these elements are more expensive, but they last much longer. (See p. 77 of the "Organic and Inorganic Soil Amendments" section for more detailed information on these three amendments.)

LAST WORD ON SOIL AMENDMENTS

Dr. Carl Whitcomb has completed another interesting study on soil prep in the intervening years since 1990, when I first talked with him. He and his cohorts dug several test holes with a tree spade—and no other soil preparation—then transplanted a tree into each using the same spade. With another batch, large rectangular holes were dug, much larger than the tree spade diameter, and soil was loosened within the holes —again, with no other soil preparation.

He tested the soil density of the larger holes in March, when the test began, and in September of the same year. He found that the increased growth of the trees in the loosened-soil holes at the end of the first growing season was astonishing. Even more amazing was that by then, the soil in the test holes had settled back to the identical density of the surrounding soil! "Apparently," says Dr. Whitcomb, "you can't significantly change how the soil particles settle down and group together again [at least without amendments], but just the amount of loosening we did at planting time made a huge difference in getting the transplants off to a good start." Word to the wise!

Organic and Inorganic Soil Amendments

The following is a partial list of soil amendments useful for xeriscaping. They fall into two categories — organic and inorganic. Each has its uses in improving soils of various types.

ORGANIC AMENDMENTS

The important thing to remember about organic amendments is that they are a temporary measure. The nutrients and bulk available in them will eventually be broken down by the organisms that digest them. They will get lawns off to a good start, but can't be relied on indefinitely. However, they're invaluable in the right setting to provide nutrients and improve soil structure.

Advantages: Change chemistry of soil. Enhance physical structure. Add nutrients. Hold water. Are fairly inexpensive.

Disadvantages: Temporary fix.

Compost

A lively population of soil organisms, including worms, bacteria, and fungi, along with the organic matter helps regulate plant growth by increasing nutrient supplies. This is called "living soil." Chemicals such as fertilizers, fungicides, pesticides, and the other –cides damage the community of beneficial soil organisms and kill the living soil. Compost can help restore it.

Compost is the most cost-effective soil amendment because you simply recycle organic matter from your own landscape, thereby keeping the nutrients on-site instead of hauling them away. It's also commercially available nationwide, and a certification process documenting pH, nutrients, textures, and many other standards is in the works.

Composting allows microbes to break down plant trimmings sufficiently so that the nutrients in them are released for the use of living plants. It basically speeds up what nature already does with all dead organic material.

The idea is to layer — or mix, for faster results, according to research from *Organic Gardening* magazine —various types of organic materials that will break down fairly easily (within two to six months) in a heap or bin of some type up to 4 feet tall. Try to balance dried materials (called "browns" in the composting world), and freshly cut yard wastes ("greens") for a good mix of carbon and nitrogen in the compost.

Keep the pile suitably moist but not too soggy, and turn the material every other week with a pitchfork or spading fork to aerate, which keeps the pile "working" aerobically instead of anaerobically (much less smelly). You can cover it with a plastic tarp most of the time, which will keep the moisture and temperature where they're supposed to be.

About 20 percent of what goes to a landfill is yard waste that could be composted. In Denver alone this amounts to about 50,000 tons annually. So save yourself

Compost bins can fit into many landscape styles from extra-organized to rustic, and they all will help you turn a pile of garden leftovers into a rich, dark soil amendment well worth having.

some bucks on lawn bags and organic soil amendments and use what's available to you.

There are books, pamphlets, websites, classes, and demonstration gardens available with all the how-to on composting. If dozens of people haven't gotten their Ph.D.s in composting, I'll eat my hat. The information is definitely out there.

Manure

Barnyard manure has long been a favorite soil amendment. The type of manure is not important, though poultry manure is much higher in nitrogen, so it should have been aged for at least a year. Basically, if it smells, it's risky to use in your landscape. Xeriscape pioneer Ken Ball saw a complete failure of a show-home landscape with under-aged poultry waste. It was stinky in more ways than one.

Fresh manure is too high in ammonia. Avoid it or allow it to lie fallow in the soil for at least six months before applying, or you run the risk of burning the plant

Organic Amendments (continued)

roots. Heat-treating kills weed seeds that might be in manure. Heat-treated, dried manure is available in bags for home garden use.

Dairy barnyard manure might be available free from a commercial stable, but it could be moderately salty; it should be composted thoroughly before use. Steer manure is often very salty.

Colorado State University advises us that home composting systems rarely reach the necessary temperatures (130–140 degrees) needed to kill pathogens in fresh manure, so better to use home-composted manure only on nonfood gardens.

Leaf Mold

Leaf mold is especially useful for woodland wildflower gardens because it helps build soil similar in structure to the plant's native environment. Leaves can take up to two years to decompose into soft, spongy leaf mold suitable for amending the soil.

A quick way to create leaf mold is to chop the leaves up by running over them with a lawnmower that has a bag attachment to catch the small pieces. Create a bin by driving four 5-foot grooved metal posts a foot deep into the soil in the shape of a square. Then surround the posts with 4-foot-wide, 1-inch-square chicken wire. Layer chopped-up leaves with acid soil, if available, hollowing out the top each time to hold water.

This method makes turning the leaf mold easier and can be used for regular compost piles, too. You simply lift the wire cage off and set it to one side, fork the material to aerate it, and replace the cage.

Sawdust and Other Wood Products

Clay soils are helped by the addition of sawdust or bark chips, which open the soil without holding water. Nitrogen must be added when raw wood products are used because they use up a lot of nitrogen in their decomposition. If you're using raw wood products, add 2 to 3 pounds of high-nitrogen fertilizer to each 1-inch layer spread over 100 square feet, or add ½ pound of actual nitrogen per 10 cubic feet of wood product.

Most commercial sources of wood products for soil amendment have been fortified with nitrogen to prevent this problem. Bark products have less of a nitrogen-robbing effect on the soil.

If not chopped small enough, wood chunks will take a long time to decompose, which may suit your needs.

Topsoil

In the semiarid West, commercial topsoil could fall under the category of "nice work if you can get it." Given the extreme thinness of topsoil in general, it's hard to imagine that companies are able to locate sources for tons of real topsoil per year. The only time true surplus topsoil might

Fallen leaves: the easiest way to create leaf mold. (Iris reticulata likes it!)

be made available is when an area is being excavated for paving over, or for a building.

Often, "topsoil" is just the layer that is currently "on top," which is stripped and sold. No standard exists for defining "topsoil."

Some companies may produce a reasonable facsimile out of soil and composted manure mixed together, but you should be a little skeptical about claims of "true topsoil." Inquire where it came from. If the excavated area was formerly farmland or an industrial area, it could have some unwanted chemical residues or weed seed.

Shredded Newspapers

These break down fairly quickly to provide nutrients in a compost pile when mixed with aged manure, but will take longer when mixed in regular soil. Newspapers are printed with soy ink these days, even color sections, so are safe for use in compost.

You could even use shredded office paper straight from your company or home shredders. Then they'll never find the evidence!

Peat Moss

The nutrient value of peat moss is very low; it's used primarily as a water-holding and soil-loosening agent. Sphagnum, not mountain meadow, peat is recommended because mountain peat moss decomposes too rapidly and may be more than 50 percent mineral solids, not just peat. In addition, mountain meadows, sometimes thousands of years old, are destroyed to mine it.

Peat moss comes dry in bundles and should be thoroughly wetted before being incorporated into the soil.

Pure Humic Acid

Pure humic acid (leonhardite) is a byproduct found in the soil layer over coal deposits that are stripped from coal mining areas. The material decomposes in sunlight to produce humic acid, which is taken into the soil by precipitation. It helps soil structure and soil chemistry, being the material produced by bacteria in the breakdown of organic matter. This is the chemical that is said to bind soil particles together, forming aggregates.

Surfactants

Also called wetting agents (or soaps), these additives break down the surface tension of water to help it move easily into the soil. They are either sprayed on as a liquid or spread on top of existing soil as a granule. CSU is willing to recommend these, having found them to be of value.

Biosolids, Kelp, Vitamins, Mycorrhizal Inoculants

The use of biosolids — sewage treatment byproducts — is acceptable even for food gardens, if Grade 1 materials are used; however, CSU advises avoiding them for root crops that contact the biosolids directly. Heavy metals, pathogens, and salt are the concern with biosolids, and are not a problem with the Grade 1 types. Don't use a grade lower than Grade 1.

Plants will undoubtedly use the micronutrients provided by kelp and these other relatively new products, but CSU has not found definitive answers as to their value, or the need for them. The vitamins themselves are not of much value to a plant, but whatever medium they are carried in often has some nutrition to it. Mycorrhizae are natural fungi that are said to help the plant take up more nutrients. They are common in undisturbed soils, and are added to disturbed soils to improve the biological balance. They seem to work better in garden/landscape settings where artificial fertilizers are not used simultaneously.

INORGANIC AMENDMENTS

It's a rare soil that doesn't need some improvement in physical structure. Inorganic soil amendments are used to open up heavy soils and increase the water-holding capacity of "light" (sandy) soils.

Advantages: Improve soil structure without adding unwanted nutrients. Have long lives because not broken down by microbial action.

Disadvantages: Don't add nutrients, where they may be needed, though certain types will store nutrients. Expensive compared to organic amendments.

Vermiculite and Perlite

Vermiculite (heat-treated mica) and perlite (heat-treated limestone) are inert, very lightweight, hollow particles used to increase aeration in soil. Their cost is such that they're only practical for use in potting soil for seedlings.

Sand

As I described earlier in this chapter, sand is not really a practical soil amendment. Some companies have had success with builder's sand, which is very coarse and doesn't turn clay to adobe.

Cross-Linked Polyacrylamide

Cross-linked polyacrylamide (CLP), also called water-absorbing polymer, hydro-gel, and soil polymer, comes in the form of inert rock-salt-sized granules. When dry, the granule swells to a ¼- to ½-inch-wide gel particle, soaking up and storing as much as 400 times its weight in pure water (rainwater and snowmelt). It stores 200–300 times its weight in irrigation water because salts present in the water temporarily limit the absorption until the salts are flushed out by rainwater.

A plant's root hairs grow right into the gel particles and draw out water as needed. The polymer helps loosen clay soil because it is always making tiny expansions and contractions as it absorbs water and the plant roots draw it out. This provides aeration and improved drainage in clay soil, soaking up excess water so roots don't become water-logged.

Inorganic Amendments (continued)

Polyacrylamide also improves the water-holding capacity of sandy soils by reducing evaporation from the soil, by providing "storage space" that doesn't dry out quickly, and by catching water and nutrients that would ordinarily drain down out of reach in sandy soil.

I've been working with cross-linked polyacrylamide for about 15 years, primarily researching what it can be used for, after hearing about it at a Xeriscape conference in Denver. Cross-linked polyacrylamide's long life (an application could last five to 10 years or longer) and safety (rated non-hazardous by the Occupational Safety and Health Administration) make it a useful soil amendment for Xeriscape.

Make sure the product you're using is labeled "94 percent cross-linked polyacrylamide." Many companies have produced inferior-quality polymers and are passing them off as the same product. For instance, some types known as starch polymers are biodegradable, disappearing in about six months.

Recently, people with chemistry backgrounds have become alarmed at the word "acrylamide" in the scientific name for the product, having understood it to cause cancer in rats. They worry that when the polymer breaks down, as it does when exposed to sunlight in its hydrated form, acrylamide is present for a time, before the polymer completely breaks down to its final form of carbon dioxide and water.

However, polyacrylamides are often used in papermaking and water purification, and recent research has shown that many common food products such as bread, French fries, pancakes, and potato chips have high concentrations of acrylamide in them, apparently to no ill effect.

The polymer is very stable when used correctly. It should be tilled into the soil and covered with at least ½ inch of soil. When used this way, it doesn't break down and is even safe for food plants, as none of the chemical is taken up in plant tissues. I recently spoke with someone who had installed polymer in his lawn 13 years ago, and he said it was still there when he dug up a shovelful of dirt recently.

CLP has been used successfully for several years to help establish stands of grass and reduce the transplant shock of trees and shrubs by providing them with a ready source of water. It appears to increase yields of certain crops such as tomatoes and other garden produce.

So far it seems to be most helpful in very dry situations, especially container gardens, which dry out quickly. When combined with the use of UV-blocking weed-barrier fabric, what amounts to a virtual no-water, no-weed garden can be achieved. I do this with every situation I can, tilling the polymer in dry, and also mixing a handful of hydrated (wet) polymer with each plant. It works for everything except where the plants will increase by reseeding or by underground runners.

CLP is applied either dry or wet at the general rate of 7–12 pounds per 100 square feet, tilled in at least 4–6 inches deep. In talking to dozens of landscape contractors around the West, I've found that this rate seems to have enough margin of error to allow for variations in water-absorption due to soil and watering conditions, and the ability of the gardener to get the material mixed in thoroughly.

If you have a large area to treat, better to till it in dry, as 7–12 pounds soaked up with water is a really big amount of shiny, slippery crystals, and is not easy to mix into the soil that way. (CLP is very slippery when wet, so clean up spills of either the dry or the wet material from any walkway, as it can pose a hazard.)

This also works for shrubs and tree plantings. CLP does not appear to have the same effect organic amendments do (that is, dwarfing plants) when placed only in individual planting holes (see the "Trees, Shrubs, and the Limits of Organic Amendments" section of this chapter, p. 72).

When you're creating a container garden, or have some other small-scale use for the polymer, soak about ⅓ cup of it (a pound is about 2¾ cups) in 5 gallons of water. Let it sit for a couple of hours, then mix 1 part hydrated polymer to 2 parts soil. It's always better to let the polymer swell before mixing it with the soil. If you don't, the swelling of the granules may push the plants back out of the pot. Like fertilizer, CLP is a material where more is definitely not better!

In lawns, the recommended rate is 15 to 30 pounds per 1,000 square feet. For trees and shrubs the polymer may be incorporated at low rates for survival (½ to 1 teaspoon dry volume or 1 to 2 cups wet) for a small seedling, or at higher rates for added water storage and faster growth.

A test at CSU in the early 1990s showed no advantage to using polymer in turf. I'm still scratching my head over this, as I continue to hear reports from landscape contractors and individuals about how it helped their lawns to get established and stay green. I've even had a few people tell me they got in trouble with the "water police" for allegedly watering too much because their lawns were so much greener than those of their neighbors. In fact, they had not been watering at all.

I can only speculate that the heavy clay nature of the soil at CSU's test site might have had an impact. The highest rate tested there was 8 pounds per 100 square feet, and, as mentioned before, I've heard in intervening years that 7–12 pounds per 100 square feet seems to be a minimum, so perhaps the original test didn't go far enough. CSU agrees that they continue to see definite benefit in using polymer for container-garden-type settings, and that polymer may be more useful for turf in sandier soils.

SOLVING PH AND SALINITY PROBLEMS

CHANGING THE PH

If you've had your soil tested to determine its pH (see the "Or Use a Pro!" section in the last chapter, p. 62) and have decided to try to alter it, as opposed to choosing plants that like the soil as is, here's what to do.

To lower your soil's pH to 6.5, add the following pound amounts of sulfur or ammonium sulfate per 1,000 square feet of soil, according to your soil type:

Current Soil pH	Sandy Soil	Clay Soil
7.0	10 lbs.	20 lbs.
7.5	30 lbs.	45 lbs.
8.5	45 lbs.	70 lbs.

To raise your soil's pH to 6.5, add the following pound amounts of limestone per 1,000 square feet of soil, according to your soil type:

Current Soil pH	Sandy Soil	Loamy Soil	Clay Soil
6.0	15 lbs.	40 lbs.	55 lbs.
5.5	30 lbs.	80 lbs.	110 lbs.
5.0	40 lbs.	105 lbs.	155 lbs.
4.5	50 lbs.	135 lbs.	195 lbs.

To lower the pH for individual plants or planting areas one-half to one point, say from 7.5 to 7.0 or 6.5, add ½ pound of ground sulfur or 3 pounds of iron sulfate per 100 square feet.

To raise the pH by one point, use 5 pounds of ground limestone per 100 square feet. If done at planting, the powder can be spaded into the soil and water will carry it down to treat the lower soil. You can also spread the powder on the ground and water it in. Keep your lawn and pine tree areas separate because the acid from the pine needles will eventually kill the grass. Actually, this is advice that requires no action on your part: It will happen whether you like it or not.

Take soil pH readings every few years, especially if the plants begin to develop pale green leaves with dark veins, and add soil amendment as needed. Again, take the local advice of the Cooperative Extension Service or other soil lab.

SALINITY SOLUTIONS

If you've decided to amend for salt, know that two popular soil amendments, composted manure and compost, are not recommended at all for soils already high in salt (above 3.0 mmhos/cm). Also, do not use these amendments when growing any of the sensitive plants mentioned in the "Got Salt?" section of the previous chapter (see p. 65). Instead opt for sphagnum peat or ground leaves.

It's OK to use a high-salt amendment—up to, but not more than, 10.0 mmhos/cm—if your soil is at 1.0 mmho/cm or less. Ask for an analysis of the amendment you're considering. If it's not available, have a small sample tested before ordering a large amount.

In any case, don't add more than 3 cubic yards of these organic soil amendments per 1,000 square feet at one time to prevent salt buildup in the soil:

- Sphagnum peat
- Grass clippings
- Straw
- Compost
- Manure
- Biosolids
- Sawdust

CSU's Cooperative Extension Service even recommends re-testing the soil before deciding whether to add more soil amendment. Organic amendments are recommended if your soil tests out at less than 3 percent organic matter.

These organic amendments are *not* recommended in Colorado:

- Wood ash. High not only in salt, but also in pH, two common problems in Colorado soils — problems that wood ash will magnify.
- Mountain peat. High in pH and too finely textured to be of much use. As well, according to CSU CES's Fact Sheet on Soil Amendments (#7.235), "Mountain peat is mined from high-altitude wetlands that will take hundreds of years to rejuvenate, if ever. The mining is extremely disruptive to hydrologic cycles and mountain ecosystems. Sphagnum peat is harvested from bogs in Canada and the northern United States. The bogs can be re-vegetated after harvest and grow back relatively quickly in this moist environment." So be a friend to the mountain environment and stay away from mountain peat.

CHAPTER 5

PRACTICAL TURF AREAS I:
GRASS

*Where to use turfgrass, what to use,
and how you're going to keep it healthy
without draining the water supply.*

ABOVE: *A practical area of turf reduces water use, as opposed to blanketing the whole yard with grass.*
OPPOSITE: *Rosebushes are planted just outside this small turf area to take advantage of irrigation over-spray and runoff. Photo by Connie Ellefson.*

Yummy, scrumptiously green, and thick Kentucky bluegrass (KBG) is what most of us are used to, but it needs about three times the water we get naturally in Colorado. So, it makes sense to really think it out: where to use turfgrass, what to use, and how you're going to keep it healthy without draining the water supply. That's what this chapter is all about.

WHEN TURF MAKES SENSE

LARGER AREA, HEAVY USE
The idea is to limit the use of turf to functional areas—those you can actually get some use out of. If the area is impractical—such as narrow strips and sloping areas—it's better to find a drought-tolerant alternative. We went into site analysis in some detail in Chapter 1, but here's a brief summary of how to determine what grass area will be practical for your needs. In certain situations, there's no good substitute for grass. Practical turf uses include any play areas for tots, sports, or pets. Grass is one of the few groundcovers (barring asphalt and the like) that not only stands up to the wear, it is comfortable and inviting, too.

DESIGN AND AESTHETICS
Turf is also a key design element. Here are just some of its benefits (if used wisely):

- Providing unity as a design element, both in your own landscape and with the neighbors', if you care to conform to some extent.
- Providing simplicity—a landscape of all eye-catching, varied plants can be too, too much without something with simple lines to rest your vision on.
- Reducing air and water pollution.
- Preventing erosion.
- Harvesting water and recharging groundwater—second only to undisturbed forest in its ability to do the same.
- Reducing heat reflection to adjacent buildings (house, garage, gazebo, and the larger and smaller potting sheds) when compared to concrete or rock mulch.
- Providing an oasis on a hot summer day.
- Soothing the soul and allowing you to roll around on the ground—no other groundcover quite gets it, you know?

ABOVE: *Turf is minimal in this beautiful back yard, where low-water perennials and no-water deck take center stage.* Photo by Connie Ellefson.
OPPOSITE: *Managing turf in this narrow, shady strip would be difficult without sweet woodruff* (Galium odoratum), *which does well in shade and thrives with little supplemental water.*

THE MAINTENANCE TRADEOFF

Turf means a different commitment to the maintenance. You need to decide if you'd rather:

- Pick a few weeds from shrub and flower beds (or a few hundred if you didn't mulch and maintain to shut them out) OR

- Water two to three times a week and run the mower around once a week. (A thick stand of turf resists weed invasion, Denver Xeriscape designer and lecturer Lise Mahnke notes. "The easiest way to maintain your yard," she says, "is to plant sod fence-to-fence and hire a mowing company to handle it. Of course, most of us want something a little more interesting!")

WHEN TURF DOESN'T MAKE SENSE

Decided you still want some turf? The key is to create, well, *practical* turf areas: big enough to serve your purposes, but avoiding the inconvenient locations. Try to find something besides turf for the following REALLY impractical areas:

- Sloping areas. What a pill to keep watered. If you must have grass here, use a low-water species.

- Anything narrower than 8 feet. Whether you have an automatic irrigation system or not, somebody might have one there someday, and these narrow strips don't fit the units that standard sprinkler systems are designed to water—therefore, mucho wastage. Besides, what the heck can you do with a 6-foot-wide strip of grass anyway—besides water, fertilize, edge, and mow? If, for some bizarre reason, you must still have grass in one of these strippety-strips, you could choose a lower-water-using turf, or grade a wee depression along the center to catch water instead of shedding it.

- Irregularly shaped areas. These places have the same problem as narrow areas: It's terribly hard to water them efficiently. In fact, whether it's a square area or a rectangular area can even make a big difference. John Olaf Nelson of the North Marin Water District in California made a study of the water requirements of areas based on shape. He found that *irrigated areas with the same square footage need increasingly more water as the perimeter increases.*

  For instance, the standard 10-by-50-foot rectangular area between houses contains 500 square feet and has a perimeter of 120 feet. A 23-by-23-foot square area has a little over 500 square feet and a perimeter of 92 feet.

  Nelson found that more irrigation water was applied to the rectangular area than the square one to keep it green. This is because sprinklers work best in overlapping patterns for complete coverage, and this is really difficult to achieve in the narrow sections, hence lots of over-watering. People have all sorts of different ideas about what constitutes a perfectly shaped or sized lawn. I've even heard about the celebrated "commercial-sized lawn," just the right size to mow during a commercial break in a TV sports broadcast.

- Areas along the fence. These places are hard to both mow and water. Try using tree, shrub, and flower beds along the perimeter of your site; it enhances the feeling of privacy and enclosure that we subconsciously seek in a satisfying landscape.

- Areas under trees or shrubs. The trees compete with the grass for water and nutrients, so neither does very well. It's better to keep them separated. If grass does grow under trees or shrubs, it's hard to mow.

Your goal should be to give as much thought to the amount of turf you really need in your Xeriscape as you do to the amount of hardscape. Realize that the low up-front cost of grass masks many years of ongoing maintenance costs, not only in terms of water, but also mowing time, fertilizer, and gas for mowers.

Rather than blanketing your lot with turf because you can't think of anything else to cover it with, try to have a specific purpose you can state to yourself for each section of turfgrass in your design.

A tiny turf area gives a nod to the rest of the neighborhood, but lavish Xeriscape perennials make the most of Arun Das' small front yard.

Now that you've identified your practical turf areas, you just have to decide which kind of grass to put in that practical turf area. There are always options in Xeriscape, and the following is no exception.

BLUEGRASS OR NOT?

CHOICE 1: Love and keep your bluegrass. Guess what? This water-loving lovely stands up to wear as well as or better than any other turfgrass! It also responds to short-term drought better, going dormant when it gets too dry. According to Arkansas Valley Seed Solutions (AVSS) in Denver, KBG has been known to recover even after nine months without water. Areas planted with bluegrass in the great drought of '02 (2002, of course) greened up more reliably when moisture started arriving in the fall; some other cool-season grasses never recovered!

Many people who grew up in the East have told me that they never irrigated their lawns there because the higher rainfall keeps grass green most of the summer. Here in Colorado, people expect (or should expect) their grass to get all dried-up and brown in late July and August, and don't sweat it, as it's considered normal.

Can you deal with that?

If you can't imagine not having some semblance of the velvet greensward in the mid- to late-summer days, you'll have to water quite a lot. Whether by hand or by automatic irrigation system, to realize water savings, this is where you really have to pay attention.

Refer to the Irrigation and Maintenance chapters for how to deal.

CHOICE 2: Install a turfgrass whose water use more closely matches our natural rainfall. This includes both cool-season grasses, which green up in spring and fall as does KBG, and warm-season grasses, which stay dormant until late spring, then green (or blue-green) up in the hot summer. Several varieties of both are discussed in the following pages.

With the exception of 'Ephraim' crested wheatgrass, which makes a pretty good cool-season substitute for KBG, most of these water-thrifty grasses will have an appearance that is different from KBG.

CHOICE 3: Sneaked this one back in. If this is starting to look too complicated, you could always fall back on the idea of eliminating turf completely and replacing it with alternative groundcoverings!

ABOVE: *This area is so far from the house that turf is neither practical nor necessary.*
TOP: *Ann Seymour's lawn of thyme* (Thymus spp.) *makes a naturalistic complement to the dry streambed. Stepping stones accommodate foot traffic.*

ALTERNATIVES TO KBG

Selecting a lower-water-using turfgrass or a drought-resistant cultivar for our region isn't really that hard because the number of different grasses used for lawns is remarkably limited. You've got your Kentucky bluegrass, crested wheatgrass, fescues, and ryegrasses (cool-season), and your buffalograss and blue grama grass (warm-season). Detailed listings of these grasses—sort of an index to all your choices—conclude this chapter.

The next few years should bring improved cultivars of many of these species, as breeding new strains of grass for drought tolerance is high priority. Useful strains of bermudagrass, tufted hair grass, and saltgrass are in the works. The research into this area is, like, *intense,* man, not only at seed companies, but at many universities, too.

If you're going to seed the lawn, contact your county extension service to get the names of several turfgrass cultivars that are highly rated for drought tolerance. It's their job to keep up on this type of research. Then you'll have a couple of options when buying seed, in case one strain isn't available.

With cool-season grasses, mixtures are recommended. The planting is then no longer a monoculture, so if a disease hits one strain it might not affect the others and will have greater difficulty spreading. In addition, the shortcomings of one type of turfgrass could be balanced by the strengths of another. For instance, fescue is a bunch-forming grass with a lower water requirement than KBG, but it doesn't form a tightly knit sod unless sown very thickly. It might be mixed with a grass with a sod-forming habit of growth to create a better turf.

In KBG-mad Colorado the *only* way a xeri-advocate can make headway with a xeri-skeptic is to show that it's still possible to have a blue-grass-like lawn. Efforts to promote the more water-thrifty grasses are met with the perennial wail, "But it doesn't look like *real* grass!"

Imagine my surprise, then, in visiting south Texas and Florida, to see people actually living with and seeing no shame in lawns of St. Augustinegrass and Bahiagrass that have blades up to ¼ inch wide! My feeling is, if these people can bravely hold their heads up and not think anything amiss with a non-bluegrass look, then perhaps we should be able to rethink our prejudices about alternative grasses.

In the early 1990s, KBG accounted for 92 percent of the sod sold. But a push in the late '90s to builder-provided "landscapes" drove the market back up and away from fescues and other lower-water-requiring turfgrasses. Nowadays KBG makes up 98 percent of the sod sold. It's too bad, since, as Tony Koski, Colorado State University horticulture professor and turf extension specialist, points out, there's really no "best turfgrass."

It just depends on what you want. Some people go strictly for aesthetics, others balance the look of the grass and the effort it takes to maintain it, and some couldn't care less how it looks as long as it takes care of itself. I, personally, get a little sick of all the green that goes on in the summer, and enjoy the variety of some buff, tan, brown, or blue-green thrown in for contrast.

One of the cool things about Xeriscape is that many of the native American grasses are being scrutinized for adaptation to turfgrass use (most traditional turfgrasses are imports). Names such as beachgrass, alkaligrass, and saltgrass may be

During autumn, the contrast between cool-season grass (background) and warm-season grass (foreground) becomes apparent. Photo by Connie Ellefson.

A turf of buffalograss (Buchloe dactyloides) *and blue grama grass* (Bouteloua gracilis), *such as in Macy Dorf and Jacquie Kitzelman's landscape, can be fertilized lightly in the spring, mowed once a month, and watered twice a month during the growing season.*

appearing on the marquee of turfgrasses in the future. (Exciting, eh?) Buffalograss and blue grama grass are have been starring in landscapes for years.

These and many other wild grasses, including species introduced from Eastern Europe and Russia, have appeared in low-maintenance areas such as roadside parks and highway rights-of-way. They've long been valued for their extreme drought tolerance and ability to survive untended.

Drawbacks of some of these species for their use in home lawns include a coarse texture, low wear tolerance, and a color more gray-green than deep green. But, thanks to the increasing public interest in prairie restoration and native grasses, they're beginning to be appreciated in their own right despite—or perhaps because of—their different appearances. Now they are showing up in urban landscapes.

are going to fit into the Denver water picture in the next 10 years, you're not the only one....

One way to use native or other low-water grasses in large yards is to raise two separate lawn areas. A more traditional turf area can be planted close to the house or in the front yard and used intensely for recreation or decoration. A section farther out or in the back yard could be given over to the lower-maintenance grasses, creating a more natural look.

WARM VS. COOL

Part of the varying appearance of native grasses stems from the fact that they are often warm-season grasses—that is, they are green only during the growing season when air temperatures rise well above freezing. The rest of the year they are a warm, tan color, very beautiful in the right setting, but rather startling to eyes accustomed in northern climates to seeing cool-season turf-grasses at their greenest in spring and fall.

Warm-season grasses come out of dormancy only when the temperature is above 50 degrees Fahrenheit, and grow vigorously when the temperature is between 80 and 95 degrees, with-standing even temperatures above 100 degrees. When the temperature drops below 50 degrees they start to turn tan; when it drops below freezing, they turn brown—signifying they are in cold dormancy.

Cool-season grasses grow best in spring and fall when daytime air temperatures range from 60 to 75 degrees. They will likely turn brown in the heat of summer, but they stay green through much colder temperatures in the winter because they don't lose chlorophyll as warm-season grasses do when the temperature dips below 50 degrees.

Overseeding an annual cool-season grass on top of a warm-season grass is sometimes done to give winter color to the lawn, but this takes extra water. So for Xeriscape you're better off picking a season that you can bear to see brownish lawn and go with the best locally adapted warm- or cool-season grass. Unless one is an annual grass, one of the species will take over the other in patches, and it will just look strange.

Dr. James Beard, consultant and retired turf-grass specialist at Texas A&M University, ranked the drought tolerance of turfgrasses as shown in the chart on p. 90. Future improvements in specific cultivars might rearrange this ranking.

If you're wondering why I keep bringing up prairie gardens, it's because, well, most of us in Colorado actually *live* on a prairie. You may have forgotten that fact, thanks to the influence of short-sighted politicians and homeowners' associations that insist that 50 percent of a land-scape be covered with KBG, but it's a true story.

If you're wondering how a million more people and their 50 percent sod-covered lots

BUNCH VS. SOD

Bunchgrasses grow as individual plants that spread over time. They may completely fill in the grass area if the seed is sown thickly enough. Divots and patches worn bare by dogs, kids, or four-wheeler rallies will not fill in on their own as would happen in a bluegrass lawn. To prevent this problem, make sure your grass mixture includes some self-healing, sod-forming grasses from the start.

Sod-forming grasses send out runners above ground (stolons) or below ground (rhizomes) that colonize, knitting the grass tightly together and forming new plants at nodes along their length. Sod-formers will repair themselves with time, once the damaging influence (like heavy traffic) is removed.

The thing is, once it really sinks in to you that the native grasses need watering only about once a month, after establishment, and one to zero mowings per season, you may find that you can really cope with the differences in appearance!

To see how some of these grasses look in person, visit the Denver Botanic Gardens, the Denver Water Xeriscape Demonstration Garden, any of several Xeriscape demonstration gardens around the state (check the Web for "Xeriscape Colorado"), the Centennial Garden just north of Elitch Gardens in Denver, and the CSU Horticulture Farm in Fort Collins.

Sandy Snyder, a professional gardener in Littleton, Colorado, found a perfect solution for her warm-season/cool-season dilemma by planting hundreds of spring-flowering bulbs in her warm-season buffalograss lawn. Her experience is described later in this chapter under "Sandy Snyder's Bulb Lawn," p. 93.

MOWING HIATUS

I'll bet you didn't know that if you decided to go on a mowing strike with your Kentucky bluegrass, it would grow about 18 inches tall and would have beautiful, feathery seed heads; it would also need much less water. This could be a simple way to get the prairie garden effect without too much work. Just mow the grass with a curving edge for lawn area and let the rest grow.

This approach works better if your turf's weed population isn't too high. Mowing once in the fall will help. To keep the grass green all summer, you'll still have to irrigate some, though not as much as for a highly maintained turf.

This works best with buffalograss, blue grama grass, crested wheatgrass, bluegrass, and fine fescues. Tall fescue and perennial ryegrass tend to develop too much leaf area and not enough of the attractive seed heads. Their growth is more "rank" (weedy-looking) than ornamental.

Grasses allowed to go to seed should be thought of as ornamental grasses. They can withstand some traffic, but not continual wear from romping dogs and kids. Be aware that KBG, especially, squashes down when walked on and won't stand back up. The following charts indicate the mature height for suitable grasses if left unmowed.

Each grass description includes a map of its native or adapted range, depending on available information. The adapted range of the native grasses is not entirely known, but given the toughness of most grasses, the ranges could probably be extended considerably. As always, the microclimate for the plant is key.

Now's the time to take a quick look at the turfgrass choice listings (opposite), arranged in order from lowest to highest water use.

Turfgrass Drought Tolerance

DROUGHT TOLERANCE	COOL-SEASON GRASSES	WARM-SEASON GRASSES
Excellent	None	Blue grama grass Buffalograss
Good	Crested wheatgrass Hard fescue Chewings fescue Sheep fescue Tall fescue Red fescue	None
Medium	Kentucky bluegrass Canada bluegrass	None
Fair	Perennial ryegrass Meadow fescue	None
Poor	Rough bluegrass	None

Top Turfgrass Choices for Colorado (pages 91–99)

WARM-SEASON GRASSES

Blue Grama Grass (*Bouteloua gracilis*)
Bunchgrass, Southern U.S.; Sod-forming, Northern U.S.

RAINFALL RANGE: 12–24 inches optimum; 8–50 inches possible (flexible!); doesn't need supplemental irrigation once established

SOIL: Sandy to clayey optimum; tolerates saline soils

PH: Neutral to alkaline soils

PROPAGATION: Seed at 1–1½ pounds Pure Live Seed (PLS) per 1,000 square feet

EXPOSURE: Sun

GERMINATION TIME: 5–30 days, during frost-free season; sod occasionally available

MOWING HEIGHT: May be left unmowed (12–18 inches maximum height) or mowed at 3 inches periodically after sod is well-established to encourage a dense cover

ADAPTED RANGE:

ABOVE: *Unmowed blue grama grass lawn.*
BELOW: *Attractive seed heads of blue grama grass.*

Blue grama grass (BGG) is a native American grass, often seen in the wild with buffalograss. It has a bluish-purple cast and is very drought-tolerant. It has an exceptional ability to go dormant during drought, then recover when more moisture is available.

Not that we care too much, but it forms bunches in the South and sod in the North. Sod-formation improves with regular mowing (or grazing, if you can recruit somebody's goats for that). Shade tolerance is slim to none, but its roots can grow 5–7 feet deep, so it's great for erosion control and on slopes—(bank stabilization!).

BGG copes well with windy, arid areas of the Great Plains, tolerates wide temperature and soil variations from sandy to clayey, and does well in alkaline soil. What a champ, eh? But don't look for it on even weakly acid soil: You'll be so disappointed!

BGG is best for lawns in cool, dry areas. It can be left unmowed, thanks to its cute seed heads—they look like downward-curving combs about an inch long—and it grows thickly to exclude weeds. Mature height is 12–18 inches, and 6–8 inches if water is scarce. (This is a hint for you. You can make it scarce by not irrigating.)

The best way to establish a lawn of blue grama grass is to seed when night temperatures drop to 60 degrees Fahrenheit, but the soil is still warm (between 60 and 90 degrees). It can be started with plugs, but coverage is faster and more uniform with seed. Planting can be done from May to mid-August for lawns, and from September 15 until you can't plant any more for non-irrigated areas.

Keep soil moist until germination seems mostly complete, and then allow it to dry out between deep waterings to encourage deep roots. BGG is drought-tolerant and turns brown—dormant—during prolonged droughts, as do so many of its colleagues.

Buffalograss (*Buchloe dactyloides*)
Sod-forming

RAINFALL RANGE: 12–24 inches best; 10–35 inches possible; doesn't need supplemental water once established, but a little extra water during extended dry spells will keep it looking better

SOIL: Silty to clayey ideal; sandy soils not as good

PH: 6.0–7.5; 'Prairie' cultivar, 4.7–8.0

PROPAGATION: Seed at 3–5 pounds PLS (burs) per 1,000 square feet

EXPOSURE: Sun; won't tolerate more than a half day of shade

GERMINATION TIME: 7–10 days for treated seed; up to 3 years for untreated; sod and plugs becoming more readily available

MOWING HEIGHT: You can leave it unmowed (6–8 inches maximum height) or mow it at 3–5 inches every month or so

ADAPTED RANGE:

(doesn't grow well above 6,500–7,000 feet in elevation)

ABOVE: *Mowed buffalograss lawn in the dry heat of August.*

LEFT: *Buffalograss spreads by stolons (shown) atop the ground and by rhizomes under the ground.*

Warm-Season Grasses (continued)

Buffalograss is one of the outstanding native and Xeriscape grasses. Able to survive on as little as 10–12 inches of rainfall a year, it still adapts to 30 inches or more annually. It's well-adapted to heavy clay, alkaline soil. In fact, it grows in a wide range of soil conditions, though it fails to thrive in sandy soil or shade. It can be mowed two or three times a summer or left unmowed for a prairie look (sounds better than "lazy look").

Buffalograss has soft, light green foliage and interesting seed heads. About half the plants are female and produce seed burs near the ground. The other half, the male plants, produce comblike seed heads held above the plants. These are so pretty that some people grow buffalograss just for that effect.

Buffalograss is native to much of the upland Great Plains, and is the most northerly surviving of warm-season turfgrass type grasses, growing as far north as Montana. The first turf-type buffalograss was released through Texas A&M in 1989. Called 'Prairie,' it is vegetatively propagated, meaning no seeds are available, and it must be produced from existing sod or plugs. It and other popular cultivars such as '609' and 'Legacy' are "all-female-plant" selections. No male flowers occur, so it appears "neater" with less mowing.

Other types of buffalograss can be seeded or sodded, though sod is sometimes hard to locate and is expensive because it must be cut fairly thick. Whereas bluegrass sod is cut ½–¾ inch thick, buffalograss sod is cut 1½ inches thick to include more of its root system. It can't be rolled, so it must be cut into squares or slabs, and the extra weight adds to transportation and installation costs. Buffalograss has to be re-sodded or seeded at the sod farm, making it more expensive still (doesn't regenerate as easily as KBG).

Buffalograss seed is usually treated to enhance germination. The seed will have a green coating if treated,

and that's just what you want. Plant from mid-May to June for seeding. Then you can still get full coverage in one season.

Suzanne and Bill and Their Buffalograss Sod

Denver amateur gardeners Suzanne and Bill purchased and installed buffalograss sod one year in early June. Suzanne first used a spade to cut a rounded edge around their roughly square lawn, then Bill thoroughly rototilled the existing bluegrass lawn (the rounded edge helped keep the tiller from going into the adjacent flowerbed).

Suzanne systematically screened the top layer of soil from the whole yard. She put all the roots and grass leaves into the compost heap and reused the soil. This way the organic matter in the soil was retained.

On her 1,200-square-foot area, Suzanne spread six bales of peat moss and 20 wheelbarrow loads of compost from the stockpile she had been working on for several years. After incorporating the amendments she raked it smooth and firmed it by walking on it in a circular pattern. She didn't use fertilizer because it can kill new grass if applied incorrectly, and she didn't want to risk it.

Because the sod came in 18-inch squares, Suzanne cut a piece of plywood slightly larger than that to carry the sod. (She deems this the most backbreaking work she has ever done.) To avoid making permanent footprint depressions in the lawn, Suzanne put down boards as paths to move around on while filling cracks between the squares with dirt and peat moss. (Note: Suzanne's heroic efforts to improve the soil could have been scaled back, given buffalograss' reputation for growing in poor soil, but they undoubtedly helped the grass take off and fill in quickly.)

She drenched the lawn with water when all this was completed, then soaked it again five days after that, then one week later, then two weeks later. After that she

Smooth-textured buffalograss turf contrasts with the rough-textured shrub rose border.

watered the lawn every one to two weeks. The grass grew very well and so did weeds, wildflowers, and other grasses.

Suzanne realized there were undoubtedly seeds in the existing soil and in the compost, but thinks there were probably some in the sod, too. She spent the summer picking out these intruders, gathering several bushels full, but says there were none left by the end of the summer.

The grass wasn't cut until the end of the summer, when it was cut as tall as possible. The male seed heads appeared in mid- to late July. Suzanne says at least 50 people walking by her corner lot stopped to comment on how much they enjoyed seeing her beautiful, unusual lawn.

The grass gradually started going dormant in September, with some green and some tan color. By first frost it was all tan.

Sandy Snyder's Bulb Lawn

Sandy Snyder, a gardening consultant in Littleton, has put in buffalograss in no less than three different ways. Wanting to replace a 2,000-square-foot vegetable garden with a low-maintenance, low-water grass, she and her husband decided to seed buffalograss.

They used 2½ pounds of "Sharps New Improved" seed per 1,000 square feet, keeping the seedbed moist until the grass sprouted about two weeks later. They didn't use any soil amendments because the ground had already been improved during its "agricultural" phase when it was a garden, and she reasoned that the grass was adapted to heavy clay soil anyway.

Sandy Snyder spent so many hours hand-weeding that summer that, if she had it to do again, she would let the ground lay fallow for a year, killing weed seeds with a pre-emergent herbicide and sprouts with a contact herbicide. She would also sow the seed at twice the rate to give them a better chance against the weeds.

The following spring, Snyder discovered the difference between warm- and cool-season grasses in Denver. Her lawn was still brown two months after the neighbors' yards had greened up. Her friend, Panayoti Kelaidis, curator at the Denver Botanic Gardens, suggested she plant spring-flowering bulbs in the lawn to add spring color and greenery. The flowers and leaves die down before the grass starts growing in early summer, so the spent bulb foliage can be mowed without harming the plants.

That fall, she and her family planted 2,000 crocus, iris, tulip, and other bulbs. The result the next spring was so spectacular that Snyder has turned another area of her yard over to the buffalograss specifically to provide more room for bulbs. The bulbs have multiplied 40-fold over the years, giving a better show each year. (Note: It's important to plant species, rather than hybrid, bulbs for this technique. The foliage of the hybrids remains green and tall too far into the summer, whereas the species bulb foliage dies down in a timely fashion so the grass can be mowed before it gets too long.)

Sandy Snyder's lawn of bulbs and buffalograss.

Snyder believes that if a person wanted to leave the grass unmowed and has the time to keep up with the weeding, it would be possible to do such "naturalizing" with bulbs flowering all summer, perhaps in a smaller area.

Even though the weeds continue to be a problem, Snyder says she still spends far less time maintaining her lawn than any of her neighbors do.

Although buffalograss is said to be the most wear-tolerant of the native warm-season grasses and certainly the most soil-compaction-tolerant (remember how all those buffalo tromped through the prairies), Snyder found that it doesn't take wear well when dormant because of its brittleness at that stage.

She fertilizes just once a year during midsummer at a quarter the rate recommended for bluegrass. She waters only during very hot or dry spells and just enough to keep the grass its normal light green color, not enough to encourage the weeds. She especially tries to avoid watering during spring and fall to discourage the cool-season weeds.

A few years later, Snyder converted another area to buffalograss by installing 2-inch plugs of grass 8 inches apart in all directions. One section had bare ground to start with, and the other was prepared with the interesting approach of killing the existing sod with glyphosate, waiting a decent interval, and simply planting the plugs in the dead sod. She says both methods gave a complete coverage by July 1, but she had far less trouble with weeds in the areas where plugs were planted in the dead sod.

Warm-Season Grasses (continued)

Other Buffalograss Cultivars

- *'Roadcrest'* (the latest and best), 'Cody,' and 'Bowie' are three recent buffalograss seed cultivars designed to fill in with a thicker turf faster and to stay green a little longer.
- *'609'* is available as sod or plugs. It doesn't green up any earlier than older cultivars, but does stay green later into the fall, and thus uses more water.
- *'Legacy,'* also a sod/plug choice, takes foot traffic well and has a very soft texture. Like '609' and 'Prairie,' this cultivar is propagated by cuttings and is one of the female genotypes (no high seed heads). If you want to be able to skip mowing, you might like this

one. It fills in well and is very fast-growing and vigorous. In 2001, a lawn in southeast Aurora was planted with plugs of 'Legacy,' 12–16 inches apart, on Memorial Day. By Labor Day, the lawn was fully meshed together as if sod had been planted. While the cost savings was not great for plugs vs. sod, the homeowners picked the plugs up at the nursery and transported them in the back of their car, rather than having to arrange for a huge truck delivery. A bunch of friends helped plant the plugs in one day using "dibble sticks"—anything to poke a correctly sized hole with, in this case a board whittled down to a wide cone with a bolt attached a few inches up to stop it at the right depth.

COOL-SEASON GRASSES

'Fairway' Crested Wheatgrass

(*Agropyron cristatum* 'Fairway') Bunchgrass

RAINFALL RANGE: 10–16.5 inches optimum; 8–19 inches possible

SOIL: Somewhat sandy to somewhat clayey; tolerates saline soil

PH: Adapted to weakly acid soil

PROPAGATION: Seed at 5 pounds Pure Live Seed (PLS) per 1,000 square feet

EXPOSURE: Sun

GERMINATION TIME: 21 days

MOWING HEIGHT: 3+ inches; if left unmowed, height is 12–18 inches

ADAPTED RANGE:

'Ephraim' Crested Wheatgrass

(*Agropyron cristatum* 'Ephraim') Sod-forming

RAINFALL RANGE: 10–14 inches optimum; 8–25 inches possible

SOIL: Somewhat sandy to somewhat clayey; tolerates saline soil

PH: Wide range; moderately high alkaline tolerance

PROPAGATION: Seed at 5 pounds PLS per acre

EXPOSURE: Sun

GERMINATION TIME: 21 days

MOWING HEIGHT: 3+ inches; if left unmowed, height is 6–16 inches (6 inches if water is very scarce)

ADAPTED RANGE:

'Fairway' crested wheatgrass (FCW) is a low-maintenance grass sometimes used as a Kentucky bluegrass lookalike, though it makes a better meadow grass. Easily established from seed, it still requires the same care as any other lawngrass to get going.

FCW won't germinate if the ground is dry (well, none of them do, do they?), so start it in the spring when the weather is cooler and it's easier to keep up with the watering. After it germinates, taper off the watering as quickly as possible without killing the sprouts; this will discourage weed growth.

'Fairway' crested wheatgrass is very drought-tolerant, though it may go dormant during hot and dry summer weather, and it tolerates cold well (it's native to Siberia), so is well adapted to the Rocky Mountains. Although its roots can go as deep as 2–3 feet, it also has a dense root system near the surface that helps it compete easily with weeds.

This is one grass that thins out if watered too much because, as a bunchgrass, it's less able to withstand the invasion of water-loving, sod-forming grasses. Keep irrigation to a minimum and don't plant it in regions that get more than about 20 inches of precipitation annually.

'Ephraim' crested wheatgrass (ECW) started out a native of the dry, gravelly, clay soil in Ankara, Turkey. It was tested and developed near Ephraim, Utah, specifically for its sod-forming characteristics. Many crested wheatgrasses are bunchgrasses, so they lack the erosion prevention capability of a sod-forming grass. Left unmowed for an "E-Z prairie meadow," ECW has a wiry texture, less pleasing than the fine fescues.

Jim Smith and his 'Ephraim' Crested Wheatgrass

After experimenting with this cultivar for several years in Cherry Hills Village and Englewood, Jim Smith, a Denver landscape consultant and installer, is sold on it for a turf-grass. He has even had success with overseeding ECW on Kentucky bluegrass without having to kill or till the bluegrass, using the following method:

1. Mow bluegrass lawn as short as possible.
2. Rent a verticutter for the seeding. It makes a shallow slit in the ground, drills in the seed, and covers it lightly.
3. Use 3–4 pounds grass seed per 1,000 square feet.

4. If possible, water every day for 10 days at about 6 p.m. for just 3–5 minutes, to keep soil moist.

5. Then you can spread out waterings to twice a week, or whatever you're allowed.

Jim says ECW has a slightly lighter green color than bluegrass and takes about one-third the watering time after it's established. He uses a lawn fertilizing service, having them do the regular fertilization in spring and fall, then substitute a soil surfactant—wetting agent—for the two summer applications. Obviously, you could do the same thing yourself. He mows the grass once a week and says it looks better in the heat of late July than any other type of grass he works with.

Smooth Bromegrass (*Bromus inermis*)
Sod-forming

Oops. This bad boy has fallen from Xeriscape grace. Once touted as a drought-tolerant turfgrass option, it has been found to be so invasive that it's just fluttering on the wings of being classified as a weed in Colorado. Native to China, Siberia, and Europe, bromegrass has long been used for erosion control along highways, but probably not for much longer. Horticulturist Jim Borland calls it "the nemesis of natural areas in foothills and low mountains everywhere!"

For all four fine fescues below:

SOIL: Silty to clay optimum; will tolerate sandy to heavy clay

PH: 5.5–6.5

PROPAGATION: Seed at 5 pounds per 1,000 square feet

EXPOSURE: Sun and shade

GERMINATION TIME: 5–21 days

MOWING HEIGHT: 2 ½ inches; mowing of fine fescues makes them more susceptible to fading out in periods of extended heat

Sheep Fescue (*Festuca ovina*)
Bunchgrass

RAINFALL RANGE: 9 inches minimum for survival in meadows; 20–30 inches for lawns

UNMOWED HEIGHT: 8–16 inches

ADAPTED RANGE:

Hard Fescue (*F. ovina* var. *duriuscula*)
Bunchgrass

RAINFALL RANGE: 13 inches minimum for survival in meadows; 25–30+ inches for lawns

UNMOWED HEIGHT: 12–18 inches

ADAPTED RANGE:

Chewings Fescue (*F. rubra* var. *commutata*)
Bunchgrass

RAINFALL RANGE: Approximately 20+ inches for survival in meadows; 30 inches for lawns

UNMOWED HEIGHT: 16–40 inches

ADAPTED RANGE:

Red Fescue (*F. rubra*)
Sod-forming

RAINFALL RANGE: Approximately 20+ inches for survival in meadows; 30 inches for lawns

UNMOWED HEIGHT: 16–40 inches

ADAPTED RANGE:

Fine fescues such as the four listed here are fine-textured grasses that cover much the same range, and respond to the same regimen of maintenance, as Kentucky bluegrass. They are better adapted than bluegrass to shade, poor soil, and dry locations, but are less wear-tolerant. *Fine fescues are the best choice for creating "meadow lawn." They are super for higher elevations—foothills, mountain (high elevation), and sub-alpine (very high elevation) areas, and shady forest sites.*

Often used in mixtures with bluegrass, they tend to be more aggressive when these harsher conditions prevail, and are dominated by bluegrass when the soil is more fertile and conditions are more favorable to bluegrass. Thatch can be more of a problem in fine fescues than in some other grasses.

Fine fescues are often planted for bank stabilization and, when left unmowed, have a delicate, windblown appearance. Chewings fescue is the best-looking for lawns, though the average person would have a hard time telling the fescues apart.

Red fescue is the most shade-tolerant of the good "lawn" grasses, but is more susceptible to disease when overwatered. It makes a thick groundcover in naturalized areas. Hard fescue is favored for its deep green color, and

Cool-Season Grasses (continued)

hard fescue and sheep fescue are often found in wild-flower mixes because they make good, resilient meadow grasses.

All fine fescues fare more poorly in hot, humid weather than bluegrass, so their range doesn't extend quite as far south. They also resent overfertilization, becoming more prone to disease (ditto with high humidity). The rate of fertilization should be about half that of Kentucky bluegrass.

Turf-Type Tall Fescue (*Festuca arundinacea*)
Bunchgrass

RAINFALL RANGE: 18 inches minimum for survival in meadows; 21–25+ inches for lawngrass

SOIL: Silty to clay optimum; sandy to heavy clay possible

PH: 4.7–8.5

PROPAGATION: Seed at 7 pounds per 1,000 square feet, or sod

EXPOSURE: Sun and shade

GERMINATION TIME: 7–12 days

MOWING HEIGHT: 3 inches

ADAPTED RANGE:

Turf-type tall fescue (TTTF) is adapted from tall fescue, a cool-season bunchgrass from Europe. Easily established, it grows well in irrigated soils or in areas that get about 18 inches of precipitation a year. It performs best in clayey sands, clayey loams, and clay soils, and it tolerates salt. Turf-type fall fescues gave the best performance and bluegrass-like appearance at Denver Water's Xeriscape Demonstration Garden during the first five years of its test of five mixtures. An earlier mixture of TTTF and bromegrass is now completely TTTF.

Many of the newest strains of tall fescue have been developed specifically for wearability. For the best turf appearance, fescue should be seeded generously to fill in, being a bunch-type grass. Where it gets thin from wear, it tends to become thick-bladed and have bare spaces between the "bunches" where weeds can move in. Avoid mowing at less than the recommended height or there's going to be more bunchiness. Note that naturally occurring endophytes (fungi) — see the following discussion under "Perennial Ryegrass" — that have been bred into some strains of TTTF tend to reduce weed growth.

Fescue is more tolerant of shade than either KBG or buffalograss. It is used in the Eastern U.S. for mined-land reclamation, in part because of its wide range of pH tolerance. (In fact, it has naturalized and about taken over some areas of the East, but in arid and semiarid regions it requires moist or irrigated sites.)

Turf-type tall fescue has been in place at Denver Water's Xeriscape Demonstration Garden since 1983, enduring drought and a minimum of attention.

Turf-type tall fescue has a dense root system concentrated in the top 12 inches of soil, but if irrigation is deep and infrequent, it may send roots down as far as 4 feet in sandy soil, which helps it survive drought. TTTF actually has a higher evapotranspiration rate (rate at which it removes moisture from the soil through evaporation and transpiration) than KBG, but its deep root system leads it to need less water under the right soil conditions. If TTTF is grown in clay soil, the roots may be limited to 2 feet, lowering its drought tolerance to not much better than KBG.

TTTF is green longer than bluegrass—and needs little or no fertilizer. Don't fail to mow weekly, though, or it will get out of hand. It doesn't have the drought-dormancy mechanism that KBG has, so if it becomes too stressed it will croak.

Perennial Ryegrass (*Lolium perenne*)
Bunchgrass

RAINFALL RANGE: Approximately 15+ inches

SOIL: Wide range; best on neutral to slightly acidic, fertile

PH: 6.0–7.0; the cultivar 'Norlea' performs well up to pH 8.5

PROPAGATION: Seed at 7 pounds per 1,000 square feet

EXPOSURE: Sun to light shade

GERMINATION TIME: 3–7 days

MOWING HEIGHT: 2½–3 inches

ADAPTED RANGE:

Perennial ryegrass is a rapidly developing grass, finer in texture than annual ryegrass, and is sometimes used to overseed warm-season grasses. It has excellent wearability, doesn't produce thatch, and tolerates some shade.

On the minus side, perennial ryegrass is a high-maintenance grass with marginal winter-hardiness, it doesn't recuperate well from drought, it requires frequent watering, and has only fair drought tolerance. That's a lot of minuses, isn't it?

Perennial ryegrass' main claim to fame is that back in the 1980s, it was discovered that certain fungi called endophytes, which the grass hosted without harm to itself, actually repelled some grass-infecting insects such as weevils, bluegrass billbugs, and sod webworms. These endophytes are contained within the cells of the grass and are passed to the new generation of grass through the seeds. Some perennial ryegrasses have multiple disease resistance as a result.

Because of its poor drought tolerance, perennial ryegrass is not highly recommended for Xeriscape, though it does grow well in the cool-climate areas of the West. Perhaps its most useful contribution is the endophytes, which are now being bred into strains of the more drought- tolerant tall fescues.

Annual Ryegrass (*Lolium multiflorum*)
Bunchgrass

RAINFALL RANGE: 18+ inches

SOIL: Tolerates a wide range

PH: 6.0–7.0

PROPAGATION: Seed at 9 pounds per 1,000 square feet

EXPOSURE: Sun

GERMINATION TIME: 3–7 days

MOWING HEIGHT: 1 inch

ADAPTED RANGE:

Annual ryegrass has little going for it in xeriscaping, needing frequent watering and having poor drought tolerance. Although it has some usefulness as a fast-germinating cover crop that can provide protection for slower-to-start perennial grass seed when sown together, it's not generally recommended for home lawns.

Annual ryegrass is just that, an annual, which will die out over the winter. If it constitutes more than 20 percent of a grass seed mixture, bare spots will result when this grass dies.

The clever Xeriscape gardener might use annual ryegrass the way the pros (reclamation experts) do, as a temporary cover crop to prevent erosion in anticipation of a permanent seeding the following growing season. It can also be used as a "green manure" crop to be turned under and allowed to lie fallow for several weeks to add nitrogen to the soil before a permanent groundcover is planted.

Rough Bluegrass (*Poa trivialis*)
Sod-forming

RAINFALL RANGE: 25–30+ inches

SOIL: Wet, clayey, poorly drained

PH: 6.0–7.0

PROPAGATION: Seed at 1–1½ pounds per 1,000 square feet

EXPOSURE: Sun or shade

GERMINATION TIME: 21 days

MOWING HEIGHT: 1–2 inches

ADAPTED RANGE:

Also called rough-stalk bluegrass, this bluegrass is noted primarily for its shade tolerance. It has the bright green color and fine texture of KBG, but requires frequent watering and is not drought tolerant. It also has poor wearability and can get weedy. It's probably not a good choice for Xeriscape unless you have a shady area that naturally receives a lot of water.

Cool-Season Grasses (continued)

Annual Bluegrass (*Poa annua*)
Bunchgrass
Not recommended for lawns because of its unattractive, low-growing tufted habit. (It looks like a weed, man!)

Kentucky Bluegrass (*Poa pratensis*)
Sod-forming
RAINFALL RANGE: 35–56 inches optimum; 20 inches minimum (enough for survival only—and it thins out in this range to look like a bunchgrass)
SOIL: Moist, well drained, fertile, medium-textured
PH: 6.0–7.0
PROPAGATION: Seed at 3–4 pounds per 1,000 square feet, or sod
EXPOSURE: Sun to light shade
GERMINATION TIME: 6–30 days
MOWING HEIGHT: 2½–3 inches; unmowed height 12–36 inches
ADAPTED RANGE:

Kentucky bluegrass (KBG) is the fine-bladed cool-season favorite of the northern United States and Canada. Most varieties of Kentucky bluegrass available today originated in the cool, humid regions of the world.

Bluegrass is popular not only because of its texture, color, and excellent wearability, but also because of its ease of handling for sod growers. The sod can be rolled up easily, and new grass will grow from the exposed roots after the top sod layer is cut. KBG seed is usually sold as mixtures of two or more varieties of bluegrass, and this is recommended.

If the intended grass area will be used for children's play or athletic activities, it might be worth the investment in water to maintain it in bluegrass. Otherwise, for areas that receive less than 30 inches of rainfall per year, or not much rainfall in the summer, there are better choices for a low-water yard, or section of the yard, than KBG.

Much of the landscape water use and abuse in semi-arid climates comes from trying to keep KBG green through the summer. Because it's a cool-season grass with low drought avoidance (turns brown quickly when drought occurs), the natural tendency for Kentucky bluegrass is to turn brown in summer's heat.

We lose our faith in its ability to revive when cool weather and more precipitation come along, and it's hard, hard, hard to resist the temptation to give it lots of water when it starts going dormant. And the fact is, KBG does need at least 18–20 inches of water per year just to survive, so if you live in an area that gets less than that you'll have to water some.

If you keep it mowed (which most of us will be doing, of course), it will need more watering to keep it thick and resistant to weed invasion. Just keep the waterings deep and infrequent, and try not to panic if it gets a little brown in between.

Kentucky bluegrass is fairly "forgiving," making a decent turf on poor soils, but it will often develop thatch and disease problems later. KBG is one grass for which it will really pay off to amend the soil as well as possible before installation.

Perennial ryegrass is often mixed with bluegrass to improve the drought avoidance of the lawn (meaning its ability to stay green during drought). This also improves disease resistance because grass is not a "one-crop field." If disease invades, it will be limited to one species or the other, but not both.

These cultivars of Kentucky bluegrass are said to be somewhat drought-tolerant: 'America,' 'Apollo,' 'Brilliant,' 'Classic,' 'Compact,' 'Livingston,' 'SR2000,' 'Showcase,' and 'Unique.

OTHER GRASSES

Alkaligrass is useful primarily where the soil is very saline. It can provide good turf quality, similar to that of fine fescue in appearance. It tolerates a range of mowing heights, likes moisture, and, oddly enough, is not competitive with weeds and other grasses if the salinity level is too low.

Annual cover crops such as **triticale, winter rye, wheat, oats,** and **barley,** as well as **annual ryegrass,** are notable for Xeriscape only in the fact that they can be used as temporary cover when drought restrictions are in effect. These grasses will be able to germinate and produce some erosion protection, even with only two waterings a week, and they all can be mowed to about 3–4 inches high.

Creeping bentgrass is not suitable for the home lawn, being a very high-maintenance, high-water grass. The only reason it's around these parts is that it can tolerate extremely short mowing heights (½ inch), so is used for golf greens and grass tennis courts.

Zoysiagrass is the drought-tolerant warm-season grass of the South, but suffers winter dieback every year in Colorado. It's very difficult to establish here, and is thatchy and invasive. It will be several years before cultivars are developed for Colorado.

Bermudagrass, a warm-season grass that performs well in the South and Southwest is not as hardy here. Some experimental varieties show better cold hardiness, but the grass is invasive, aggressive, and very difficult to eradicate once started. "If you have it, your neighbors have it," I've heard on more than one occasion.

Canada blue fescue is a newly developed grass combination available as sod in Colorado. It is a blend of Canada bluegrass with four types of fescue (Chewings, hard, red, and blue), said to need 50 percent less water and fertilizer than straight KBG within two months of

Creeping veronica (Veronica pectinata) *makes a nice lawn substitute for a low-traffic area in Mary Ellen Keskimaki's Xeriscape.*

laying the sod. These savings continue in succeeding years, making this blend as drought-tolerant as buffalo-grass or blue grama grass. It needs mowing only once every two weeks, at a height of approximately 5 inches. It tends to fade during heat if too frequently mowed. It works well for alternative "meadow lawns," and as a substitute for seeded fine fescue if instant green is needed.

Tall fescue (dwarf hybrids) is blend of hybrids that uses 20–30 percent less water than KBG because of its deep root system, and 50 percent less fertilizer, after one season. The roots continue to grow deeper in the second year, and need the two years of growth to attain their ultimate growth, and thus, drought tolerance.

SHADE TOLERANCE

In the past, home landscapers were advised to pick among fine fescues, particularly red and Chewings fescues, if they had excessive shade in their yards. However, studies have shown that the following cultivars of other grasses performed well in the shade, too:

KENTUCKY BLUEGRASS: 'A-34,' 'Alpine,' 'Apex,' 'America,' 'Blacksburg,' 'Bristol,' 'Classic,' 'Freedom,' 'Georgetown,' 'Glade,' 'Limousine,' 'Mystic,' 'Nugget,' and 'Ram-I'

TALL FESCUE: 'Rebel' and 'Kentucky 31'

PERENNIAL RYEGRASS: 'Pennfine' and 'Linn'

With shade tolerance, as with drought tolerance, it's best to consult with a county extension agent or other local expert as to the best species and cultivars for your area.

PRACTICAL TURF AREAS II:
INSTALLATION

Now that you've wracked your brains to figure out what kind of lawngrass to grow, you still have to decide how to put it in.

ABOVE: *Blue grama grass has a feathery texture.*
Photo by Connie Ellefson.
OPPOSITE: *A mixture of groundcovers and trees makes an excellent low-water treatment for this "hell strip."*

BASIC PLANTING OPTIONS

You can seed, sod, or plug (plugs come from sod). Lucky for you, depending on your grass choice, you might not need to make a decision; some grasses are available only as seed or sod. Others offer options....

There are pros and cons for each method. For the adventurous xeriscaper, seeding adds dozens of grass varieties and strains to choose from, letting you tailor the lawn to your own taste, as well as specific site conditions. Grasses available for sod are severely limited. Seeding is less expensive initially than sod, and, with the right equipment, it can spread quickly over a large area.

However, there's one key point to remember for xeriscaping: *If what you want is lawngrass growth that will cover the ground in a reasonably short amount of time, say within a few weeks, seeding, in general, takes more water and more time.* It takes water to keep the ground constantly moist until germination (may need sprinkling one to four times a day for two to three weeks), and to keep the tender sprouts from drying out (more watering for another week or two). Then it must be watered regularly for several more weeks until fully established.

A sodded lawn, by contrast, may need water daily initially, then two or three weeks of twice- to thrice-weekly watering to become established. Sometimes the cost of the seed added to the cost of the water and the time to water equals or exceeds the initial cost of sod. Sod has additional advantages in that it can be installed on slopes without washing away, it provides instant cover, and keeps mud tracking inside to a minimum. It can be installed almost anytime during the growing season, and it smothers weeds near the surface.

Weeds are a discouraging, though not unnatural, presence in the seeded lawn. They are not only the "plants with the greater will to live;" they're actually part of an orderly plant succession in the establishment of mature grassland. If left to itself, an area of bare ground will be thick with annual weeds the first year or two, followed by perennial weeds that crowd out the annuals,

CHAPTER 6:
PRACTICAL TURF AREAS II: INSTALLATION

and finally perennial grasses that eventually eliminate the perennial weeds. This process can take seven or more years if left to nature alone. Dang! That's a long time!

By maintaining a lawn, you're actually keeping the grass in a suspended and somewhat "immature" state, reducing the perennial grasses' dominance, so those childish annual weeds just keep right on appearing.

Newly seeded lawns often contain annual weeds, including weedy grasses that sprout from seed in the ground and from the grass seed itself. After the turf becomes established and is mowed several times, most of these disappear. However, perennial grass weeds should be removed before the grass is seeded. If you're trying to establish a new buffalograss lawn, for example, Kentucky bluegrass remnants are considered a weed.

Eliminating weeds as much as possible before seeding or sodding helps to bring about a thick stand of grass such as this.

You have some choices in seeding to keep the weeds *and* watering down to a minimum:

- Sow the grass seed anytime, knowing it won't germinate for weeks or months until conditions are just right. This saves water, but birds might eat the seeds, and weeds will still really grow.
- Allow the weeds to grow along with the grass the first year—sounds strange, but the weeds provide shade and protection for grass seedlings, which cuts down on watering. In early spring of the second year, apply a pre-emergent herbicide to the lawn to knock out the weeds before they get started. The result will be a thick stand of grass achieved with little or no pain, and limited use of herbicide. You can avoid the herbicide completely, but you'll be doing some serious hand-weeding in the second growing season. This method is not as successful as the next option.

- Get the weeds under control before starting the lawn. According to Warren Schultz, author of *The Chemical-Free Lawn: The Newest Varieties and Techniques to Grow Lush, Hardy Grass* (Rodale Press, 1989) and co-author of *Ortho's All About Lawns* (Ortho Books, 1999), one of the best ways to get a new or improved lawn off to a good start is to reduce the weed population as much as possible before sodding or seeding. This will cut down as much as anything on the amount of time you have to spend maintaining the lawn later. This choice is recommended by Colorado State University turf experts, as well (http://csuturf.colostate.edu).

Several ways to control weeds are listed in the next few sections, and under "Stand Establishment" in the "Prairie Gardens" section of Chapter 7 (see p. 122). (Soil sterilization is *never* recommended because beneficial soil organisms are killed, as well as all the plants.)

Realize that it's not possible to eliminate all the weed seeds, some of which are viable for scores of years. Dan Johnson, native plant specialist at Denver Botanic Gardens, bought a house with a 60-year-old concrete driveway in the middle of the back yard. He had the driveway removed, and before long noted prickly poppy weeds sprouting! Typical soil contains about 5,000 weed seeds in the top 6 inches of soil per square foot. Bringing in animal manures and imported topsoil can chip in—ha!—a few more.

REMOVING EXISTING SOD

People devise some interesting methods for removing existing sod from an area to be replaced with a more drought-tolerant species or other groundcover. They work for weed cover on a new site as well as removing grass from an existing landscape. No way is perfect, but knowing what you'll replace the grass with helps.

The "easiest" way to get rid of existing lawngrass is to rent a sod cutter (or better yet, hire someone else to do it!) and remove the top layer of grass and roots. If you're planning to install native grasses that are adapted to poor soil, this method is just fine, though it does leave some rhizomes that will re-sprout. Compost the removed sod for other use in the landscape.

If you want to put in a perennial bed, though, retain as much of the nutrient value of the sod as you can. You can still use this method, just save all the grass and attached dirt and compost it for

One method of reducing turf area is to outline the new edge by cutting a small trench and spraying the unwanted turf area with glyphosate. Then cover the old area with a thick layer of mulch. *Photos by Don Buma.*

later use in the garden. (For additional considerations and information, look at the "Home Lawn Care" section of http://csuturf.colostate.edu, especially the "information on starting a new lawn or repairing a lawn damaged by drought.") I have detailed some other methods in the following section.

RIPPING OUT I

Use a sod cutter, shovel, or sod spade (with a square, sharp edge) to cut the roots of the grass at a depth of ½–2 inches. Then you can either give the sod away, haul it away, or compost it.

ADVANTAGES: Removes most intense competition from existing grass roots and a thick layer of weed seeds.

DISADVANTAGES: Hard, hard work. Sod cutters are heavy and so is sod. In poor soil this method removes the most nutrient-rich soil layer (unless composted and returned, which takes a lot of time, too).

RIPPING OUT II

Essentially start out the same as "Ripping Out I," but this time turn slabs of sod upside down in place and let them stay there until the grass is dead. Then rototill or spade broken-up slabs into the soil along with your soil amendments.

ADVANTAGES: Keeps nutrients in soil. May take shorter amount of time than the tilling method described next. This is possibly the best compromise.

DISADVANTAGES: Still back-breaking. Weed seeds remain present (but then they always will be, no matter what you do). Grass at the pieces' edges could arise from the deep and continue to grow.

TILLING UP

With this option, you first rototill the area. Then you let the lawn sit four to six weeks to allow the grass and weeds to re-sprout and dead grass and weeds to decompose, then till the area again. You might have to do this more than once.

ADVANTAGES: Lets the rototiller do (most of) the work. Retains the nutrients and organic matter of the grass.

DISADVANTAGES: Tiller could still be hard to handle. Ground is "under construction" for a long time.

REPLACING WITH A TOUGH GROUNDCOVER

This is an easier approach than any mentioned previously. First, plant an aggressive groundcover such as juniper or purple-leaved wintercreeper in good-sized holes right in the grass. Mulch with 3–4 inches of wood chips or other mulch. The plants will eventually take over the grass.

ADVANTAGES: Doesn't take chemicals or too much labor, just enough to dig the holes for the plants.

DISADVANTAGES: Expensive if you have to buy all new plants. Might take one or two years to cover the grass.

USING SOIL SOLARIZATION

Here's another easier approach. About a month before planting, just deeply water the area to be redone. Then cover the area completely with clear or black plastic and anchor the plastic with rocks or soil around the edges. Leave the plastic on until the grass is dead. (About one to two months— summer months, I mean. They're the only ones that work for this method.)

ADVANTAGES: Grass and sprouting weeds are killed by intense heat under plastic. Easy technique.

DISADVANTAGES: Doesn't seem to work well where nights are cool (Colorado). Not enough heat generated to kill weeds. Plastic must be anchored or it will blow around.

KILLING GRASS WITH HERBICIDE

There are chemical alternatives to consider in removing old turf. This method is only recommended if you're getting rid of lawn in order to put in prairie grass or non-turf alternatives. If you're preparing the area for a different turfgrass, you have to do additional work, which is included in the next method. To kill grass with herbicide, first follow the directions for spraying the area to be de-sodded, using "mild" herbicide such as glyphosate. Always remember to keep watering the area before applying the herbicide, as these chemicals only work on actively growing plants. Allow the lawn to dry for a day after spraying it and then continue watering for 10 days. Continue to spot spray any weeds or grass remaining green.

If you're preparing the ground for prairie grasses, you might need to take a whole summer to eliminate the weeds in this way. During the rest of the growing season, you'll need to do a check to chase down and spray any green that appears with glyphosate, especially about two weeks before the first frost, when weeds are most actively absorbing nutrients (and herbicide) into their roots.

ADVANTAGES: Little labor involved. Kills annual weeds, as well. Will not harm nearby existing trees and shrubs if used correctly.

DISADVANTAGES: You might just not want to use chemicals. Glyphosate is not a harmless substance; otherwise it wouldn't work. Repeated use of herbicide near existing trees and shrubs may damage them over the long run. However, glyphosate is acknowledged to be one of the safest herbicides.

RENOVATION USING CORE AERATION AND SEEDING

Most of this info is from the Colorado State University turf website, http://csuturf.colostate.edu. It assumes you want to take the shortest route to getting rid of the old lawn, i.e., spraying it with glyphosate. Aside from the convenience and relative safety of this method, it also allows

Cool-season grasses green up early in spring.

you to take advantage of the shading and mulching provided by the remnants of the dead sod. Here are the steps:

1. Kill the existing vegetation with herbicide, as described in the previous section.

2. After it's dead, mow the site to about ½ inch in height and remove the cuttings by raking or using a mower bagging unit.

3. If there is existing thatch (matted layer of organic material on the surface) deeper than 1 inch, it should be removed from the lawn using a sod cutter. A shallower thatch layer doesn't need to be removed, but you still have to expose the soil surface

by either (a) core cultivating with holes 1 to 3 inches deep and 2 inches apart in all directions or (b) power raking deep enough to expose the soil, run over the lawn in two directions, and removing debris by raking or bagging.

4. Seed at the recommended rate, dividing the seed into two batches, making passes in two directions with a drop spreader.

5. Rake lightly to work seed into the soil.

6. If desired, apply a starter fertilizer at the rate recommended on the label, or check out the "Fertilizer" section later in this chapter (see p. 109). Some experts recommend only adding nitrogen to areas previously planted with turfgrass, as Colorado soils may already have enough phosphorus and potassium from their first go-round.

7. Look at the after-care recommendations in the last paragraph of the "Mixtures" section for your next moves (see p. 111).

SMOTHERING WITH MULCH

Mulch can also be used to remove lawn. First, cover the area with a layer of newspapers several sheets thick. It's OK to use color-advertising pages, too, because newspapers are printed with non-toxic vegetable-based ink these days. Then cover the newspapers with several inches of an organic mulch, such as shredded bark. (Don't use gravel mulches as they will tear the newspaper and let weeds through too easily.) Once you've mulched, you can just leave the area alone to compost the grass until next year, or dig planting holes for flowers, trees, or shrubs.

ADVANTAGES: Extremely inexpensive and easy. I tried this one. A year later, instead of scrawny grass and compacted soil there was a thin black layer of compost from the newspaper and a thicker brown layer of decomposed grass and roots. Areas that were impenetrable with a shovel before then were easy to turn over.

DISADVANTAGES: Newspaper must be well covered with mulch or it will be a sight. Weeds can still come up through gaps or tears. Don't try to spread out the newspapers while the wind is blowing, unless you like a lot of excitement!

After a winter of being smothered by newspapers and mulch, this former bluegrass lawn is ready for tillage and buffalograss seed.

LET IT BE

Last, but certainly not least, for the xeriscaper most inclined to be economical with his or her time is the simple method of just leaving the grass there. Before you expend the energy to remove

it, make sure it's not filling some important function for which grass is best suited. Then devote your time to renovating the grass itself for improved water thriftiness by aerating, overseeding, and/or fertilizing (or *not* fertilizing), and by being a better-informed "irrigator" as explained in Chapter 10: Irrigation. Or let it go to seed and become a grassy meadow.

ADVANTAGES: Easier in terms of upfront labor, but you might spend more time down the road aerating, overseeding, and irrigating.

DISADVANTAGES: You still have a turf you might not want.

WHEN TO SOD OR SOW

The best time to plant a new lawn is when both temperature and moisture are favorable for seed germination and the growth of seedlings or plugs, but not for weed growth. Most weeds germinate in the spring, languish in the summer heat, and sprout to a lesser extent in the fall.

For seeding or plugging a new lawn, you need six to eight weeks of favorable weather for the grass to become sufficiently established; for sodding, a month is needed.

For cool-season grasses, late summer to early fall is the recommended time to seed a turfgrass. Less water will be needed then because evaporation slows from the soil with cooler temperatures. You can lay sod anytime during the growing season, but you may use considerably more water by starting midsummer. By laying sod in the spring, you can sometimes take advantage of spring rains to eliminate some of the watering.

For warm-season grasses, mid-spring to midsummer is the best time for seeding because this is when soil temperatures are most favorable for germination.

At high elevations—above 7,000 feet— don't use warm-season grasses at all. Instead, seed cool-season grasses beginning in spring when temperatures start to warm up.

Grasses for Overseeding and Renovation

When changing out your type of turf, the idea is to match the appearance of the old grass with the new, thus:

OK	Not OK
Changing to ryegrass from bluegrass	Changing to turf-type tall fescues from bluegrass
To fine fescue from bluegrass	To buffalograss from bluegrass, ryegrass, or turf-type tall fescue
	To bluegrass, turf-type tall fescue, or ryegrass from buffalograss

Xeriscape is right at home even in the most exclusive neighborhoods.

in whatever moisture zone you find yourself in throughout the Rocky Mountain region.

To make picking your plants easier, first roughly define your goal. Do you want a no-water landscape (after establishment, of course, as even Xeriscape plants are thirsty when first planted), a low-maintenance yard, year-round color, a landscape attractive to wildlife? Do you want to re-create a particular plant habitat, create locations for favorite plants, or, you know, like, what do you WANT???

In this chapter we look at selecting ornamental grasses and groundcovers (other than turf), with some details on how to choose, install, and/or propagate them.

In choosing plants, keep in mind one of the fundamental truths about Xeriscape:

- You can water your plants to your heart's delight. If you don't drown them, they may flower more, they may be a little more fiercely green, and they may grow a little or a lot larger than in past years.

- Or you can do your best to choose the right plants, give them appropriate homes, and never water them after they're established. They may flower indifferently, they may have a subdued rather than brilliant green color, and they may not grow an inch over last year, but they probably won't die! (Though they die in a forest fire or break in a snowstorm if too drought-weakened, so don't get too carried away with the tough love.)

PICKING AND CHOOSING

Recently a group of Colorado garden center owners gathered to decide how to break out their list of X-rated plants: X being drought-tolerant, XX being very drought-tolerant, and XXX being really, really drought-tolerant.

After scratching their heads for a good while, they ruefully concluded that they really didn't know for sure. Plants that had always appeared on the moderate water lists were found by some to have sailed through the big drought of '02 looking very good. The professionals had to conclude it's just a guess.

While there has been extensive research into the water needs of turfgrasses, little such research has been done on ornamental plants. So we're left with the experience of amateur and professional gardeners for guidance in plant water use.

Are you shocked? Well, there are thousands of plants to research and choose from, and let's face it, we've all been busy.

You must always remember that no matter how triple X-ed a plant is rated, *any NEW plant, whether started from seed or transplant, undergoes an initial period of establishment during which it needs a higher quantity of water to survive than it will after it has settled in.*

If rainfall doesn't provide this water, then we must. We don't leave new plants to fend

Siberian peashrub (Caragana arborescens) *has leaves divided into small leaflets, one of the characteristics of certain drought-tolerant plants.*

for themselves any more than we expect young children to tough it out on their own.

Thus you might be startled to see your water consumption actually increase the first year if you have introduced a large number of new plants into the landscape. Don't despair; in the second year you should see a marked decrease in water consumption for trees and shrubs.

In the third year you should be able to eliminate additional watering (except, perhaps, during a dry fall and winter). With drought-tolerant perennials, the period of establishment is shorter, and with appropriate annuals, it is a matter of weeks. For many water-thirsty species, however, we might be tied to watering them as long as we want the plant to live, if we don't find the perfect spot for it.

NATIVES

The most obvious place to start looking for plants for Xeriscape is in the category of natives: plants that thrive in your region on the amount of rainfall given to them by nature. They need less fertilizer because they get required nutrients from the native soil. They are usually more resistant to pests and diseases, so fewer chemicals are required to prevent these problems. Many people think native means less colorful, but the fact is there are brilliantly hued flowers and foliage among the natives of all regions.

Native plants will usually withstand any record-breaking extremes of weather, especially long cold spells, which may kill non-native plants. Over time, droughts are interspersed with ideal

General Characteristics of Drought-Tolerant Plants

Many drought-tolerant species share common characteristics that have to do with how they adapt to and survive drought:

- One rule of thumb (though not an ironclad one) is that the larger the leaf size, the more water the plant needs, and the easier it will scorch in the sun. (A notable exception is the catalpa, a splendid Midwest native drought-tolerant tree with huge heart-shaped leaves. I still haven't figured this out, except maybe it just shows what a good sense of humor God has.)
- Grayish, fuzzy, or finely divided leaves usually mean the plant is drought-tolerant.
- Low-growing plants may be drought-tolerant. They hug the ground to stay out of drying winds.

moisture conditions and flooding. Natives are adapted to most of these seasonal variations (although the big drought of '02 brought up the sobering realization that our natives are adapted to summer rains, and some of them couldn't withstand the bone-dry season we had then).

Southwest native plant specialist Judith Phillips recommends studying not only which plants grow easily in the wild near your home, but also where and with what other plants. Phillips recommends asking yourself the following questions about how natives naturally grow where you live:

- Does the plant grow in wide-open areas or in a well-sheltered spot?
- Does it grow along stream banks or on rocky hillsides?
- Is it thriving where the soil has been undisturbed for centuries or does it spring up prolifically like sunflowers do, where the soil is recently disturbed, as in road cuts?
- Does it like sunny, south-facing slopes or cooler, moister, north-facing slopes?
- Do you find it in groups, as isolated plants, or with a particular other species?

Phillips emphasizes the practicality in thinking this through. If your goal is a self-sustaining landscape, it's especially important to choose plants with soil and exposure requirements that your site can meet. The plant that can thrive on natural rainfall, as well as be tolerant of drought, is less likely to weaken and be susceptible to diseases and pests.

Grouping plants that grow together in the wild gives them a better chance to help each other in the same ways they do naturally, whether providing shade for protection, increasing humidity, or moderating temperature. This will reduce the nursing that *you* have to do on your plants.

By using native plants you can provide food or cover for native birds, and thus, in a small way, help preserve the habitat for a wider variety of species. Think of it as a step toward taking monotonous and foreign habitat (nonstop velvet greensward of the 'burbs) out, and putting complex, diverse habitat in. It's good for the 'hood, and I bet you feel better already.

NON-NATIVES

When I first started writing about Xeriscape, I heard a lot of whining around the country as to how Xeriscape plants should *not* be equated with native plants! People clutched at

my sleeve and fervently begged me to reassure the budding xeriscaper that if they don't favor natives, that's OK, and that many beautiful non-native plants work well, especially those adapted to periods of drought and/or poor soil. So here it goes.

Species native to the Mediterranean area, China, Australia, and New Zealand are often successful in American Xeriscapes. Also, many adapted non-native plants were brought over so long ago (like 300 years) that it's hard to say what's native and what isn't.

ABOVE: *For her Xeriscape, Phoebe Lawrence has chosen 'Carol Mackie' daphne (Daphne burkwoodii 'Carol Mackie,' background) and 'Ruby Glow' daphne (Daphne cneorum 'Ruby Glow,' foreground). Although non-native, they are appropriate for moderate water zones in any Xeriscape and are beautiful in the spring.*

RIGHT: *In contrast, native dotted gayfeather (Liatris punctata) packs a magenta punch to the dry water zone of Xeriscapes in the latter part of the summer.*

More important than a plant's parentage, native or not, are the following considerations:

- SUITABILITY. Is the plant native to the specific microclimate/environment you want to put it into? A plant native to creek-bottom areas will not thrive on your dry, rocky slope. Some natives depend on ample moisture.

- AVAILABILITY. Some natives are hard to grow under nursery conditions, and digging plants up from the wild is the fastest way to endanger them. Fortunately, the number of native plant nurseries is on the rise.

- NATURAL GROUPING. When using natives, group them with plants of similar horticultural needs—not just water requirements, but soil nutrition and soil texture, too. Obviously, this is going to be easier if they are natives that grow together in the wild.

Natives may be just too "wild and woolly" for your taste. You may not like the untamed look or coarse features some of them have. Well, they may look untamed because they are, and untended, too. If placed in your landscape and given the same care you give other plants, they might clean up real nice.

INVASIVENESS

"Invasiveness" is a term that often crops up in xeriscaping, mainly because some of the most drought-tolerant species are pretty tough plants. It's one of the reasons they survive drought. But problems can occur when certain plants "escape cultivation." Such plants start to take over if removed from their original environment—away from the attendant pests, diseases, and competition from other nearby

Don't Ever Plant These, as They're Invasive in Our Land

BOTANICAL NAME	COMMON NAME
Anthemis arvensis	Scentless chamomile
Chrysanthemum leucanthemum	Ox-eye daisy
Clematis orientalis	Chinese clematis
Elaeagnus angustifolia	Russian olive
Euphorbia cyparissias	Cypress spurge
E. myrsinites	Myrtle spurge
Hesperis matronalis	Dame's rocket
Lathyrus latifolius	Perennial sweet pea
Linaria dalmatica	Dalmatian toadflax
L. vulgaris	Yellow toadflax
Lythrum salicaria	Purple loosestrife
L. virgatum	Wand loosestrife
Potentilla recta	Sulfur cinquefoil
Salvia aethiopis	Mediterranean sage
Saponaria officinalis	Bouncingbet
Tamarix gallica	Tamarisk
T. parviflora	Saltcedar
T. ramosissima	Saltcedar
Tanacetum vulgare	Common tansy

SOURCE: Adapted from Colorado Native Plant Society brochure and "Best Perennials for the Rocky Mountains and High Plains," CSU Bulletin 573A, Tannehill and Klett, Dec. 2002 (more of a book than a bulletin, and an excellent source of in-depth perennials info).

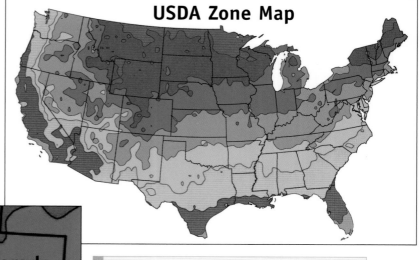

USDA Zone Map

Colorado

The USDA Zone Map groups areas of similar cold-hardiness into zones. Colorado has four zones: 3, 4, 5, and 6 (most of the state falls under zones 4 and 5). Refer to this map while reading this book's plant lists, most of which include references to various zones.

| Zone 3 | Zone 4 | Zone 5 | Zone 6 |

species—to a more hospitable one with more rainfall or irrigation and less competition.

Russian olive is an unfortunate example of this phenomenon. It's a great little picturesque, gray-foliaged, drought-tolerant tree that has the sweetest-smelling June flowers west of the Pecos, and mildly apricot-flavored seeds delicious to birds. It was introduced in the late 1800s, touted as a windbreak and an ornamental species.

Alas, the bird droppings spread the seeds far and wide, and the species escaped cultivation in Minnesota, other parts of the Midwest, and even in the Rockies. It has crowded out some natives that provide nesting sites for birds and has taken over pastureland. Ten years ago, the Russian olive didn't appear on the "Don't Ever Plant These, as They're Invasive in Our Land" list for Colorado and the Rockies, but now it does, sad to say. See the list (opposite) of these insidious monsters.

One of the advantages of living in the near-desert states is that invasiveness into the natural environment is often less of a problem than in higher-rainfall areas of our country. (So are some of the more disgusting bugs and diseases.) Some plants are called invasive because they'll just take over your yard (not the entire Western Hemisphere) if you don't keep them confined.

COLD HARDINESS

Plants available from local nurseries usually fall within the local hardiness zone (see map on the opposite page to figure out your zone). If you order plants from some distant source, you'll need to pay attention to the hardiness zones listed.

Panayoti Kelaidis, curator at the Denver Botanic Gardens, stresses that cold-hardiness, with

For simplicity and elegance, it's hard to beat maiden hair grass (Miscanthus sinensis).

respect to perennials, has been overemphasized. Kelaidis says that in Denver and in other parts of the country he has seen smaller plants, particularly the more drought-tolerant ones, survive in much colder areas than they're "supposed to."

In xeriscaping we look for plants that can survive the minimum amount of precipitation a region can expect. A plant that can survive both drought and other extremes of weather ranks among the truly tough.

GUERRILLA XERISCAPING

Some of my previous gardens were just big Xeriscape experiments, in that I purposely did not water plants, wanting to see how far they could be pushed. For example, I once had two tea rose bushes in my back yard on the west side of a fence downhill from the lawn. They were never fed, watered (beyond the runoff from the grass), or pruned in seven years, beyond cutting off a few blooms. They even endured bitter cold spells without being mulched. Each year they produced beautiful blooms on schedule.

Horticultural research seems to be showing that many, many more plants are drought-tolerant than was previously thought. Often they have just never been given the chance to show what they can do, as gardeners are so addicted to watering. Our recent droughts have given this research a big boost, so I encourage you to live on the edge a little.

THE NON-FLOWER CHOICES

ORNAMENTAL GRASSES

Ornamental grasses are a natural for Xeriscape because they not only require little water (if placed appropriately), but also little maintenance. They need no deadheading (removal of spent flowers to promote continued bloom) or mowing. They are very pest- and disease-free, and they don't need a lot of fertilizer, which will make them grow too quickly and die out in the center of the plant. They also accommodate a wide range of soil types.

Ornamental grasses add needed winter interest to the landscape because they don't need to be cut down until spring, and the golden remains of the plant are very lovely. In summer they provide sound and movement with every breeze, and blend well with other types of plants.

The more drought-tolerant grasses (listed on p. 120) will make do with average soil, but the ones that need slightly higher moisture will do much better with excellent soil preparation. Most of these plants can be found in local nurseries. Others can be started from seed or divided from existing plants.

PRAIRIE GARDENS

Growing up in the West, seeing only the grazed-over desiccation of the former prairie and grass-land, I was unprepared for the lushness and splendor of the reconstructed tallgrass, midgrass, and shortgrass prairies that I saw one day on an Indian-summer visit to the Denver Botanic

Gardens. The "understory" grasses were thick on the ground, and the taller grasses ranged over them in an endless weaving of delicate gold silhouettes. In 10 seconds I came to see why devotees of prairie gardens labor patiently, sometimes for years, to re-create this scene.

Prairies are mixtures of grasses and wildflowers (see the next chapter for a detailed discussion on wildflowers) in varying ratios, but usually about 60 to 90 percent grasses. They once covered thousands of square miles of the central United

Ornamental grasses look good year-round. Here they star with bright-blooming asters.

Ornamental Grasses for Xeriscape

XXX-rated plants (Perennials established for at least a year and annuals established for several weeks need to be watered up to ½" every two weeks during the growing season, above and beyond natural precipitation.)

BOTANICAL NAME	COMMON NAME	HEIGHT	ZONE
Agropyron cristatum	Crested wheatgrass	12–18"	3
Agrostis nebulosa	Cloud grass	8–20"	Annual
Andropogon gerardii	Big bluestem	4–6"	3–9
A. saccharoides	Silver beard grass	3'	4–9
Bouteloua curtipendula	Sideoats grama	1–2'	3
B. gracilis	Blue grama grass	1–2'	3
Nassella tenuissima	Silky thread grass	18"	5
Oryzopsis hymenoides	Indian rice grass	18"	5
Panicum virgatum	Switch grass	4–6'	5–9
Schizachyrium scoparium syn. *Andropogon scoparius*	Little bluestem	2–5'	4–9
Sporobulus heterolepsis	Prairie dropseed	18–24"	3–8
Triticum turgidum	Bearded wheat	2–4'	Annual

XX-rated plants
(need ½" applied water every week during growing season)

BOTANICAL NAME	COMMON NAME	HEIGHT	ZONE
Festuca ovina glauca	Blue fescue	4–10"	4–9
Helictotrichon sempervirens	Blue avena grass	4'	4–9
Imperata cylindrica	Japanese blood grass	16–20"	6–9
Phalaris arundinacea 'Picta'	Ribbon grass	1–3'	4–8
Sorghastrum nutans	Indian grass	3–4'	3–8

X-rated plants
(need 1" applied water every week during growing season)

BOTANICAL NAME	COMMON NAME	HEIGHT	ZONE
Calamagrostis x *acutiflora*	Feather reed grass	3–5'	5–9
C. arundinacea 'Karl Foerster'	Karl Foerster feather reed grass	2–4'	4
Chasmanthium latifolium	Northern sea oats	3–4'	4
Deschampsia caespitosa	Hairgrass	12–18"	5–9
Erianthus (Saccharum) ravennae	Hardy plume grass	9–12'	4–9
Festuca arundinacea	Tall fescue	1–2'	2
Miscanthus sinensis (and cultivars)	Maiden hair grass	Varies	4–9
Pennisetum alopecuroides 'Hameln'	Hardy fountain grass	2–3'	5–9
P. setaceum 'Rubrum'	Purple fountain grass	2–3'	Annual

States, blanketing the ground in what truly must have been a blaze of glory. Prairies were a very stable and complex ecosystem, impossible to replicate, but relatively easy to approximate.

Once established, which could take three years or more, prairie gardens are model Xeriscapes: They are drought-tolerant, low-maintenance, and require no watering, fertilizing, or mowing. They are an ideal way to take advantage of a full-sun environment (what they prefer) and also attract birds and butterflies.

Native grasses grow naturally on soils moderately low in nitrogen. They often tolerate soils high in clay and slow to drain. Prairies are found in climates that get lots of winter precipitation, and less in summer. This is why they thrive in our climate, which has a similar precipitation pattern, with little or no irrigation.

TYPES OF GRASSLANDS

According to grass historians, a new type of prairie developed with the advance and retreat of each of the estimated 25 ice ages that have occurred in the earth's history. However, they are grouped into three main categories. Tallgrass prairies covered the eastern part of the American grasslands, where higher rainfall supported larger

plants, some as high as 8 or 9 feet. Typical dominant species included big bluestem (*Andropogon gerardii*), Indian grass (*Sorghastrum nutans*), and switch grass (*Panicum virgatum*).

Re-creating a tallgrass prairie may include seeding or setting out individual plants at intervals. Weeds will probably grow in the spaces between plants for several years until the grasses become tall enough to shade them out. Check local zoning codes that may restrict your prairie. Some cities prohibit anything that even resembles a weed over 6 inches tall in front yards, but let you have your way in the back, as long as neighbors don't complain.

Farther west were midgrass prairies dominated by grasses about knee-high, such as needle-and-thread (*Stipa comata*), little bluestem (*Schizachyrium scoparium*), and western wheatgrass (*Agropyron smithii*). Needle grasses are aggressive and leave sharp seeds on the ground for a couple of months in the summer, so midgrass prairie is a less desirable planting to emulate.

There is debate over whether shortgrass prairie is really a climax prairie or simply the result of overgrazing. But, in any case, a blue grama grass (*Bouteloua gracilis*) and buffalograss (*Buchloe dactyloides*) prairie is fairly simple to re-create because of seed availability, and the way these grasses form a dense cover.

STAND ESTABLISHMENT

Is this straightforward, or what? It means the successful establishment of a good stand of whatever you're trying to raise, whether native grass, wildflowers, or a crop. This section covers suggestions for how to establish your prairie garden, especially shortgrass.

Native grass expert Rick Brune says that the single most important factor in successful prairie gardening is to get the weeds under control BEFORE you do anything else. If you don't, you'll have an ongoing and perhaps overwhelming battle trying to establish prairie grasses and wildflowers in the midst of the more aggressive weeds. The number of weeds you have in the existing groundcover will dictate which of the following methods for establishing a hearty stand will be more successful for you.

Seeds of some prairie grasses and flowers have a low germination rate, having evolved their little ways of making sure their seeds won't sprout until conditions are just right. In some cases seeds must be helped to germinate by scarifying them—rubbing them with rough sandpaper to create cracks for water to get in and induce germination. I kid you not; people actually do this! But I guess you probably will, too, because if you're putting in a prairie garden, you're not one to shirk the tough duties.

Wildflowers dot the shortgrass prairie re-creation at the Denver Botanic Gardens. Photo by Connie Ellefson.

Method 1: Few weeds present

1. If you have a fairly weed-free sod, except for a few dandelions, you can rent a sod cutter and remove the sod, which has the advantage of removing many of the weed seeds, as well. Because buffalograss and blue grama grass are adapted to poor soil, removing the richest layer of humus isn't as disastrous as it would normally be.

2. Remove all rhizomes (runners) of bluegrass or quackgrass in the remaining soil. If you are not sure they are all out, water and wait two weeks, digging out any grasses that sprout. Then till and level the seedbed. (Buffalograss and blue grama grass like lumpy soil for establishment, so you don't have to get rid of every little clod.)

3. You can plant wildflower seedlings started indoors (more cost-effective than broadcasting seeds) at the same time as you sow the grass seed, if you have a fairly weed-free base. To give them a head start on competition from the grass, lay out 6-inch cardboard circles or bottoms of tin cans where you will plant the flowers, and sow the grass seed around these protected areas.

   After several years of following the tradition of sprouting seeds in soil-less medium, transplanting them to soil, then finally planting them in the ground, it dawned on prairie garden sage Rick Brune that the prairie wildflowers were probably used to tough conditions and a short growing season. So now he just sets them out in the seedling stage and has had very good success.

4. Brune has found planting prairie grass seeds between May 1 and mid-June to be most successful in Colorado. (Check with your county extension agent for exact planting time, as it could be later in your area.) Plant later than mid-June and the heat and drought of summer may kill many of your seedlings. Also, the cool-season weeds sprout early in spring, so you get a last chance to nail them before planting.

   Buffalograss is planted ½ to ¾ inch deep. Make furrows about an inch deep and 6–12 inches apart. Broadcast the seed and rake it in across the furrows. This way more of the seed is buried deeper than if you just raked it in. Blue grama grass can be broadcast over the area just seeded with buffalograss, and raked in, too.

   Blue grama grass is usually more abundant in shortgrass prairie than buffalograss (about six to one). With the relative numbers of seed per pound and germination of the two grasses, a ratio of half a pound of blue grama seed and one pound of buffalograss seed is close enough for this purpose. It produces a turf thick enough to crowd out weeds the second year, if not the first.

   Buy blue-green buffalograss seeds because they have been treated to reduce germination time from up to three years to seven to 10 days. Other shortgrass species such as side-oats grama may be overseeded for variety, but it's not necessary.

Sideoats grama grass is easily identified in prairie grass mixes.

5. After completing seeding, rent a roller and roll the entire seedbed. Planting wildflowers is done after rolling and before watering. It's OK to walk on the newly seeded area to plant the flowers, but try to disturb it as little as possible.

   Either spread the wildflowers randomly for a natural look or group them in clumps for patches of color. Real prairies may have up to 15 flowering plants per square yard, but it's hard to realize that, as they're not all in bloom at once. With a large prairie project you might not be able to manage more than about four wildflower plants per square yard (weeding, my dear!), but you can add more later. For an established prairie garden, just dig a 6-inch-wide and 6-inch-deep planting hole through the grass sod for each plant.

6. Establishing a good cover of prairie grasses requires as much watering as a bluegrass lawn. The area must be kept constantly moist for the first three weeks, which might mean watering several times a day if it's windy and hot (get a timer!).

   After that, watering can be reduced to every two to three days, tapering to one deep watering once a week for the first year. Avoid producing drought stress in the plants, as shown by wilting, rolling leaves, or a gray appearance to the plant. From the second year, you should be able to eliminate watering, or at most water two to three times a year. (YAY!)

Another germination-enhancing technique is called stratifying, which means simulating the cool (34–41°F) and moist winter soil conditions most perennials need to go through to germinate by storing the seeds in fridge in moistened vermiculite or perlite for several weeks or months. (This I could handle.)

Brune also says he omits organic soil amendments for stand establishment of native grasses because, even though they might help the plants take hold faster, the plants then tend not to be as durable and long-lived. This gives you the perfect eco-excuse to forgo the hard labor of adding organic amendments to your prairie. Weeds like rich soil, too, so there's an extra excuse.

The addition of fertilizers is *not* recommended. Blue grama grass reacts negatively to nitrogen, and phosphorus and potassium deficiencies are rare in most Colorado soils.

Midgrass prairies feature grasses about knee-high, as replicated here at the Denver Botanic Gardens.

Method 2: Heavy weeds, man!

1. If you've got a heavy or unknown weed problem, go through several cycles of watering to germinate seeds after removing the sod, then hoe to control the weeds and get some idea of the severity of the problem. If it looks hopeless, spray with glyphosate to kill the bluegrass and susceptible weeds, and damage the bindweed and thistle.

   If you don't want to use the broadcast herbicide method, you can either plan on doing a tremendous amount of hand-weeding until the prairie grasses fill in, or till the ground every two to three weeks as new wee crops appear during the growing season. Soil solarization (see "Using Soil Solarization" on p. 103 of the previous chapter) did not work well in Denver when Brune tried the technique: Because of the cool nights, not enough heat was generated to kill the seeds.

   Bindweed (*Convolvulus arvensis*) and thistle (*Cirsium vulgare*) are very difficult to eradicate. Hand-pulling bindweed is said to stimulate further growth, and thistle will grow back if only a tiny amount of root is left in. You might have to resort to spot-killing these pests, but even if you only want to hand-weed, make sure you don't let them overrun your planting area.

   One intriguing technique for killing bindweed involves covering the plant with glyphosate, gathering up as much as you can into a plastic food-storage bag, and securing it with a rubber band. Leave this attractive tent on for a couple of weeks to really keep the chemical fresh, as well as to cook the plant a little; it's said to be very effective.

2. You might want to plant grass seed the second year (after your year of weed control) and wait another year to plant wildflowers. This leaves the option open for spraying for weeds during the grass-growing year, if your yard's problem is severe. You'll have to water the wildflowers individually when you do plant them, and help them beat back the competition from grass runners.

3. Proceed, as in Method 1, with seeding, rolling, and watering grass seed, and then add wildflowers the following spring.

GROUNDCOVERS

God bless groundcovers, I say, as do a lot of other xeriscapers! They're a mainstay of Xeriscape because they fulfill many of the functions of grass, except wearability. They can duplicate the lush, green feeling of lawngrasses for those who love the "sea of grass" look, without the high maintenance and watering costs. They can be used in many places where lawngrasses are impractical.

Suitable places for groundcovers include:
- Narrow strips between sidewalks and structures
- Steep slopes where mowing is difficult
- Hot, dry exposures where grass is hard to keep watered
- Dense shade under trees and behind buildings
- Any front yard that's too small to be anything but a nuisance to raise a lawn in

A well-behaved groundcover should do the following:
- Provide cooling for adjacent buildings
- Have year-round color
- Spread by itself
- Have a compact growth habit
- Be dense enough to keep out weeds
- Be (generally) low-maintenance
- Have a dense, fibrous root system (good for erosion control)

Still not convinced? Well, they're also just so excellent for:
- Providing a variety of textures and colors
- Serving as transitions between lawn areas and shrub or flower borders
- Replacing areas previously covered by gravel

Prairie Grasses for Xeriscape

Low water zone (12–20" annual precipitation)

BOTANICAL NAME	COMMON NAME	HEIGHT	ZONE
Agropyron smithii	Western wheatgrass	2–4'	3–9
Andropogon gerardii	Big bluestem	4–6'	3–9
A. hallii	Sand bluestem	2–5'	3–9
A. virginicus	Broomsedge	2–4'	4
Bouteloua curtipendula	Sideoats grama	1–2'	3
B. gracilis	Blue grama grass	1–2'	3
B. hirsuta	Hairy grama grass	6–24"	3–9
Bromus kalmii	Kalm's chess	2–4'	3–8
Buchloe dactyloides	Buffalograss	6–12"	3
Calamagrostis canadensis	Bluejoint	2–5'	3–7
Calamovilfa longifolia	Prairie sand reed	2–6'	3–6
Elymus canadensis	Canada wild rye	2–5'	3–8
E. virginicus	Virginia wild rye	2–4'	3–9
Eragrostis spectabilis	Purple love grass	18–24"	5–9
E. trichodes	Sand love grass	2–4'	5–9
Festuca ovina	Sheep fescue	1–2'	3–9
Hordeum jubatum	Squirreltail grass, Foxtail barley	1–2'	4–9
Koeleria cristata	Junegrass	1–2'	3–9
Panicum scribnerianum	Scribner's panicum	1–2'	3–9
P. virgatum	Switch grass	3–6'	4–9
Phalaris arundinacea	Reed canary grass	2–5'	4–8
Poa glaucifolia	Glaucous bluegrass	1–2'	3–9
P. interior	Inland bluegrass	1–2'	3–9
Schizachyrium scoparium syn. Andropogon scoparius	Little bluestem	2–5'	4–9
Sorghastrum nutans	Yellow Indian grass	3–7'	6
Sporobolus asper	Longleaf dropseed	2–4'	3–9
S. heterolepis	Prairie dropseed	1–3'	3–9
Stipa comata	Needle-and-thread	1–2'	4–9
S. spartea	Porcupine grass	2–3'	3–6
Tridens flavus	Purpletop	3–5'	4

Moderate water zone (20"+ annual precipitation)

BOTANICAL NAME	COMMON NAME	HEIGHT	ZONE
Festuca rubra	Red fescue	2–3'	5–8
Hystrix patula	Bottlebrush grass	2–4'	4–9
Phragmites communis	Common reed grass	6–8'	3
Spartina pectinata	Cord grass	3–7'	5–9

Himalayan border jewel (Persicaria affinis) *turns from green to brilliant red as fall approaches, remaining a russet color throughout the winter.*

Most drought-tolerant groundcovers thrive in full sun, but there are species adapted to dry shade, as well. They might sound perfect, but, in fact, they do take a little work to get started, like all plants do. Also, most can't take much of being walked on, so if you're expecting some heavy foot traffic, install walkways of concrete or stepping stones first.

PLANTING GROUNDCOVERS

Loosen and improve the soil for groundcovers as much as you can, with two exceptions:

- If the ground is definitely sloping, try to disturb the native soil as little as possible to minimize erosion.

- If the area is infested with perennial weeds, tilling will help propagate them. Leave the soil alone and treat individual weeds with glyphosate, or spray the whole area if the weeds are overwhelming.

Normally, the soils should be generously improved before planting. Most groundcovers spread by offshoots or runners, and they'll be more apt to fill in quickly where the soil has good aeration, organic matter, and drainage. Heavy clay soils should be improved extensively

throughout the bed or over-excavated, as they are not suitable even for groundcovers that can survive in poor soils.

It's important to control as much of the weed-cover as possible before planting, especially perennial weeds. Annual weeds can be hoed out, pulled out, or chemically controlled. Glyphosate kills most weeds, but use it sparingly, for only the most intractable ones such as bindweed.

Incorporate at least 3 cubic yards of compost or well-rotted manure into each 1,000 square feet of area. This is a good place to include hydrogels because they help improve drainage, as well as store water. Use 7–10 pounds per 100 square feet, tilling in at least 4–6 inches deep. After soil amendments have been incorporated, water the area and fill in any low spots that develop.

The spacing between plants varies tremendously, from 6 inches to 10 feet, depending on the species. Study groundcover books to determine the spacing and the best plant to use for your location.

This is a good place to utilize the local talent and discuss it with nursery people. You'll be using just one type of plant to cover a large area. Because there are usually only a few options for each situation, they can probably recommend just the right one in short order.

Plant groundcovers early in spring if you can, so they can have the most time to get established before cold weather. If you plant in summer, they'll be stressed by heat and will need close attention to watering.

When setting out the plants, treat them as trees and shrubs (well, itty-bitty trees and shrubs

—see Chapter 9). Dig holes just to the depth of the root mass, letting larger plants actually sit on a plateau with a little trench around them.

If you're putting them on a slope, give each plant a wee terrace with its own watering basin (slightly depressed trench) behind the plant. A handful of hydrated hydro-gel with the backfill gives them some extra immediate water storage.

Groundcover areas are good candidates for drip or underground irrigation systems, thanks to the regular spacing of the plants. To avoid over- or under-watering, use the knuckle method: Stick your finger in the ground down to your first knuckle. If the soil is dry to this depth, go ahead and water; otherwise, wait until it's dry.

Groundcovers for Xeriscape

XXX-rated plants (Plants established for at least a year need to be watered up to ½" every two weeks during the growing season, above and beyond natural precipitation.)

BOTANICAL NAME	COMMON NAME	HEIGHT	ZONE
Achillea tomentosa 'Nana'	Dwarf yarrow, Woolly yarrow	2"	3
Antennaria spp.	Pussytoes	3–20"	4
Artemisia frigida	Fringed sage, Mountain sage	12–18"	3
Atriplex gardneri	Gardner's saltbush	8–16"	4
Callirhoe involucrata	Purple poppy mallow	6–12"	4
Cerastium tomentosum	Snow-in-summer	6–8"	4
Oenothera caespitosa	Evening primrose	1'	5
O. speciosa	Sundrops	6–18"	5
Penstemon pinifolius	Pineleaf penstemon	12–15"	5–9
P. strictus 'Bandera'	Rocky Mountain penstemon	2'	4
Sphaeralcea coccinea	Scarlet globe mallow	3'	3
Zauschneria garrettii	Hummingbird trumpet flower	1'	4
Zinnia grandiflora	Prairie zinnia, Golden paperflower	3–9"	5

XX-rated plants

(need ½" applied water every week during growing season)

BOTANICAL NAME	COMMON NAME	HEIGHT	ZONE
Aegopodium podograria 'Variegatum'	Snow-on-the-mountain (invasive if not confined)	6–12"	4
Aubrieta deltoides	Purple rockcress	6–12"	4
Delosperma cooperi	Purple iceplant	2–3"	5
D. floribundum 'Starburst'	Starburst iceplant	2–4"	5
D. nubigenum	Yellow iceplant	2–4"	5
Dianthus gratianopolitanus 'Tiny Rubies'	Cheddar pinks	3–8"	5
Fragaria americana	Wild strawberry	2–4"	4
F. frel 'Pink Panda'	Pink panda strawberry	6–8"	4
Galium odoratum	Sweet woodruff	8–10"	4–8
Gazania linearis 'Colorado Gold'	Hardy gazania	8–12"	5
Gypsophila repens	Creeping baby's breath	4"	3
Lavandula vera syn. L. angustifolia	Lavender	1–3'	5–9
Nepeta spp.	Catmint	1–2'	3
Persicaria affinis	Himalayan border jewel	8"	3
Phlox subulata	Creeping phlox	4–6"	3
Potentilla verna var. nana	Creeping potentilla	2–6"	3

BOTANICAL NAME	COMMON NAME	HEIGHT	ZONE
Santolina spp.	Lavender cotton	12–18"	4–8
Saponaria ocymoides	Rock soapwort	9"	2
Sedum spp.	Sedum, Stonecrop	3–18"	3
Sempervivum arachnoideum	Cobweb houseleek	1–2"	4–8
Symphoricarpos x chenaultii 'Hancock'	Hancock coralberry	18"	3
Teucrium chamaedrys	Germander	10–12"	5
Thymus pseudolanuginosus	Woolly thyme	1–2"	3
Veronica liwanensis	Turkish veronica	1–2"	3
V. pectinata	Blue woolly speedwell	3–6"	3
Waldsteinia ternata	Barren strawberry	4–6"	6
Zauschneria californica	California fuchsia	1–2'	6

X-rated plants

(need 1" applied water every week during growing season)

BOTANICAL NAME	COMMON NAME	HEIGHT	ZONE
Ajuga reptans	Bugleweed	8–10"	4
Arctostaphylos uva-ursi	Kinnikinnick, Bearberry	4–6"	2
Aster spp.	Dwarf Michaelmas daisy	12–18"	5
Ceratostigma plumbaginoides	Plumbago	6–12"	5
Cotoneaster dammeri	Bearberry cotoneaster	1–4'	5
Duchesnea indica	Mock strawberry (invasive if not confined)	4"	5
Euonymus fortunei var. colorata	Purple-leaf wintercreeper	6–18"	5
E. f. 'Kewensis'	Kew wintercreeper	2–3"	5
Geranium spp.	Geranium (perennial)	1'	4
Hedera helix	English ivy	6–12"	4
Lamiastrum galeobdolon	Yellow archangel	12–18"	3
Lamium maculatum	Dead nettle	8–12"	4
Lysimachia nummularia	Moneywort, Creeping Jenny	2–4"	4
Mahonia repens	Creeping mahonia	6–12"	4
Ranunculus repens	Creeping buttercup	1'	4
Sedum hybridum	Hybrid sedum	4–6"	3
S. spectabilis meteor	Meteor stonecrop	12–22"	3
Sempervivum tectorum	Hen-and-chicks	4–12"	5
Thymus praecox	Mother-of-thyme	2–6"	4
T. vulgaris	Common thyme	6–12"	3
Verbena canadensis	Clump verbena	6–10"	5–6
Vinca minor	Periwinkle, Myrtle	3–6"	5

CHAPTER 8

APPROPRIATE PLANT CHOICE II:
FLOWERS, FLOWERS, FLOWERS

*You knew they had to have a chapter
unto themselves: Flowers! Whether
by bulb or seed or seedling, flowers
make our hearts soar! And there are
so many choices. Let's get right to it.*

ABOVE: *Miniature daffodils* (Narcissus triandrus) *and
drumstick primrose* (Primula denticulata) *sparkle in the
early spring.*
OPPOSITE: *Double-flowered tulips* (Tulipa *spp.*)
bloom mid-spring.

BULBS

Here's something I'll bet you didn't realize.
Because of their growth pattern, spring-flowering
bulbs are naturals for Colorado Xeriscape. No
matter how dry the year here, there's almost
always some moisture in the spring, which is
when bulbs do their flowering and growing.
They go dormant in summer when it gets hot
and dry, and, in fact, they go dormant anytime
the going gets tough, whether from drought or
heat; they're survivors!

HOW TO USE BULBS

Early spring bulbs such as crocuses, grape
hyacinths, daffodils, and species tulips can be
scattered through lawns (a practice called naturalizing) as long as the plants will have ripened
and the foliage died down before it's time to start
mowing the grass. This works especially well
in warm-season grasses (such as buffalograss),
which don't green up until late spring.

Plant bulbs close to the house and/or highly
visible from windows to give your spring fever

a boost. They're often the first flowering plants
most people notice in the spring, and, boy, do
they make you look garden-organized.

Solid blocks of color are more striking from a
distance than a mixture of colors and bulb types.
The planting area should receive adequate sunlight, as this is how they store food for next year's
bloom. Use bearded irises! These tough beauties
never cease to amaze me. I've seen them thriving
with neglect in little strips between fence and
sidewalks. They bloom in their show-stopping
way each spring and provide striking foliage the
rest of the season.

Drought-Tolerant Bulbs

Spring-Flowering Bulbs

Water these bulbs only if the spring season is dry; they're dormant during the summer and require no special watering. For the purists among you, I just want you to know that not all of these plants are true bulbs. Among them are also corms, tubers, rhizomes, and tuberous roots. Some are even sold as potted plants. But they all grow similarly, and they're all sweet.

BOTANICAL NAME	COMMON NAME	COLOR	HEIGHT	ZONE
Allium spp.	Ornamental onion	Purple, blue, red, yellow, pink, white	9"–5'	4
Anemone blanda	Greek anemone	Purple, pink, red, white	4–6"	6
Crocus spp.	Crocus	Purple, white, yellow	2–6"	3
Eremurus spp.	Foxtail lily	White, pink, yellow, orange, peach, cream	3–9'	5–9
Erianthus spp.	Winter aconite	Yellow	2–4"	4–9
Erythronium spp.	Fawn lily, etc.	White, yellow, purple	6–24"	3–9
Fritillaria imperialis	Crown imperial	Orange, red, yellow	2–4'	5
F. meleagris	Guinea hen flower	Purple-white (checkered pattern), white	1'	5
F. michailovskyi	Michael's flower	Bronze-maroon	8–12"	5
Galanthus spp.	Snowdrop	White	3–8"	3–9
Hyacinthoides (Scilla) hispanica	Spanish bluebell	Blue, white, pink	1'	4
Hyacinthus orientalis	Dutch hyacinth	Blue, purple, yellow, pink, white, red, cream, apricot	8–12"	4
Ipheion uniorum	Spring starflower	White	6"	6
Iris reticulata	Reticulate iris	Blue, lavender, purple	6"	3–8
Leucojum spp.	Snowflake	White	9"	4
Muscari spp.	Grape hyacinth	Blue, white	4–12"	2
Muscari botryoides	Grape hyacinth	Purple, pink	4–6"	4
Narcissus spp.	Daffodil	White, gold, yellow, orange, apricot	3–24"	4
N. bulbocodium	Miniature daffodil	Yellow, orange, white	6–14"	4
Ornithogalum umbellatum	Star-of-Bethlehem	White-green stripes	1–2'	4
Scilla siberica	Siberian squill	Blue, pink, white	6"	1–8
Tulipa spp.	Tulip	Red, cream, salmon, orange, yellow, gold	6–20"	3
T. (Dutch)	Tulip	Every color except blue	18–30"	3–7

Summer-Flowering Bulbs

Water only during prolonged summer drought. These high-zone plants need to be dug up before the first frost and stored each fall if you want them to survive.

BOTANICAL NAME	COMMON NAME	COLOR	HEIGHT	ZONE
Acidanthera bicolor	Abyssinian gladiolus, Peacock orchid	White	18–24"	7
Crocosmia syn. *Montbretia* spp.	Crocosmia, Montbretia	Yellow, orange, scarlet	2–4'	8
Gladiolus spp.	Gladiolus	All colors	1–5'	8
Ranunculus asiaticus (requires dry soil in summer)	Buttercup	All colors but green and blue	18"	8
Sparaxis spp.	Harlequin flower	Red, yellow, blue, purple, white	12–18"	9
Zephyranthes spp.	Rain lily, Fairy lily, Zephyr lily	White, pink, yellow, apricot	6–8"	7

ABOVE: *Species tulips such as these* Tulipa tarda *are great for naturalizing.* BELOW: *If only this long-blooming red valerian* (Centranthus ruber) *was catmint!*

Loose, well-amended soil is important for bulbs, especially in heavy clay soil (up to one-third organic matter by volume). Plant bulbs at a depth roughly four times their height (except bearded iris, which I'm told aren't really bulbs; they go just below the soil surface).

According to *Flowering Bulbs Indoors and Out* by Theodore James (Macmillan Publishing, 1991), it was thought for many years that bonemeal and a 5-10-5 fertilizer was best for bulbs, but a study by the Netherlands flower bulb industry revealed these treatments were a waste of time and money. Instead the study found the best formula for bulb food was a 9-9-6 ratio (nitrogen-phosphorus-potassium) at a rate of 4 cups per 50 square feet (1 tablespoon per square foot). This ideal bulb food, called "Holland Bulb Booster," is available at most garden centers.

Plant the bulbs growing tips up when you install them and water them in at planting. If the fall or early spring is very dry, a little extra water will encourage a better display of flowers. After they put on their show for you, remove spent flowers and add additional fertilizer before the leaves wither; this will increase bulb size the following year.

To keep the size of the plant from each bulb increasing each year, make sure the bulb has

adequate moisture and sunlight during its time of ripening, between its flowering and when the leaves yellow and die down. The bulb is storing food for next year's use, so don't cut the leaves off while they're still green.

PERENNIALS AND ANNUALS

Flowers are super for Xeriscape and for the Rockies. The sunny summers and non-soggy winters, along with low humidity that thwarts many pests and diseases, make for the perfect environment for these babies.

With the right soil preparation and zoning for water needs, flowerbeds can actually use far less water per square foot than highly maintained turf. One of my favorite xeriscaping contacts, Wilbur Davis, an amateur gardener in Austin, Texas, liked to say, "If part of my lawn is giving me trouble, I just turn it into a flowerbed."

Perennials are the darlings of the flower gardening world. Praised for their toughness, tenacity, refined beauty, and, well, "perennial-ness," they are beloved by gardeners everywhere, especially those who aspire to elegance.

On the other hand, try talking perennials to an annuals fan like amateur gardener Pat Hoeft, and you might hear, "Oh, yes, *perennials.* They take forever to cre-e-e-p across the landscape." Replanting each year is OK with Pat, apparently.

The good news is there's no real need for this *versus* stuff because both perennials and annuals have advantages for the Xeriscape flower garden. Annuals are often well able to withstand the extremes of heat and drought that can occur in summer. Research at Colorado State University shows that many perennials are as able to live without supplemental watering after their second years as trees and shrubs.

Both have an endless variety of flower and foliage texture and color, and there are flowers for every condition of soil moisture, from desert-dry to boggy. The flower list that follows is divided into dry, low-water, and moderate-water use perennials and annuals (best guesses, of course!).

Cool-season annuals grow best in the cooler weather of spring and fall. You can put out bedding plants earlier in the spring, and you can even plant seeds in the fall, which will emerge in early spring, if the birds haven't eaten them yet.

Warm-season annuals need summer heat to flower and thrive, not to mention survive. Put them out before last frost and you'll have to put blankets over them when the early-May snow happens—or they'll croak.

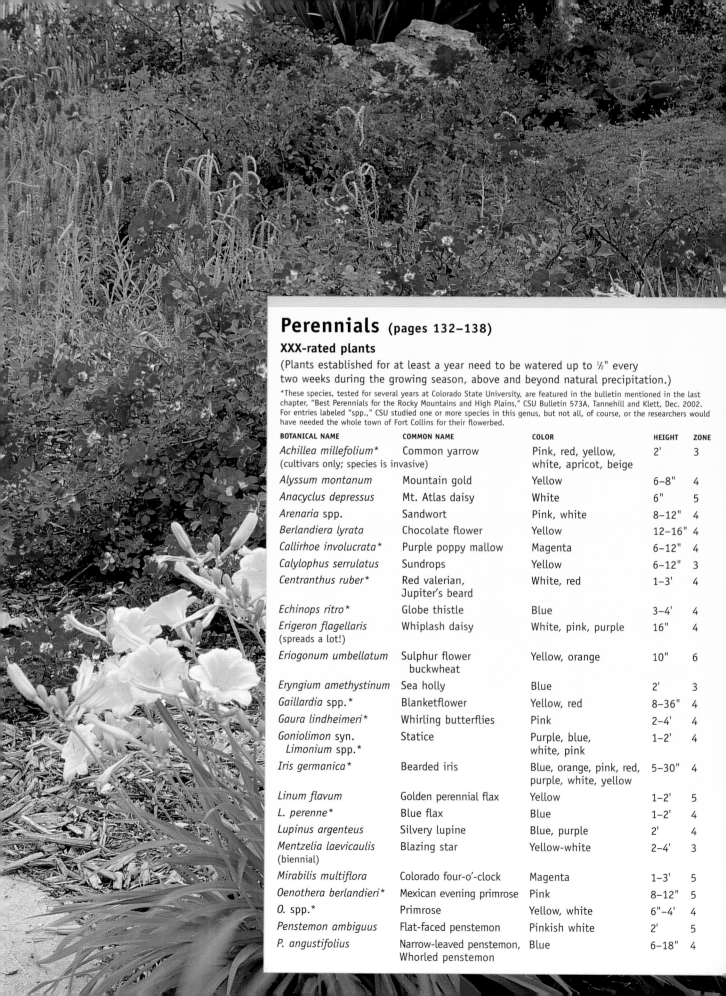

Perennials (pages 132–138)

XXX-rated plants

(Plants established for at least a year need to be watered up to ½" every two weeks during the growing season, above and beyond natural precipitation.)

*These species, tested for several years at Colorado State University, are featured in the bulletin mentioned in the last chapter, "Best Perennials for the Rocky Mountains and High Plains," CSU Bulletin 573A, Tannehill and Klett, Dec. 2002. For entries labeled "spp.," CSU studied one or more species in this genus, but not all, of course, or the researchers would have needed the whole town of Fort Collins for their flowerbed.

BOTANICAL NAME	COMMON NAME	COLOR	HEIGHT	ZONE
Achillea millefolium* (cultivars only; species is invasive)	Common yarrow	Pink, red, yellow, white, apricot, beige	2'	3
Alyssum montanum	Mountain gold	Yellow	6–8"	4
Anacyclus depressus	Mt. Atlas daisy	White	6"	5
Arenaria spp.	Sandwort	Pink, white	8–12"	4
Berlandiera lyrata	Chocolate flower	Yellow	12–16"	4
Callirhoe involucrata*	Purple poppy mallow	Magenta	6–12"	4
Calylophus serrulatus	Sundrops	Yellow	6–12"	3
Centranthus ruber*	Red valerian, Jupiter's beard	White, red	1–3'	4
Echinops ritro*	Globe thistle	Blue	3–4'	4
Erigeron flagellaris (spreads a lot!)	Whiplash daisy	White, pink, purple	16"	4
Eriogonum umbellatum	Sulphur flower buckwheat	Yellow, orange	10"	6
Eryngium amethystinum	Sea holly	Blue	2'	3
Gaillardia spp.*	Blanketflower	Yellow, red	8–36"	4
Gaura lindheimeri*	Whirling butterflies	Pink	2–4'	4
Goniolimon syn. Limonium spp.*	Statice	Purple, blue, white, pink	1–2'	4
Iris germanica*	Bearded iris	Blue, orange, pink, red, purple, white, yellow	5–30"	4
Linum flavum	Golden perennial flax	Yellow	1–2'	5
L. perenne*	Blue flax	Blue	1–2'	4
Lupinus argenteus	Silvery lupine	Blue, purple	2'	4
Mentzelia laevicaulis (biennial)	Blazing star	Yellow-white	2–4'	3
Mirabilis multiflora	Colorado four-o'-clock	Magenta	1–3'	5
Oenothera berlandieri*	Mexican evening primrose	Pink	8–12"	5
O. spp.*	Primrose	Yellow, white	6"–4'	4
Penstemon ambiguus	Flat-faced penstemon	Pinkish white	2'	5
P. angustifolius	Narrow-leaved penstemon, Whorled penstemon	Blue	6–18"	4

Above: Silver groundsel (Senecio longilobus).
Opposite: Scarlet Pfeifer's early summer border features perennials such as daylily
(Hemerocallis 'Stella d'Oro'), Red Meidiland™ 'Meineble' rose, and silver speedwell
(Veronica incana).

Evergreen candytuft (Iberis sempervirens).

BOTANICAL NAME	COMMON NAME	COLOR	HEIGHT	ZONE
P. barbatus	Beardlip penstemon	Scarlet	2–3'	5–9
P. cardinalis	Cardinal penstemon	Scarlet	3'	5
P. cyananthus	Wasatch penstemon	Bright blue	3'	4
P. eatonii	Firecracker penstemon	Red	2'	5
P. grandiflorus	Large-flowered beardtongue	Lavender	4'	4
P. jamesii	James penstemon	Purple	1'	5
P. mexicale*	Mexicale penstemon	Purple/pink	1–2'	5
P. palmeri	Palmer's penstemon	Light pink	2–3'	3–9
P. pinifolius*	Pineleaf penstemon	Red, yellow	18"	5
P. pseudospectabilis	Desert beardtongue	Pink	3–4'	6
P. secundiflorus	Sidebells penstemon	Pink	2'	4
P. speciosus	Royal penstemon	Rose	2'	5
P. strictus*	Rocky Mountain penstemon	Blue	2'	3
P. virgatus	Wand penstemon	Purple	2–4'	5
Perovskia atriplicifolia*	Russian sage	Blue	2–4'	4
Petalostemon purpureum	Purple prairie clover	Purple	2'	3
Potentilla recta 'Macrantha'*	Sulphur cinquefoil	Yellow	1–2'	4
Psilostrophe tagetina	Paperflower	Yellow	2'	5
Ratibida columnifera	Prairie coneflower	Yellow	1–3'	3
Senecio longilobus	Silver groundsel	Yellow	1–3'	5
Stanleya pinnata	Prince's plume	Golden yellow	1–3'	3
Tanacetum densum amani	Partridge feather	White	8–12"	4
Thelesperma megapotamicum	Cota, Navajo tea	Yellow	1–3'	4
Townsendia exscapa	Easter daisy	White	2–12"	4
Tradescantia spp.	Spiderwort	Blue, pink, purple, white	18–26"	4
Verbena bonariensis	Purple verbena	Purple	3–4'	6–9
Zauschneria arizonica	Hardy hummingbird trumpet	Red-orange	1–2'	4
Zauschneria garrettii	Hummingbird trumpet flower	Orange-red	1'	4
Zinnia grandiflora	Prairie zinnia, Golden paperflower	Yellow	3–9"	5

Blackberry lily (Belamcanda chinensis).

Pineleaf penstemon (Penstemon pinifolius) shows
off bright red flowers and evergreen foliage.

Perennials (continued)

XX-rated plants (need ½" applied water every week during growing season)

BOTANICAL NAME	COMMON NAME	COLOR	HEIGHT	ZONE
*Achillea filipendulina**	Fernleaf yarrow	Yellow	3–4'	4
Agastache spp.*	Hyssop	Pinkish purple, pinkish orange	2–4'	4
Alcea spp.*	Hollyhock	Lavender, pink, white, salmon, purple, yellow	2–6'	4
Allium cernuum	Nodding onion	White, pink, purple	1'	3
*Anaphalis margaritacea**	Pearly everlasting	White	20"	4
*Anemone sylvestris**	Snowdrop anemone	White	6–18"	4
Anthemis tinctoria	Chamomile, Golden marguerite	Yellow	3'	4
Arabis caucasica	Rock cress	White, pink	8–12"	4
*Armeria maritima**	Thrift, Sea pink	Pink	18–24"	4
Artemisia spp.	Artemisia	Foliage, some have yellow flowers	4'	Varies
Asclepias tuberosa	Butterflyweed	Orange, red, yellow	1–3'	3
*Aurinia saxatilis**	Basket-of-gold	Gold	6–12"	4
*Baptisia australis**	False indigo	Blue	3–6'	3
Belamcanda chinensis	Blackberry lily	Orange, yellow	1–3'	4
*Boltonia asteroides**	False chamomile, Boltonia, False aster	Pink, white	2–4'	3
Campanula spp.*	Bellflower	Purple, blue, white	6–12"	4
*C. rotundifolia**	Harebell	Blue	6"–1'	3
Catananche caerulea	Cupid's dart	Blue, white	18–36"	4
*Centaurea montana**	Perennial bachelor's button, Mountain bluet	Blue, white	18–24"	4
*Chamaenerion (Epilobium) angustifolium**	Fireweed, Willow herb	Pink, purple, white	2–8'	3
Chrysanthemum x *morifolium*	Garden mum	Orange, purple, yellow, white, pink, bronze, red	1–3'	4

Above: Oriental poppies (Papaver orientale) peek through a fence to delight passersby.
Below: Hollyhocks (Alcea rosea or Althaea rosea) are considered biennial or short-lived perennials.

German statice (Goniolimon tataricum).

BOTANICAL NAME	COMMON NAME	COLOR	HEIGHT	ZONE
Coreopsis lanceolata	Lanceleaf coreopsis, Tickseed	Yellow	2–3'	4
Dianthus spp.*	Pinks	White, red, pink, orange, yellow	9–18"	4
*D. plumarius**	Cottage pinks	Pink, white	6–12"	4
Diascia integerrima 'Coral Canyon'	'Coral Canyon' twinspur	Pink	15"	4
*Dictamnus albus**	Gas plant, Dittany	Blue, pink, red, white	2–3'	4
Erigeron compositus	Cutleaf daisy	White	2–10"	3
Erigeron spp.	Daisy fleabane	White, blue, purple	Varies	3
Erysimum asperum (biennial)	Western wallflower	Yellow	30"	3
Gazania spp.	Hardy gazania	Orange, red, brown, pink, yellow	8–12"	5
*Geum coccineum**	Avens	Orange	8–12"	5
*G. triflorum**	Geum	Reddish pink	6–18"	3
Gutierrezia sarothrae	Snakebroom, Snakeweed	Yellow	6"–3'	3
*Gypsophila paniculata**	Baby's breath (perennial)	Pink, white	18–36"	4
Helianthemum apenninum	Silver sun rose	White	12–18"	5
*H. nummularium**	Sun rose	Orange, pink, white, yellow	9–12"	5–6
Helianthus maximiliani	New Mexican sunflower, Maximilian's daisy	Yellow	5–8'	3
*Heliopsis helianthoides**	False sunflower	Yellow	4'	4
Hemerocallis spp.*	Daylily	Orange, pink, yellow, purple, red	2–3'	3
*Iberis sempervirens**	Evergreen candytuft	White	1'	4
*Knautia macedonica**	Red pincushion	Purple, red	2–3'	5

Iceland poppy (Papaver nudicaule) *and painted daisy* (Tanacetum coccineum).

Snowdrop anemone (Anemone sylvestris).

Perennials (continued)

BOTANICAL NAME	COMMON NAME	COLOR	HEIGHT	ZONE
*Kniphofia uvaria**	Red hot poker	Yellow, orange, red	2–4'	5
*Lavandula angustifolia**	Lavender	Lavender, purple	1–3'	5
*Lavatera thuringiaca**	Tree mallow	Pink	2–4'	4
Liatris punctata	Gayfeather	Magenta	1'	3
*L. spicata**	Blazing star	White	2–5'	3
*Limonium latifolium**	Sea lavender	Lavender, purple	2'	3
Linum perenne lewisii	Lewis' flax	Blue	1–2'	4
Lupinus 'Russell Hybrids'*	Russell hybrids lupine	Blue, orange, white, pink, yellow, purple	3–4'	4–9
Lychnis coronaria	Rose campion	Pink	18–36"	4
*Malva alcea**	Rose mallow	Pink	2–4'	4
*Nepeta faassenii**	Catmint	Purple	1–2'	3
Oenothera serrulata	Tooth-leaved evening primrose	Yellow	6–12"	4
Origanum spp.	Oregano, Marjoram	Pink, purple, white	30"	4
Paeonia hybrids*	Garden peony, Chinese peony	Red, white, yellow, pink	2–4'	5
Papaver alpinum	Alpine poppy	White, pink, yellow, orange	6–12"	5
P. nudicaule	Iceland poppy	Orange, red, pink, white, yellow	1–2'	3
*P. orientale**	Oriental poppy	Red, orange, pink, purple, white	2–3'	5
Penstemon alpinus	Alpine penstemon	Blue, purple	3'	3
Phlomis cashmeriana	Jerusalem sage	Lilac	2–4'	4
*Platycodon grandiflorus**	Balloon flower	Blue	18–30"	4
*Polemonium caeruleum**	Jacob's ladder	Blue	1–2'	4
*Pulsatilla vulgaris**	Pasqueflower	Purple, white	6–12"	4
Ruta graveolens 'Blue Mound'*	Common rue, Herb-of-grace	Yellow	2–3'	5
Salvia officinalis	Garden sage	Purple	18–24"	4
*S. pratensis**	Meadow clary	Blue, pink	3'	5

Black-eyed Susan (Rudbeckia fulgida 'Goldsturm'), *annual cosmos* (Cosmos bipinnatus), *and spike speedwell* (Veronica spicata).

Shasta daisy (Leucanthemum maximum *or* L. x superbum), *snow-in-summer* (Cerastium tomentosum), *bachelor's buttons* (Centaurea cyanus), *and Oriental poppy* (Papaver orientale).

BOTANICAL NAME	COMMON NAME	COLOR	HEIGHT	ZONE
S. x superba*	Perennial sage, Violet sage, Perennial salvia	Blue, purple	18–36"	4
Saponaria ocymoides	Rock soapwort	Pink	9"	4
Scabiosa spp.*	Pincushion	Blue, lavender	1–2'	4
Solidago spp.	Goldenrod	Yellow	2–4'	4
Stachys byzantina*	Lamb's ears	Pink	18"	5
Tanacetum niveum	Snow daisy	White	2'	4
T. parthenium	Feverfew	Yellow, white	1–3'	5
Thermopsis montana* (invasive)	Golden banner	Gold	2–4'	4
Veronica spicata*	Spike speedwell	Blue, pink, white	12–18"	3

X-rated plants (need 1" applied water every week during growing season)

BOTANICAL NAME	COMMON NAME	COLOR	HEIGHT	ZONE
Amsonia hubrichtii	Blue star	Blue	2'	4
Anemone vitifolia*	Japanese anemone	Pink	3–4'	5
Aquilegia caerulea*	Rocky Mountain columbine	Blue	2–3'	4
Aquilegia spp.*	Columbine	Red, pink, white, blue, yellow, purple, salmon	1–3'	Varies
Asclepias speciosa	Showy milkweed	Pink	2–4'	3
Aster alpinus	Dwarf alpine aster	Dark violet	6–12"	4
A. novi-belgii*	New York aster, Michaelmas daisy	White, pink, purple	1–4'	4–9
Calamintha grandiflora	Large-flowered calamint	Blue, pink	10–12"	5
Campanula carpatica*	Carpathian harebell	Blue-purple	6–12"	4
Chrysanthemum x morifolium*	Hardy or Garden chrysanthemum	Red, orange, lavender, yellow, white, bronze	1–4'	5
Clematis integrifolia*	Solitary clematis	Blue, purple	2–5'	3
Coreopsis spp.*	Tickseed	Yellow, pink	2–4'	4
Coreopsis verticillata*	Threadleaf coreopsis	Yellow	18–30"	4
Delphinium spp.	Delphinium	Pink, blue, purple, white, green	3–5'	4
D. elatum	Candle larkspur	Blue, pink, purple, white	6'	4

'Coral Canyon' twinspur (Diascia integerrima 'Coral Canyon') and First Love dianthus (Dianthus 'First Love').

Perennials (continued)

BOTANICAL NAME	COMMON NAME	COLOR	HEIGHT	ZONE
Dianthus deltoides	Maiden pink	Pink, purple, red, white	4–12"	4
D. plumarius*	Cottage or Grass pink	Pink, white	9–18"	4
Dicentra spectabilis*	Common bleeding heart	Pink, red, white	1–2'	3
Digitalis spp.*	Foxglove	Pink, purple, yellow, brown, white, red	1–2'	4
Echinacea purpurea*	Purple coneflower	Purple, white	2–3'	4
Geranium spp.*	Geranium (perennial)	Magenta, pink, white, lavender, rose	1'	4
Geum quellyon*	Sweet avens	Orange, red, yellow	2'	5–6
Helenium autumnale	Sneezeweed, Helen's flower	Brown, red, orange, yellow	3–5'	4
H. hoopesii	Orange mountain daisy	Orange, yellow	3'	3
Heliopsis helianthoides var. *scabra**	Heliopsis, False sunflower	Yellow	5'	4
Helleborus spp.	Lenten rose	Pink, white, red, green	18"	5
Heuchera sanguinea*	Coral bells	Pink, white, red	6–12"	4
Hosta spp.*	Plantain lily	Purple, white	1–2'	4
Hypericum calycinum*	Creeping St. John's wort	Yellow	1–2'	4
Iris missouriensis	Western blue flag	Blue-purple, white	2'	3
I. sibirica*	Siberian iris	Blue, white, lavender, purple, cream, rose	2–4'	4
Leontopodium alpinum	Edelweiss	White	6–12"	4
Leucanthemum x *superbum**	Shasta daisy	White	1–3'	5
Lilium spp.*	Garden lily	Orange, red, white, pink, yellow	2–6'	Varies
Lychnis chalcedonica*	Maltese cross	Red, salmon, white	1–3'	4–9
Monarda fistulosa	Wild bergamot, Bee balm	Rose-purple, lavender	3–4'	3
Myosotis scorpioides	Dwarf forget-me-not	Blue	12–18"	5
Oenothera hookeri	Yellow evening primrose	Yellow	2–6'	5
O. tetragona	Common sundrops	Yellow	18"	5
Penstemon cobaea	White wild snapdragon	White, lavender	12–18"	5
P. hirsutus	Dwarf hairy beardtongue	Blue	1–3'	3–9
Physostegia virginiana*	Obedient plant, False dragonhead	Pink, purple, white	2–3'	4
Prunella laciniata	Self heal	White, purple	6–12"	4
Pulmonaria spp.*	Lungwort	Blue, pink, white	6–12"	4
Rudbeckia spp.*	Coneflower	Yellow	8"–6'	Varies
Rudbeckia fulgida 'Goldsturm'*	Orange coneflower, Black-eyed Susan	Golden yellow	2–3'	5
Solidago virgaurea*	European goldenrod	Yellow	3–4'	4
Tanacetum coccineum	Painted daisy	Pink, red, white	1–3'	4
Verbena canadensis	Clump verbena	Purple	6–10"	5–6
Veronica prostrata*	Harebell speedwell, Rock speedwell	Blue	6"	3
Viola corsica	Corsican violet	Violet	6–10"	5

Top right: Periwinkle (Vinca minor).
Bottom right: A mix of yarrows (Achillea spp.).
Far right: Desert beardtongue (Penstemon pseudospectabilis).

Annuals (pages 141–146)

XXX-rated plants (Plants established for several weeks need to be watered up to ½" every two weeks during the growing season, above and beyond natural precipitation.)

BOTANICAL NAME	COMMON NAME	COLOR	HEIGHT
Abronia villosa	Sand verbena	Pink	2'
Argemone mexicana	Mexican poppy, Prickly poppy	White	2–3'
Baileya multiradiata	Desert marigold	Yellow	20"
Calandrina umbellata	Rock purslane	Pink	6"
Echium lycopsis	Viper's bugloss	Blue, white, purple, rose	2'
Eschscholzia californica	California poppy	Yellow-orange, red	8–12"
E. mexicana	Mexican gold poppy	Yellow	1'
Gomphrena globosa	Globe amaranth	Magenta, pink, white, yellow, orange	10–20"
Ipomopsis rubra (biennial)	Standing cypress	Scarlet, yellow	2–3'
Lesquerella gordonii	Bladderpod	Yellow	1'
Lupinus arizonicus	Arizona lupine	Purple	1'
Mentzelia lindleyi	Lindley blazing star	Yellow	1–4'
Orthocarpus purpurascens	Owl's clover	Purple/white	18–24"
Phacelia campanularia	California bluebell	Blue	18–30"

XX-rated plants (need ½" applied water every week during growing season)

BOTANICAL NAME	COMMON NAME	COLOR	HEIGHT
Anagallis arvensis	Scarlet pimpernel	Red, white	18"
A. monellii	Flaxleaf pimpernel	Blue	9–12"
Antirrhinum majus	Snapdragon	Blue, red, white, pink, orange, purple, yellow	6–36"
Aster bigelovii	Purple aster	Purple	3'
Borago officinalis	Borage	Blue	16–24"
Celosia spp.	Cockscomb	Orange, pink, red, yellow	10–18"

Left: Annuals in containers set against a background of perennials create a moveable feast for the eyes.
Below: California poppies (Eschscholzia californica).

Annuals (continued)

BOTANICAL NAME	COMMON NAME	COLOR	HEIGHT
Centaurea cyanus	Cornflower	Blue, pink, purple, white	20"
Cheiranthus cheiri	Wallflower	Yellow	2–3'
Chrysanthemum carinatum	Tricolor chrysanthemum	Orange/red/yellow	2–3'
Clarkia spp.	Godetia	Pink, red, purple, white, combos	1–3'
Cleome hasslerana	Beeplant	Pink, white, rose-purple	3–5'
Consolida ambigua	Rocket larkspur	Violet, rose, blue, white	1–2'
Convolvulus tricolor	Dwarf morning glory	Blue, white	12–18"
Coreopsis tinctoria	Tickseed, Calliopsis, Plains coreopsis	Yellow/orange/red	18–40"
Coriandum sativum	Coriander	Pink	3'
Cosmos bipinnatus	Cosmos	Pink, red, yellow, white, orange	1–3'
Crepis rubra	Hawks-beard	Pink, white	8–18"
Cynoglossum amabile	Chinese forget-me-not	Blue, pink, white	16–24"
Datura inoxia	Angel's trumpet	White	3'
D. metel	Downy thorn apple	White	2–5'
Dimorphotheca pluvialis	Rain daisy, Cape marigold	Orange, white, yellow	16"
D. sinuata	African daisy	Salmon, yellow, buff, orange	1'
Dyssodia tenuiloba	Dalhberg daisy	Yellow	8–12"
Gaillardia pulchella	Blanket flower, Indian blanket	Yellow/red, red	1–2'
Gilia spp.	Gilia	Blue, violet	1–2'
Helianthus annuus	Common sunflower	Yellow, red, bronze, cream	10'
Hymenoxys grandiflora	Alpine sunflower	Yellow	1'
Iberis umbellata	Globe candytuft	White, pink, red, lilac	8–12"
Layia platyglossa	Tidy tips	Yellow/white	1–2'
Limonium sinuatum	Statice, Sea lavender	Blue, white, lavender, yellow, pink, red	12–18"
Linanthus grandiflorus	Mountain phlox	Purple, white	2'
Linum grandiflorum	Flowering flax	Red, white, blue, pink, purple	12–18"
Lobularia maritima	Sweet alyssum	Pink, purple, white	6–8"
Lonas annua	Yellow ageratum	Yellow	8–18"
Lupinus nanus	Sky lupine	Purple	20"
L. sparsiflorus	Arroya lupine	Purple	1'
L. texensis	Texas bluebonnet	Blue/white	1'
Malope trifida	Annual mallow	Pink, purple	2–3'
Malva verticillata crispa	Curled mallow	White	1'
Matthiola incana	Stock	White	18–36"
Mentzelia lindleyi	Blazing star	Yellow	1–4'
Mirabilis jalapa	Four-o'-clock	Red, pink, white, yellow	2–3'
Nigella damascena	Love-in-a-mist	Blue, pink	12–18"
Omphalodes linifolia 'Venus' Navelwort'	Venus' navelwort	White	1'
Osteospermum hybridum 'Salmon Queen'	Salmon Queen osteospermum	Salmon, apricot	12"

Above: Clary sage (Salvia sclarea).
Right: Sweet pea (Lathyrus odoratus).

BOTANICAL NAME	COMMON NAME	COLOR	HEIGHT
O. hyoseroides	Cape daisy	Yellow, orange	2'
Oxypetalum caeruleum	Southern star	Pink, purple	3'
Papaver rhoeas	Corn poppy, Flanders poppy	Red	2'
Pelargonium x hortorum	Zonal geranium	Red, white, pink, orange	1–2'
Penstemon gloxinioides	Border or Garden penstemon	Rose	3'
Phacelia grandiflora	Wild heliotrope	Lavender	1–2'
Phlox drummondii	Drummond's phlox	Lavender, pink, purple, white	6–12"
Pimpinella anisum	Anise	Yellow	2'
Portulaca grandiflora	Moss rose	Orange, pink, red, white, yellow	4–6"
Reseda odorata	Common mignonette	Orange, yellow, green	18"
Ricinus communis	Castor oil plant	Red	3–7'
Rudbeckia hirta	Black-eyed Susan	Orange, red, yellow	1–3'
Salvia sclarea	Clary sage	Blue, yellow, pink, white	3'
S. splendens	Scarlet sage	Red	18–24"
Senecio elegans	Purple ragwort	Magenta	2'
Tagetes spp.	Marigold	Yellow, white, orange	6"–3'

Geraniums (Pelargonium domesticum)
and *Sweet alyssum* (Lobularia maritima).

Cosmos (Cosmos bipinnatus).

Annuals (continued)

BOTANICAL NAME	COMMON NAME	COLOR	HEIGHT
Thelesperma filifolium	Showy Navajo tea, Greenthread	Yellow	1–2'
Trachymene coerulea	Blue laceflower	Blue, lavender	18–30"
Ursinia anethoides	Dill-leaf ursinia	Yellow/red	15"
Venidium fastuosum	Cape daisy	White, orange	2–3'
Verbena x *hybrida*	Verbena	Pink, purple, red, white	1'
Verbesina encelioides	Golden crownbeard	Yellow	3'
Viola tricolor	Johnny jump-up	Purple, white, yellow	3–8"
Xanthisma texana	Sleepy daisy, Star-of-Texas	Yellow	2–4'
Xeranthemum annuum	Immortelle, Everlasting	Pink, purple, red, white	2–3'
Zinnia angustifolia	Narrowleaf zinnia	Orange, white	12–18"

X-rated plants (need 1" applied water every week during growing season)

BOTANICAL NAME	COMMON NAME	COLOR	HEIGHT
Ageratum houstonium	Common garden ageratum	Blue, white, pink, purple	6–8"
Agrostemma githago	Corn cockle	Pink	1–3'
Amaranthus caudatus	Love-lies-bleeding	Red	4–6'
Ammobium alatum	Winged everlasting	White, yellow	14–16"
Anchusa capensis	Cape forget-me-not, Bugloss	Blue, pink, white	18"

Beeplant (Cleome hasslerana).

BOTANICAL NAME	COMMON NAME	COLOR	HEIGHT
Anethum graveolans	Common dill	Yellow	30"
Arctotis stoechadifolia	Blue-eyed African daisy	Blue, white, hybrid colors	30–48"
Barberea vulgaris	Wintercress	Yellow	2–3'
Calendula officinalis	Pot marigold	Orange, yellow	12–18"
Campanula medium	Canterbury bells	Blue	16–26"
Carum carvi	Caraway	White	1–2'
Catharanthus roseus	Periwinkle	Lavender, pink, white	1–2'
Collinsia grandiflora	Blue lips	Blue/purple	8–15"
C. heterophylla	Chinese houses, Innocence	Purple/white	12–20"
Cuphea ignea	Cigar flower	Red	18–24"
Dianthus barbatus (biennial)	Sweet William	Pink, red, purple, white, bicolor	1–2'
Diascia barberae	Twinspur	Pink/yellow	8–15"
Dorotheanthus bellidiformis	Livingstone daisy	Red, yellow, pink, orange, white	2–4"
Emilia javanica	Tassel flower	Red, orange, yellow	1–2'
Erysimum linifolium	Alpine wallflower	Purple	6–18"
Eustoma grandiflorum	Prairie gentian	Blue	20–28"
Felicia amelloides	Blue marguerite	Blue, purple	1–3'
Fragaria vesca	Wild strawberry	White	2–6"
Gypsophila elegans	Baby's breath (annual)	White, pink, red	10–18"
Hedysarum coronarium	French honeysuckle	Red, pink, violet	2–4'
Heliotropium arborescens	Common heliotrope, Cherry pie	Blue, lavender, white, purple	18–36"
Ionopsidium acaule	Diamond flower	Pale lilac	2–4"

Sweet alyssum (Lobularia maritima).

Annuals (continued)

BOTANICAL NAME	COMMON NAME	COLOR	HEIGHT
Lavatera trimestris	Annual mallow	Pink, rose, white	2–4'
Linaria maroccana	Toadflax	Blue, red, lavender, orange, yellow	9–18"
Malcolmia maritima	Virginia stock	Pink, purple	8"
Matthiola longipetala	Evening stock	Violet, white	12–18"
Monarda citriodora	Horsemint, Lemon mint	Pink	12–18"
Nemophila maculata	Five spot	White/blue	1'
Nierembergia hippomanica	Cupflower	Blue, purple, white	6–8"
Petunia x hybrida	Petunia	Pink, blue, red, white, yellow, green, purple	6–15"
Salvia farinacea	Mealy-cup sage	White	2–3'
Sanvitalia procumbens	Creeping zinnia	Yellow, orange	4–6"
Silene armeria	Campion	Pink	12–18"
Zinnia elegans	Common zinnia	Purple, red, pink, white, lavender, yellow, orange	1–3'
Z. haageana	Zinnia	Orange, yellow, red	1–2'

Moist-soil annuals

BOTANICAL NAME	COMMON NAME	COLOR	HEIGHT
Asclepias curassavica	Blood flower	Red, yellow	3–4'
Calceolaria integrifolia	Slipper flower	Yellow	2–4'
Callistephus chinensis	China aster	Red	18–36"
Dianthus chinensis	China pink, Indian pink	Pink, red, lilac, white	12–18"
Impatiens hawkerii	New Guinea impatiens	Red, pink, purple, orange, white	18–30"
Lobelia erinus	Edging lobelia	Blue, purple, white	3–8"
Myosotis sylvatica (can be invasive)	Forget-me-not	Blue, pink	12–18"
Salpiglossis sinuata	Painted tongue	Blue, red, orange, pink, purple, yellow	18–36"
Schizanthus pinnatus	Butterfly flower	Purple, pink, yellow, white	1–4'
S. wisetonensis	Butterfly flower	Blue, red, pink, brown, white	8–20"
Torenia fournieri	Wishbone flower	Pink, blue, purple, yellow	6–12"
Trachelium caeruleum	Throatwort	Blue, white	2–3'
Viola x wittrockiana	Pansy	Blue, pink, red, white, yellow, orange, purple	6–12"

Common zinnia (Zinnia elegans).

PLANTING YOUR FLOWERS

As you probably know by now, soil preparation depends on what you're planting. Believe it or not, some native desert wildflowers really do *poorly* if the soil is too rich. For instance, my all-time favorite annual, cosmos, produced masses of foliage and almost no flowers the year I carefully amended the soil with lots of compost.

On the other hand, if you've picked perennials that grow best in average to rich soil, soil prep is very important, especially as you won't, if all goes well, be replanting them for several years. Few "garden perennials," as distinguished from "Xeriscape perennials," do well in heavy, poorly drained, or un-aerated soil.

Double digging is recommended for these, and it's an icky, labor-intensive process that involves amending and turning over soil to about a foot's depth. You can read about it in all the perennials' books, and it may cause you decide on "Xeriscape perennials" after all, but as the French say, *"Chacun a son gout!"* (To each one's own taste.)

Organic amendment rates vary from zero for the desert natives to 3–6 cubic yards per 1,000 square feet for rich soil. Please see the Soil Improvement chapter for more information.

I plant everything with soil polymer, as I loathe watering. For flowerbeds, I spread the dry polymer over the bed and till it in with any organic

Darwin tulip mix.

material used. A good rate is 7–10 pounds per 100 square feet, tilled in 4–6 inches deep. (If you do this stuff in the fall or in early spring, the polymer can be soaking up the snowmelt and spring rain, without you lifting one finger to water, not to mention getting yourself all worn out with too much gardening at once.)

Additionally, each plant also gets a handful of hydrated polymer mixed with the immediate backfill (⅓ cup dry polymer to 5 gallons water). This gives the plants a ready water supply and makes it less critical to keep watering regularly the first few days. It's squishy fun, too; just make sure you start soaking the polymer in water at least two hours before.

WATERING

When planting, water the plants gently and thoroughly after setting them in place. If the seedlings don't have much soil attached, check two or three times a day during the first three days to make sure they haven't wilted.

After that, stick a finger into the soil up to the first knuckle every few days to check for soil moisture. If it's dry that far down, apply an inch of water (approximately ⅔ of a gallon per square foot) and don't water again until it's that dry again. This will take into account rain doing some of your watering, and will let the soil moisture, not your calendar, dictate the watering frequency.

In summer 2003, the Colorado State University Horticulture Department studied the effect of reduced watering on 20 different species of popular bedding plants (annuals) recommended for drought tolerance. Test beds of each species received varying percentages of the total ET (evapotranspiration) rate, from 0 to 100 percent.

The results had not been completely analyzed at the time of this writing, but, without a doubt, the researchers saw excellent showings in every species, even those surviving on rainfall only. Some of the species looked smaller and less floriferous at the lower levels of watering, but, according to Debi Borden Miller, a Denver horticulturist who helped duplicate the trials at the nursery where she works, "with most of the species you couldn't tell any difference among the different watering levels. Clearly, we're still watering many annuals much more than is necessary!"

The flowers studied included several that have been traditionally thought of as high-water, such as petunias, pansies, and impatiens.

I gave all my flowers the same acid test one dry summer, cutting off watering to my flowerbeds in mid-July. My yard is fairly protected from drying winds but gets a full measure of sun, and the only plants that ever even drooped mildly were the red annual salvias. The rest—cleome, celosia, nierembergia, cosmos, portulaca, stocks, linaria (all annuals); and purple coneflower, coreopsis, rudbeckia, variegated thyme, hardy ice plant, blue salvia, chrysanthemum, santolina, chocolate flower, pinks, and achilleas (perennials)—did just fine.

SEEDS

Here's God's truth about growing flowers from seeds: I've never had much luck starting flowers from seeds, either indoors or out, though I've tried many, many times. I always think I'm following the directions carefully, but somehow I rarely score.

Perhaps it's because I tried this while working full-time and raising a family, so eventually I was just too busy to keep an eye on the itty-bitty plants and make sure they were constantly comfortable. If you are the wizard at this process, my admiration for you is boundless, and please keep at it. And I will continue to grow flowers using plants already started by someone else!

SEEDLINGS/BEDDING PLANTS

Pick bedding plants that have a healthy growth of foliage rather than those that just have a pretty flower display. Too many flowers may mean the plant has been hurried along with high-nitrogen plant food, and if you don't continue to feed its habit it won't fare very well after planting.

A perennial looking a little mushy on top has probably been overwatered, and might die of rot before long, so avoid those. Also, if some root growth sticks out of the bottom of the pot, it means the plant has been growing there for a while, not just stuck in a larger-size (more expensive) pot the week before.

WILDFLOWERS

Want a carefree alternative to traditional bedding plants? Wildflowers are ideal where a more natural, less formal appearance is desired. If they're native to the area, they also have the built-in advantage of being adapted to our climate. And if they're not, they can still make a dependable contribution to a wildflower planting. Just be careful to exclude those non-natives listed as invasive in Chapter 7 (see p. 118).

As with any well-planned flowerbed, wildflowers can also provide color from April to frost, with the right mix of species. And, just think, if it gets to looking a little too wild, you have a perfect excuse: "Oh, that's my wildflower garden!"

You'd be surprised how some plants you used to think of as weeds can make a beautiful addition to a garden. I often saw poppy mallow—*Callirhoe involucrata*—(also called wine cups) trailing around fence posts on my grandparents' hardscrabble farm in Kansas. It never dawned

Prairie wine cup (Callirhoe involucrata), *Mexican evening primrose* (Oenothera speciosus), *and prairie coneflower* (Ratibida columnifera) *are perennial wildflowers somewhat organized in large, showy clusters.*

on me that they could be used in a landscape (I scorned them, in short) until I saw them looking lovely in a Xeriscape demonstration garden. They're drought tolerant, make a good ground-cover, and have beautiful flute-shaped flowers, similar to morning glories, in a stylish magenta shade, and they look just fine when properly taken care of in someone's yard.

Meanwhile, if you're into it, creating an authentic native wildflower garden is just one more way you can be an eco-star, supporting the local flora, improving diversity, and just generally being awfully knowledgeable.

The key for success is to either plant wild-flowers that are so easy to grow anywhere it would be difficult to fail, or to choose wildflowers that already naturally grow in the immediate environment.

For instance, most popular woodland flowers prefer a very light soil, and particularly dislike compacted roots. This makes sense when you examine their native soil—hundreds of years of leaf mulch and loosely packed ground litter (leaves and dead flowers plus twigs and branches) and decaying animal matter such as droppings and the occasional carcasses of forest animals.

The result is almost pure humus, what we strive to re-create with our compost piles. When we learn that common garden soil may have only 5 percent or less organic matter, we begin to see what we're up against. Fortunately, most forest wildflower roots are not particularly deep, usually no more than 12 inches, so you can over-excavate the soil for a wildflower bed if you have particularly crummy soil.

Humus-rich soil is almost constantly moist because of its huge capacity to store water. Woodland soil holds up to 10 times its weight in water, while ordinary garden soil may hold only 15–30 percent of its weight. To grow any kind of woodland wildflower, even those native to the Rockies, you will have to re-create this environment. Leaf mold as described in the Soil Improvement chapter can be used when developing soil pockets for woodland flowers. Another possibility is to incorporate a higher than normal rate of hydro-gel (see "Cross-Linked Polyacrylamide," p. 77) in the soil for the woodland flowers.

Wildflowers that grow in meadows and fields will generally grow in more "average" garden soil. The soils in these environments are lighter than the very heavy soils of semiarid lands (us) and poorer than the humus-rich soils of woodlands. Many of the species native to meadows, such as purple coneflowers (*Echinacea purpurea*), sunflowers (*Helianthus* spp.), gaillardias, gayfeather (*Liatris* spp.), and salvias are common garden favorites.

Alpine flowers thrive in rocky soil because in their native environment smaller soil particles are washed downhill by rainfall and snowmelt. To succeed with alpine flowers you need an extremely gravelly soil with a small amount of humus. You may need 12–24 inches in depth, as these plants have deep root systems, and still need drainage below the roots.

Freestanding berms are often constructed as a home for alpine wildflowers to ensure proper drainage, and because it's easier to build a berm than to excavate a deep soil area. (For the best examples around, do not fail to visit the Rock Alpine garden at the Denver Botanic Gardens. It's wildly successful and famous around these parts.)

PLANNING A WILDFLOWER GARDEN

Choose a site receiving at least six hours of sunlight a day, and a minimum of foot traffic. Ultimately, a large wildflower area is more effective than a small one, but you can start small and spread the garden over several years' time. It's easy to underestimate how much weeding will be necessary. *Remember, once you plant wildflowers, you will no longer be able to use broadleaf "weed controls" in your yard because they will have disastrous consequences for your wildflowers.*

WILDFLOWER MEADOW

In nature, most wildflower meadows include more grass than flowers, but if you just want flowers, that's cool. It will be similar to a cultivated flower garden, but more random and natural-looking. The fastest results are obtained by plugging individual plants into cleared ground.

A dense mat of wildflowers, known as wildflower sod, is available commercially. It gives instant color, flowering the first year, but in later years, one or two of the original 15 or so species in the sod may dominate and crowd the rest out. You might want to think of it as a temporary measure.

For long-term variety, a better use of the wildflower sod is to separate the plants and set them out individually with 6–12 inches in between (vary the spacing for a more natural look). This gives the less-aggressive species a better chance to establish themselves and survive competition from the dominant plants.

It's hard to think of wildflowers as domineering, isn't it? But they are. It's a no-holds-barred brawl to rule the meadow! If you're feeling nervous about this, don't worry. It happens ever so slowly, and you can wrest control back if you want to work at it.

The same fight to the finish occurs with many commercially available "wildflower mixes." They often include annual wildflower species to provide bloom the first year while the perennial species are becoming established. The annual species may or may not reseed themselves, depending on how much competition they get from aggressive perennials or the ever-present weeds.

The Denver Botanic Gardens did an experiment with these mixes long ago in which it fumigated an area—to kill *everything*, including weed seeds—then planted a so-called weed-free "wildflower mix." The resulting meadow still had

BELOW AND RIGHT: *A seeded wildflower mix is typically lively and lovely the first year. By the second year, one plant usually dominates.*

generous quantities of weeds in it, suggesting that it's virtually impossible to keep weed seeds out of mixes.

Wildflower mixes often include species that may or may not be native to your area. This is not the worst thing that can happen; your intent is usually to create a colorful palette of wild-flowers (some of the most popular species in mixes are practically "gardener proof"—anyone can grow them), and mixes give quick, if not permanent results.

If you want a true native mix of wildflowers, research what grows in your area and buy seeds from a reputable seed company. Try to choose a minimum of five perennial and five annual species.

If you want to try starting from seed, here are some tips from Rick Brune, who writes and lectures on wildflower gardening:

1. Clear the ground with a sod cutter (if it previously had turf), water, and wait for the remaining rhizomes to sprout. Dig them up as they appear. This process may take three to four weeks. Hoe or dig up weeds that appear.

2. Unless your soil is exceptionally poor, don't add organic soil amendments, as many wildflowers are adapted to poor soil. Don't till the ground unless it's very compacted, as this will increase weed germination.

3. Rake random furrows in the soil no more than ½ inch deep. Either broadcast the wildflower seed mix (which is rather waste-ful and contributes to the crowding-out process) or lightly scatter seeds of individual species in groups spread randomly over the area, with some overlap. This will give the less aggressive species a slightly better chance to establish themselves in colonies.

4. Cover the seeds with a thin layer of soil (¼ to ½ inch) and tamp lightly with the back of a rake. For the fastest germination and establishment, water gently once or twice a day, if it doesn't rain, for two to three weeks. (Germination takes 10 to 20 days.)

An alternative to the first step is to kill the grass with glyphosate in midsummer and leave it to rot over the winter. The dead vegetation can be tilled into the soil in the spring. You can supposedly plant in a sprayed area just two weeks after applying the herbicide, but there are small-print warnings about many species that can't be planted in the area for six to 12 months. These warnings indicate that there may be other

Scarlet gilia (Ipomopsis aggregata).

species, including wildflowers, that would be sensitive to the chemical.

Wildflower meadows from seed take patience. The seeds could wash away if it rains heavily, or may be eaten by birds. (If you have a slope, build dikes of small rocks across the slope, removing them after the flowers are somewhat established, or put down jute or excelsior netting designed to prevent erosion.)

The perennial wildflowers will likely not flower the first year. Count on it taking up to three years for your wildflower garden to be well established and effective.

Wildflower Caution

The Lady Bird Johnson Wildflower Center in Austin, Texas, advises asking questions of your prospective supplier to make sure it propagates its own plants rather than digging them from the wild. In the past, some wildflowers were wild-collected to the point of near-extinction.

Be sure to check out the center's website (wildflower.org) for lists of reputable suppliers in your state, plus photos of hundreds of native wildflowers and other native plants. (How I love the Internet for stuff like this!)

THE WOODLAND EFFECT

If your site is overgrown with existing trees and shrubs (Hey, it could happen!), and you want to create a wild woodland garden, keep selected mature trees and remove weak or diseased ones, plus the seedlings that will crowd the flowers. Retain some groupings of underbrush for a naturalized, layered effect.

Because woodland wildflowers like loose soil, try not to step on the ground after you've prepared it. If your wildflower beds are wide enough that you can't reach all the flowers from the edge in order to tend them, create a path with stepping-stones or small gravel set among the plants to let you and your many admiring visitors where it's safe to step.

Wildflowers for Xeriscaping (pages 153–155)

For Dry Exposures

(under 15" rainfall and/or irrigation per year)

*Native   **With filtered shade

Annuals

BOTANICAL NAME	COMMON NAME	COLOR	HEIGHT
Centaurea cyanus	Cornflower	Blue	20"
Clarkia unguiculata	Clarkia, Tickseed, Calliopsis	Pink, lavender	3–4'
Coreopsis tinctoria*	Plains coreopsis	Yellow/orange/red	18–40"
Cosmos bipinnatus	Cosmos	Pink, red, white	1–3'
Dimorphotheca aurantiaca	African daisy	White, orange	12"
Eschscholzia californica (tender perennial, often acts as annual)	California poppy	Yellow-orange	8–12"
Gaillardia pulchella*	Blanket flower, Indian blanket	Yellow/red	1–2'
Gilia tricolor	Bird's eyes	Lavender, white	1–2'
Gypsophila elegans	Baby's breath (annual)	White	10–18"
Helianthus annuus*	Sunflower	Yellow	10'
Iberis umbellata	Globe candytuft	White, pink	8–12"
Ipomopsis aggregata* (biennial)	Scarlet gilia	Red	30"
Linanthus grandiflorus	Mountain phlox	Purple, white	2'
Linaria maroccana	Toadflax	Pink, yellow, violet	9–18"
Linum grandiflorum rubrum	Scarlet flax	Red	6"
Lobularia maritima (tender perennial, often acts as annual, reseeding readily)	Sweet alyssum	White, purple	6–8"
Lupinus spp.* (some are native)	Lupine	Blue, red, pink	10–20"
Machaeranthera spp.* (some are native)	Aster	Purple	1–4'
Papaver rhoeas	Corn poppy, Flanders poppy	Pink, red, white	2'
Phacelia campanularia	California bluebell	Blue	18–30"
Sanvitalia procumbens	Creeping zinnia	Yellow	4–6"
Silene armeria (sometimes a biennial)	Campion	Pink	12–18"

Purple rockcress (Aubrieta deltoides).

Wildflowers for Xeriscaping (continued)

Perennials

BOTANICAL NAME	COMMON NAME	COLOR	HEIGHT	ZONE
Anemone patens	Pasqueflower	Purple	2–10"	1
Anthemis tinctoria (sometimes a biennial)	Golden marguerite, Chamomile	Yellow	3'	4
Artemisia spp.* (some are native)	Sage	Gray foliage	1–4'	Varies
Asclepias tuberosa*	Butterflyweed	Orange	1–3'	3
Aubrieta deltoides	Purple rockcress	Purple	6–12"	4
Castilleja spp.* (some are native)	Indian paintbrush	Red, orange, purple	9–18"	4–8
Cerastium tomentosum	Snow-in-summer	White	6–8"	4
Chamerion syn. Epilobium angustifolium*	Fireweed	Pink	2–8'	3
Erigeron speciosus*	Fleabane daisy	Violet	42"	4
Eriogonum umbellatum*	Sulphur flower	Yellow	10"	6
Erysimum spp.* (some are native)	Wallflower	Yellow	30"	3
Gaillardia aristata*	Perennial gaillardia	Yellow/red	2–3'	3–9
Liatris punctata*	Gayfeather	Magenta	1'	3
Linum perenne lewisii*	Blue flax	Blue	1–2'	4
Mirabilis multiflora*	Desert four-o'-clock	Magenta	2'	5
Oenothera caespitosa*	White evening primrose	White	6–10"	4–7
O. missouriensis	Ozark sundrops	Yellow	12"	4
Penstemon strictus*	Rocky Mountain penstemon	Blue	2'	3
Penstemon spp.* (some are native)	Penstemon	Varies	1–4'	Varies
Ratibida columnifera*	Prairie coneflower	Yellow	1–3'	3
Saponaria ocymoides	Soapwort	Pink	9"	2
Solidago rigida*	Goldenrod	Gold	2–4'	3
Thermopsis montana* (invasive)	Golden banner, False lupine	Gold	2–4'	4
Viguiera multiflora	Showy goldeneye	Yellow	10–40"	4

For Sunny to Partly Shaded, Moister Exposures

(over 15" rainfall and/or irrigation per year)

Annuals

BOTANICAL NAME	COMMON NAME	COLOR	HEIGHT
Consolida ambigua	Larkspur	Violet, white, rose, blue	1–2'
Dianthus barbatus (biennial)	Sweet William	Pink, red, white	1–2'
Eustoma grandiflorum*	Prairie gentian	Blue	20–28"
Iberis umbellata	Annual candytuft	Pink, white	8–12"
Lupinus texensis	Texas bluebonnet	Blue/white	1'
Mimulus tigrinus**	Monkeyflower	Yellow/red, yellow/orange	6–10"
Mirabilis jalapa (tender perennial, often acts as an annual)	Four-o'-clock	Red, pink, white	2–3'
Nemophila menziesii**	Baby blue-eyes	Blue	1'

Above: Fleabane daisy (Erigeron speciosus).
Below: Golden marguerite (Anthemis tinctoria).

Desert four-o'-clock (Mirabilis multiflora).

Perennials

BOTANICAL NAME	COMMON NAME	COLOR	HEIGHT	ZONE
Anthemis nobilis	Roman chamomile	White	1'	3–8
Aquilegia spp.*	Columbine	Yellow, red, blue, white	1–3'	Varies
Aster novae-angliae	New England aster	Violet	3–5'	5
Bellis perennis	English daisy	White, rose	6–8"	3
(sometimes a biennial; invasive in the Northwest)				
Leucanthemum x *superbum*	Shasta daisy	White	1–3'	5
Lychnis chalcedonica	Maltese cross	Scarlet	1–3'	4–9
*Monarda fistulosa**	Wild bergamot, Bee balm	Rose-purple	3–4'	3
Viola spp.	Johnny jump-up	White/purple	6–10"	5

Avoid seed mixes with these species

(high potential for invasiveness):

Achillea millefolium	Yarrow	*Leucanthemum vulgare*	Ox-eye daisy
Cichorium intybus	Chicory	(*Chrysanthemum leucanthemum*)	
Hesperis matronalis	Dame's rocket	*Myosotis sylvatica*	Forget-me-not

(See also "Don't Ever Plant These, as They're Invasive in our Land," p. 118.)

Primary source for wildflower list—CSU Extension Service Publication 7.233

APPROPRIATE PLANT CHOICE III:
TREES, SHRUBS, VINES, AND GARDENS

Trees and shrubs are vital to Xeriscapes, providing more than just shade.

ABOVE: *Burning bush* (Euonymus alatus) *is an attention-grabber in the fall.*
OPPOSITE: *Silver lace vine* (Polygonum aubertii) *and staghorn sumac* (Rhus typhina) *cover a fence.*

TREES AND SHRUBS

Trees and shrubs are vital to Xeriscapes because they provide:

- Drama
- Seasonal color
- Architectural interest, AND
- One of the key water-saving devices: shade!

The temperature under a shade tree may be 10–15 degrees cooler than in the open, and that cuts down on evaporation from surface plants. Trees and fences also act as wind barriers, reducing evaporation from plants as well as the top layer of soil. Some plants that will survive only in moist soil in the sun fare well in dry, dappled shade.

Because of their extensive root systems, trees and shrubs are more efficient than other plants at using whatever water reaches them, whether from precipitation or applied water. The roots of one large tree may actually take more water from the soil than an equal area of grass, but tree roots are so efficient at tapping groundwater sources or moist subsoil that they can usually survive one or two droughty seasons. They'll just grow less.

If I sound partial to trees, it's because I am; but the truth is trees are pretty slick at helping themselves to the water you put out for the nearby lawn, too. (This is one reason for watering the lawn deeply when you do water, so all the little root systems will grow deeper instead of shallower.)

Still planting trees in the lawn? There are several good reasons NOT to:

- Some lawngrasses (like Kentucky bluegrass, buffalograss, and blue grama, for starters) don't do well in shade, and will eventually die out.
- Bumping a tree with a lawnmower or "weed whacker" can seriously damage the tree ("lawnmower blight").

Saskatoon serviceberry (Amelanchier alnifolia) *in autumn.*

- If the lawn is watered frequently, it will encourage the tree or shrub to grow shallow roots and compete with the grass.
- If the tree likes acid soil and the grass favors alkaline, putting them close together will cause one of them to suffer!

If you're going to plant trees in a lawn, at the very least put a shallow ring of organic mulch to at least 18 inches away from the trunk. This will keep the mowers away, though going out to the ultimate drip line is better—the mulch breaks down and improves the soil. It's hard to believe that scrawny little tree will eventually be 15 to 30 feet in crown diameter, but it will if you wait long enough.

Better than grass under trees are shade-tolerant, low-water groundcovers, flowers, or shrubs. These choices work especially well in sandy soil because the root systems of the different plants grow to different depths, and water not used by the shallow-rooted plants drains to the deeper-rooted ones.

Research indicates many trees have much wider, shallower root systems than we once thought, especially in clay soil where the roots are gasping for air. So consider your soil type before you go

digging around in the roots that much. It might be easier just to give them some space, you know?

If you plant trees on slopes or berms, be sure to create permanent, saucer-like depressions around them to catch water.

STARTING OUT

SIZE

One of the most fun things about Xeriscape is exploding old myths, or turning things inside out. Plant size at installation is a great example of that. Who can resist the temptation to make room in your budget for the largest trees and shrubs you can afford, for that instant landscape effect?

Wait! Before you "go for it," there's a catch: The larger the plant is at transplant time, the longer it will be before the tree or shrub recovers from the transplanting process and starts growing again.

Tree expert Carl Whitcomb, Ph.D., has found that when the caliper (diameter) of a tree trunk gets larger than about 3 inches, the tree has so many twig and leaf cells to support above-ground that transplanting it at that size leaves it in shock for years. The tree expends all its energy rebuilding roots to support the top-growth again.

Meanwhile, he says, a 1- or 2-inch-caliper tree transplanted at the same time may catch up to or surpass the larger tree in size after just a few years. Also, slow-growing plants such as some of the oaks (not all) will tolerate very little change, so transplant them when small.

TIMING

Late March to mid-April is the best time to plant trees and shrubs in Colorado, where winters are cold. Do it as soon as the soil can be worked, or as we like to say here, "as soon as you can jack-hammer through the ground." This is the only time "bareroot" stock is available, so you are all set there. Balled-and-burlapped stock or container-grown trees and shrubs (see p. 161) should be planted before bud-break.

Avoid disturbing a plant that has recently broken bud and is producing new, soft growth. Balled and burlapped and container stock plants can be installed after new growth has hardened (early summer), just not during the soft-growth stage.

Container-grown stock can usually be planted all summer, but it's still best to avoid planting when the new growth is soft. For evergreens, it's safe to plant when a pine candle (new growth at branch tip—aren't plants just so poetic?!) can be broken off; this means it has sufficiently hardened.

When winters are cold, there's a greater risk of losing a fall transplant, but you can help it along by mulching with a layer of 3–4 inches of wood chips to prevent early freezing of the soil. Sometimes nurseries sell stock at lower prices in fall so they don't have to take care of them another winter. A little more money in your pocket if you're willing to keep them protected.

New root growth usually slows substantially when the soil temperature goes below 40 degrees, and mulching delays this a little.

The best scenario is to give the plant about a month to take hold before the soil temperature gets that cool. Mid-October is usually recommended as a cutoff date for fall planting.

Forget the winter. I know, I know, we do have the warm days sometimes, and the soil seems warm, but the temperatures are too erratic, so just take a break already.

TENDING THE SOIL

In all cases, when someone says "plant the tree" it means plant them with respect to your soil type. In average, sandy, or gravelly (well-drained) soil, plant the tree/shrub with the base level (i.e., where it met the ground before, marked by a color change on the stem) at the same level as the surrounding ground.

In heavy clay soil (poor drainage), plant it with the base level 2–4 inches *above* the surrounding ground. This helps prevent the roots from drowning if settling occurs. The good news is that while we used to have to excavate a few inches below where the root ball would end up, now the word is to set that root ball on undisturbed ground. This saves some backbreaking labor, but….

The bad news is that now we're advised to make the planting hole as wide as we can stand, between two and five times the diameter of the root ball. And all because some *scientists,* whom I bet were getting paid by the hour, discovered tree root growth is much more shallow and sideways than we all used to think!

Remember that one from the Soil Improvement chapter about not using organic amendments for trees and shrubs unless you can amend the whole bed area? Apparently, the complete story on that is that it can be helpful to use

ABOVE: *Setting the root ball slightly above grade prevents settling and root-drowning.*
BELOW: *Removing the wire basket and the majority of the burlap around the root ball ensures proper root development.*

organic amendments, but only if you can mix in enough to supply the plant's root zone for at least three years. For a large maple tree, for instance, this would be a 6- to 8-foot-diameter hole amended 12 to 18 inches deep.

You may be into it, but that's a little more work than I can face, so the next best thing is just to loosen the soil as much as you can through the area, and skip the organic amendments. (Even I have a hard time getting my mind around this one.)

Tree and shrub planting is a great place to use hydro-gels to ensure your plant survives the installation. Denver landscape company president Dave Tollefson reported his company cut losses on pines and spruce a few years ago from 21 percent to 13 percent after starting installation with polymer. The company tried this after learning that many of its suppliers were using polymer in raising the container stock.

A good application rate for Colorado is: one part hydrated polymer (mix ⅓ cup dry in 5 gallons water and let it sit for one to two hours) to two parts soil (backfill in the planting hole). One dry pound of polymer is about 2¾ cups.

Many landscape contractors bemoan the fact that most of the trees and shrubs they have to replace for homeowners were killed by *overwatering*, not underwatering. The polymer won't make this situation worse; in fact it actually helps soak up extra water that would drown the plant, but do pay close attention to soil moisture before watering, as described in the following section.

WATERING

Backfill the planting hole, then fill the hole with water. Let the water set to get air out of the backfill soil. Fill the hole with soil while the water is still in it. As the soil shrinks in the hole, top it off with more soil. This intense method eliminates the chance of air pockets developing, which can kill the plant as quickly as too much or too little water during establishment. Allow the water to settle the soil; don't tamp the backfill.

It can take up to three growing seasons for xeric trees and shrubs to become well-established, so don't be thinking you can go to zero watering 10 days after you plant them, unless you've done some serious plant research for just the right species, plant siting, and weather cooperation!

Two forms of species roses, Austrian copper (Rosa foetida 'Bicolor') and Persian yellow (R. f. 'Persiana'), flower once in late spring with a spectacular show of single flowers.

When watering newly transplanted trees or shrubs, you want to try to get the moisture down 12 to 18 inches each time you water. After planting and watering in, wait a week to 10 days, then dig down with a trowel at the edge of the planting hole 6 to 8 inches (just above root zone). If the soil is dry (falls apart when squeezed in your hand) at that depth, then water. If it holds together in a ball in your hand, it's still moist enough. Using this information, and taking precipitation into account, you can devise a rough watering schedule for the first season without constantly having to dig.

Trees should be watered through fall and winter when these seasons are dry. A good rule of thumb is to water them on holidays. This will get them some moisture once or twice a month.

In some cases, if the roots have dried out they can be soaked to restore moisture and survive, but most will die if roots have dried out. Many Colorado soil conservation districts have tremendously increased survival of seedling trees by dipping the roots in a slurry of a fine grind of soil polymer. (See "Cross-Linked Polyacrylamide," p. 77.)

Other options include wrapping the roots in moist peat moss and keeping them sealed in a plastic bag. In any case, leave these plants in the shade until you're ready to install them.

To plant, prune off broken, damaged, or diseased roots, and hold the plant so the base level will be at, or above (remember the soil stuff) the same level as it was previously while you are backfilling.

Balled & Burlapped

Balled-and-burlapped trees and shrubs have been dug from the field with a ball of soil attached. A huge percentage of the root system is lost with this method, and it will take the plant a while to recover from transplanting and begin growing.

Keep roots moist and plants in the shade until it's time to put them in the ground (which you'll do just as soon as you can for all plants, but it's especially critical for B&B plants.)

As mentioned before, set the root ball on undisturbed ground, then remove all wires (top ⅓ to ⅔ of wire, as much as you can), ropes, twine, pins, nails, ribbons, or barrettes that may have been used to hold the root ball together. Cutting the burlap or removing it from the top will help the roots grow out more quickly, but leave the rest of the burlap in place to biodegrade, as that is most of what's keeping the root ball from disintegrating.

Container-Grown Stock

Remove plastic pots before installing the plants in the wide, shallow hole you've slaved over.

Paper pots can be left on to keep the root ball intact. Often bareroot plants are planted out into these in early spring, just to get them available, so leave them on. Tear off the rim as much as you can and make some cuts along the sides with a utility knife to speed deterioration and root escape.

If container-grown stock has pot-bound roots at the bottom of the root mass, cut through any roots that circle more than halfway around, as

MULCH AND FABRIC

A layer of cedar mulch, wood chips, or bark up to 3–4 inches deep—keep it away from the tree trunk—can be added around the tree/shrub to reduce watering and weeding chores. The use of weed-barrier fabric dictates an even shallower layer of mulch, or the soil could stay too wet. Never use the black plastic—it cuts out air and water and can snuff your plant.

TYPES OF TREES AND SHRUBS FOR TRANSPLANTING

Bareroot Plants

The least expensive option, these plants are dug from the field in early spring when they are dormant. The roots are cleaned, trimmed, and kept moist for shipping. Bareroot stock is usually available for small deciduous trees or shrubs, as they have the longest dormancy period. (Evergreens are not dormant long enough, and they also can't stand to have roots exposed.)

these are in danger of continuing to grow in circles around the tree and deleting it (more tough talk for plant killing). The plant eventually strangles because the roots are not moving into the landscape where there's food, water, and room to grow!

STAKING

Research shows that unstaked trees develop thicker trunks with the additional movement they experience. You can take advantage of this advice if you're planting in a very protected area, but let's face it, there's lots of wind in the Rockies, and most people don't want to take the gamble. I've seen a 10-foot tall new tree askew at about 45 degrees, in what I thought was a pretty average neighborhood.

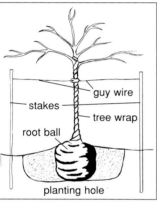

Illustration by Ian Ellefson.

guy wire
stakes
tree wrap
root ball
planting hole

Some designers and contractors stake on three sides for evergreens and two sides for deciduous trees to keep the wind from wiggling the root ball. Make sure there's a little give in the staking or the thickness of the trunk won't increase below the guying.

Stakes and wide, flexible strapping are readily available. Skip the garden hose over wire, as it still causes girdling. Straps will, too, when they're left on too long. Guy for no more than two seasons without changing the strap position.

SUNSCALD PROTECTION

Except for aspens and birches, which already have light-colored reflective trunks, thin deciduous trees should be wrapped to prevent sunscald. Bark heats up on the south side during the day from absorbed heat on warm winter days, becomes active, then gets zapped by cold night temperatures. The alternating freeze/thaw causes the bark to split.

Commercially available asphalt composite crepe paper wrap reflects the light away from the trunk. Wind it around the trunk from the base up, overlapping layers slightly, and secure with duct tape at the top—so as not to wound the tree! Leave this on from November to April the first year.

Deciduous Shrubs (pages 162–165)

XXX-rated plants (Plants established for at least a year need to be watered up to ½" every two weeks during the growing season, above and beyond natural precipitation.) *Native

BOTANICAL NAME	COMMON NAME	HEIGHT	ZONE
*Amorpha canescens**	Silvery leadplant	3'	5
*A. fruticosa**	False indigo bush	6'	5
*Caragana arborescens**	Siberian peashrub	10–15'	2–7
C. a. 'Logergii'	Fern-leaf Siberian peashrub	7–10'	2–7
C. frutex 'Globosa'	Globe peashrub	8–10'	2–7
C. maximowicziana	Maximowicz peashrub	4–7'	2–7
C. microphylla	Littleleaf peashrub	6'	2
C. pygmaea	Pygmy peashrub	3'	4
Caryopteris x *clandonensis*	Blue-mist spirea	2–3'	5
*Ceonothus fendleri**	Mountain lilac	3'	5
*Ceratoides lanata**	Winterfat	1–3'	4
*Cercocarpus montanus**	Trueleaf mountain mahogany	3–6'	4
Chamaebatiaria millefolium	Fernbush	4–5'	5
Chrysothamnus nauseosus subsp. *graveolens**	Green rubber rabbitbrush	4'	4

(Note: Here's one of your perfect species. Xeriscape expert Ken Ball planted this species as a one-gallon plant and walked away from it. Twelve years later it's still growing strong.)

C. n. subsp. *nauseosus**	Blue rubber rabbitbrush	4'	5
*C. viscidiflorus**	Sticky-leaved or Yellow rabbitbrush	20–40"	5
*Fendlera rupicola**	Cliff fendlerbush	5'	5
*Fallugia paradoxa**	Apache plume	3–8'	5
*Forestiera neomexicana**	New Mexico privet	8'	4
*Fraxinus anomala**	Singleleaf ash	25'	5
Hippophae rhamnoides	Sea buckthorn	10–20'	4
Ligustrum obtusifolium var. *regalianum*	Regal privet	4'	4–7
L. vulgare 'Cheyenne'	Cheyenne privet	6'	4–7
L. v. 'Densiflorum'	Upright privet	12–15'	4–7
L. v. 'Lodense'	Lodense privet	3'	4–7
*Purshia tridentata**	Antelope bitterbrush	4–7'	5
*Quercus gambelii** (forms a colony)	Gambel oak	20'	4–7
*Q. undulata**	Wavyleaf oak	20'	4–9
Rhus aromatica	Fragrant sumac	6'	3–9
R. a. 'Gro-Low'	Gro-low sumac	3'	3–9
*R. glabra**	Smooth sumac	10'	3–9
R. g. var. *cismontana**	Rocky Mountain sumac	6'	3–9
*R. trilobata**	Three-leaf sumac	3–6'	5
R. typhina	Staghorn sumac	10'	3–9
R. t. 'Laciniata'	Cutleaf sumac	8'	3–9
*Ribes aureum**	Golden currant	6'	2–7
*R. cereum**	Wax currant	4–5'	2–7

Rose of Sharon (Hibiscus syriacus, *foreground*) *keeps a colorful presence in this mixed border most of the summer. Once established, it is quite drought tolerant.*

BOTANICAL NAME	COMMON NAME	HEIGHT	ZONE
Shepherdia spp.*	Buffaloberry	8–10'	3

(Note: Jim Borland, horticulturist and Genesee Open Space coordinator, reported to me that there are only three Shepherdia species in the world, each with a distinctly different habitat. Two are native to Colorado.)

Sorbaria sorbifolia	Ural false spirea	6'	2–8
Symphoricarpos x chenaultii	Chenault coralberry	3–6'	4–7
S. x c. 'Hancock'	Hancock coralberry	2–3'	4–7

XX-rated plants

(need ½" applied water every week during growing season)

BOTANICAL NAME	COMMON NAME	HEIGHT	ZONE
Acer amur	Amur maple	18'	4
A. ginnala compacta spp.	Compact amur maple	8'	2
*A. glabrum**	Rocky Mountain maple	24'	4
A. tataricum	Tatarian maple	15–25'	3–7
Amelanchier alnifolia	Saskatoon serviceberry	10'	3
A. a. 'Regent'	Regent serviceberry	6'	3
Berberis thunbergii 'Atropurpurea Nana'	Crimson pygmy barberry	2'	4–8
Berberis spp.* (a few are native, most are not)	Barberry	1–4'	Varies
Buddleia alternifolia	Fountain butterfly bush	15'	5–8
B. davidii	Butterfly bush	4'	5–9
Colutea arborescens	Common bladder senna	8'	6
Cotinus coggygria	Smoke tree	10–15'	5
Cotoneaster acutifolius	Peking cotoneaster	9'	5
C. multiflorus	Flowering cotoneaster	12'	3
Euonymus alatus	Winged euonymus, Burning bush	6'	4
Forsythia spp. (some species are groundcovers)	Forsythia	1–10'	5
Hibiscus syriacus	Althea, Rose of Sharon	5–15'	5
*Holodiscus dumosus**	Rock spirea	4'	4
*Jamesia americana**	Waxflower, Mountain mockorange	6'	4–8
Kolkwitzia amabilis	Beautybush	10'	4
Lonicera korolkowii	Blueleaf honeysuckle	10'	4–7

BOTANICAL NAME	COMMON NAME	HEIGHT	ZONE
L. k. var. *floribunda* 'Blue Velvet'	Blue velvet honeysuckle	10'	3
L. maackii	Amur honeysuckle	10'	2–8
L. tatarica 'Arnold Red'	Arnold red honeysuckle	8'	4
L. xylosteoides 'Clavey's Dwarf'	Clavey's dwarf honeysuckle	6'	4
*Peraphyllum ramosissimum**	Squaw apple	6–12'	5
Perovskia atriplicifolia	Russian sage, Azure sage	5'	4–5
Philadelphus lewisii	Lewis mockorange	3–6'	5–8
*P. microphyllus**	Littleleaf mockorange	6'	6
*Physocarpus monogynus**	Mountain ninebark	6'	5
P. opulifolius and cultivars	Ninebark	4–7'	2–7
*Potentilla fruticosa**	Potentilla	2–4'	Varies
*Prunus americana**	American plum	6–25'	3–8

Top: In autumn, red barberry (Berberis thunbergii) *stands out against the deep green of mugo pine* (Pinus mugo) *and low-growing junipers. Above: Serviceberry flowers appear on bare branches. In frontier times, these earliest-blooming flowers were often employed at funeral services, hence the name.*

Deciduous Shrubs (continued)

BOTANICAL NAME	COMMON NAME	HEIGHT	ZONE
P. besseyi*	Western sand cherry	4–6'	4
P. virginiana and cultivars*	Chokecherry	25'	4–8
P. v. melanocarpa*	Native chokecherry	25'	2
Ptelea trifoliata*	Wafer ash	10–15'	5
Ribes alpinum	Alpine currant	5–8'	3
R. aureum*	Golden currant	6'	2
R. cereum*	Squaw currant	3–5'	5
R. inerme*	Whitestem gooseberry	5'	6
R. 'Red Lake'	Red lake currant	4'	5
Rosa 'Nearly Wild'	Nearly wild rose	2–3'	4
R. foetida 'Bicolor'	Austrian copper rose	6'	4
R. f. 'Persiana'	Persian yellow rose	6'	4
R. x harisonii	Harison's yellow rose	6'	4
R. 'Meidiland' (series)	Meidiland roses (various)	2–4'	4

The elongated sterile flowers of the smoke tree or smoke bush (Cotinus coggygria 'Royal Purple') generate clusters of fluffy hairs, giving the impression of smoke.

BOTANICAL NAME	COMMON NAME	HEIGHT	ZONE
R. rubrifolia	Redleaf rose	6'	2
R. woodsii*	Woods rose, Wild rose	5'	4–9
Rubus deliciosus*	Thimbleberry, Boulder raspberry	5'	4
Spiraea nipponica 'Snowmound'	Snowmound spirea	4–6'	4
S. thunbergi	Bridalwreath spirea	3–5'	4–8
S. vanhouttei	Vanhoutte spirea	6'	4
Symphoricarpos albus*	White snowberry	3–6'	3
S. doorenbosii 'Magic Berry'	Magic berry coralberry	3–5'	5–7
S. d. 'White Hedge'	White hedge snowberry	3–5'	5–7
S. occidentalis*	Western snowberry	3'	3

Festooned with single blossoms in June, nearly wild rose (Rosa 'Nearly Wild') continues to flower less profusely throughout the rest of the summer.

BOTANICAL NAME	COMMON NAME	HEIGHT	ZONE
S. orbiculatus	Red coralberry	3–6'	2
S. oreophilus*	Mountain snowberry	2–4'	4
Syringa x chinensis	Chinese lilac	10'	3–7
S. laciniata persica	Persian lilac	5–7'	4–8
S. patula 'Miss Kim'	Miss Kim lilac	4–5'	3–7
S. reflexa	MacFarlane lilac	6–10'	5–7
S. villosa*	Late lilac	10'	3–7
S. vulgaris	Common lilac	15'	3–7
Viburnum lantana*	Wayfaring viburnum	10'	4–7
V. l. 'Mohican'	Mohican viburnum	6'	4–7
Weigela florida and cultivars	Weigela	4–6'	4–8

X-rated plants

(need 1" applied water every week during growing season)

BOTANICAL NAME	COMMON NAME	HEIGHT	ZONE
Amelanchier spp.* (some are natives)	Serviceberry	6–12'	5
Aronia spp.	Chokeberry	6'	3
Chaenomeles speciosa	Flowering quince	6–10'	5
Cornus baileyi	Bailey dogwood	7'	5
C. mas	Cornelian cherry	24'	4
C. sericea*	Red-twig dogwood, Red-osier dogwood	6'	3
Hydrangea arborescens 'Annabelle'	Annabelle hydrangea	4'	3–9
Philadelphus x virginalis and cultivars	Mockorange	3–10'	5–8
Prunus x cistena	Purpleleaf cherry	6–8'	3–7
P. glandulosa	Dwarf flowering almond	6'	5–8
P. pensylvanica*	Pin cherry	8'	2
P. tomentosa	Nanking cherry	8'	3
Rhamnus cathartica	Common buckthorn	20'	3
R. frangula 'Asplenifolia'	Fernleaf buckthorn	7'	3–7
R. smithii*	Smith buckthorn	9'	3
Rubus parviflorus*	Western thimbleberry	3'	4
Spiraea spp.	Spirea	2–6'	Varies
S. x bumalda 'Froebelii'	Froebel spirea	4'	3
Viburnum carlesii	Koreanspice viburnum	6'	4–7
V. lantana	Wayfaring tree viburnum	10–15'	4
V. lentago	Nannyberry viburnum	15'	3–7
V. opulus	European cranberry bush	8–12'	3–8
V. trilobum	American cranberry bush	10'	2–7

High-water plants

(need regular watering or damp soil)

BOTANICAL NAME	COMMON NAME	HEIGHT	ZONE
Alnus tenuifolia*	Thinleaf alder	20–30'	1–7
Betula glandulosa*	Bog birch	10'	3
Lonicera involucrata*	Twinberry, Bearberry honeysuckle	3–5'	4–9
Philadelphus coronarius 'Aureus'	Golden-leaved mockorange	6'	4–8
Ribes lacustre*	Bristly currant	3–6'	2–7
Salix discolor	Pussy willow	15–20'	2–9
S. exigua*	Sandbar willow	10'	2–9
S. irrorata*	Bluestem willow	10–15'	5–9
S. purpurea nana	Dwarf arctic willow	4'	4–8
Sambucus canadensis	American elder	10–15'	4
S. racemosa*	Red-berried elder	10–12'	3–7
Sorbus scopulina*	Native mountain ash	3–10'	2–6

Evergreen Shrubs (pages 165–166)

XXX-rated plants

(Plants established for at least a year need to be watered up to ½" every two weeks during the growing season, above and beyond natural precipitation.)

BOTANICAL NAME	COMMON NAME	HEIGHT	ZONE
Agave utahensis	Utah agave	8'	5
Arctostaphylos patula*	Greenleaf manzanita	3–6'	5
Artemisia abrotanum	Wormwood sage	3–5'	5
A. cana*	Silver sagebrush	1–5'	4
A. filifolia*	Threadleaf sage, Sand sage	4'	5
A. tridentata	Tall Western sagebrush	3–10'	3–9
A. tridentata subsp. tridentata	Basin big sagebrush	6–12'	3–9
Atriplex canescens*	Four-wing saltbush	5'	4
Cercocarpus brevifolius	Little-flowered mountain mahogany	12'	3–8
C. intricatus*	Little-leaf mountain mahogany	5'	5
C. ledifolius*	Curl-leaf mountain mahogany	4–15'	4–5
Cowania mexicana*	Cliffrose	6'	5
Ephedra nevadensis	Mormon tea	3–4'	5
E. torreyana*	Torrey Mormon tea	2–3'	5
E. viridis*	Green Mormon tea	4–8'	5
Juniperus horizontalis spp.	Andorra, Bar Harbor, Blue chip, Wilton juniper	6–18"	4
Nolina texana*	Texas nolina	3'	5
Purshia tridentata*	Antelope bitterbrush	4'	5
Yucca baccata*	Banana yucca	3'	5
Y. elata	Soaptree yucca	30'	6
Y. glauca*	Soapweed	3–6'	4

Froebel spirea (Spiraea x bumalda 'Froebelii'), which enjoys full sun or part shade, flowers in late May or June.

Evergreen Shrubs (continued)

XX-rated plants

(need ½" applied water every week during growing season)

BOTANICAL NAME	COMMON NAME	HEIGHT	ZONE
Cotoneaster apiculatus	Cranberry cotoneaster	3'	5
C. a. 'Tom Thumb'	Tom Thumb cotoneaster	1'	5
C. divaricatus	Spreading cotoneaster	6'	5
C. horizontalis perpusillus	Ground cotoneaster	1'	5
Cytisus x praecox 'Allgold'	Warminster broom	10'	5
C. scoparius 'Moonlight'	Moonlight Scotch broom	5'	5
Euonymus spp.	Euonymus	2–6'	5
Juniperus chinensis spp.	Armstrong, Holbert junipers	3–4'	4
J. communis*	Common juniper	2–3'	3
J. sabina spp.	Arcadia, Buffalo, Tammy junipers	1–3'	4
Mahonia aquifolium	Oregon grapeholly	6'	5–9
M. a. compacta	Compact Oregon grapeholly	3'	5–9
Picea abies 'Nidiformis'	Bird's nest spruce	3'	2
P. pungens 'Globosa'	Globe blue spruce	3'	2
Pinus mugo and cultivars	Mugo pine	2–10'	2–7
P. sylvestris 'Glauca Nana'	Scotch dwarf pine	3'	3–7
Pyracantha spp.	Pyracantha	3–6'	5

X-rated plants

(need 1" applied water every week during growing season)

BOTANICAL NAME	COMMON NAME	HEIGHT	ZONE
Ligustrum x vicaryi	Golden vicary privet	6'	5–8
Picea glauca 'Conica'	Alberta dwarf spruce	6'	2–6
Pinus mugo 'Mops'	Mops mugo pine	5'	2–7
P. strobus 'Nana'	Eastern white dwarf pine	3'	3–7
Taxus media	Yew	3–8'	4
Thuja occidentalis	Arborvitae	3–10'	3–7

Bigtooth maple (Acer grandidentatum) *is a beautiful small tree or large shrub. Its fall leaves can be quite striking, with colors varying from year to year between yellow, pink, orange, and red.*

Deciduous Trees (pages 166–168)

XXX-rated plants

(Plants established for at least a year need to be watered up ½" every two weeks during the growing season, above and bey natural precipitation.)

BOTANICAL NAME	COMMON NAME	HEIGHT	ZONE
Crataegus ambigua	Russian hawthorn	12–20'	4
C. arnoldiana	Arnold's hawthorn	20'	4–7
C. crus-galli	Cockspur hawthorn	20'	3–7
C. c.-g. var. inermis	Thornless cockspur hawthorn	20'	3–7
C. douglasi	River hawthorn	20–30'	5–9
C. mollis	Downy hawthorn	20'	3–7
C. succulenta	Fleshy hawthorn	15'	3–6
Forestiera neomexicana	New Mexico privet	8–10'	5
Juglans nigra	Black walnut	75'	4–9
Quercus gambelii*	Gambel oak	20'	5
Q. macrocarpa	Bur oak	70–80'	2
Q. undulata*	Wavy-leaf oak	20–30'	5–9
Robinia pseudoacacia	Black locust	75'	3
R. p. 'Purple Robe'	Purple Robe common locust	50'	3

XX-rated plants (need ½" applied water every week)

BOTANICAL NAME	COMMON NAME	HEIGHT	ZONE
Acer ginnala	Amur maple	20'	2
A. grandidentatum*	Bigtooth maple	25–50'	2
A. tataricum	Tatarian maple	20'	3–7
Aesculus glabra	Ohio buckeye, Yellow buckeye	60'	4–8

Russian hawthorn (Crataegus ambigua) *in spring flower. This tree will later produce deep-red fruit, most welcome by birds.*

BOTANICAL NAME	COMMON NAME	HEIGHT	ZONE
A. hippocastanum	Horsechestnut	50'	3–7
A. pavia	Red buckeye	35'	3–7
Celtis occidentalis	Common hackberry	65'	3
Crataegus laevigata 'Paul's Scarlet'	Paul's Scarlet hawthorn	15'	6
C. phaenopyrum	Washington hawthorn	20'	4–8
C. viridis 'Winter King'	Winter King hawthorn	30'	5–7
Gymnocladus dioica	Kentucky coffee tree	45'	5
Phellodendron amurense	Amur corktree	35'	3–7
Pyrus calleryana 'Aristocrat'	Aristocrat pear	30'	4
P. c. 'Chanticleer'	Chanticleer pear	35'	5–8
P. c. 'Stone Hill'	Stone hill pear	35'	5–8
P. fauriei	Fauriei pear	25'	3–7
P. f. 'Korean Sun'	Korean sun pear	12'	3–7
P. ussuriensis	Ussurian pear	50'	4–6
P. u. 'Prairie Gem'	Prairie gem pear	30–35'	4–6
Quercus alba	White oak	70'	3–9
Q. bicolor	Swamp white oak	50'	4–8
Q. imbricaria	Shingle oak, Laurel oak	50'	4–8
Q. prinus	Chestnut oak	65'	4–8
Q. robur	English oak	50'	5–8
Q. r. 'Fastigiata'	Columnar English oak	40'	4–8

Top: Showy upright greenish-yellow flowers appear in the spring on this handsome Ohio buckeye (Aesculus glabra, *at left*). *In the fall, its yellow hue brings another dimension to the landscape.*
Above: Washington hawthorns (Crataegus phaenopyrum) *are a standout in the fall. Clusters of bright red berries, which persist well into the winter, intermingle among scarlet-orange leaves.*

Robinia idahoensis	Idaho locust	40'	4
R. neomexicana*	New Mexico locust	25'	5
Syringa pekinensis	Peking lilac	25–30'	4–7
S. reticulata	Japanese tree lilac	30'	4
Ulmus spp.	Elm	50–70'	Varies

Deciduous Trees (continued)

X-rated plants
(need 1" applied water every week during growing season)

BOTANICAL NAME	COMMON NAME	HEIGHT	ZONE
Acer platanoides	Norway maple	50'	3
Catalpa ovata	Chinese catalpa	30'	5
C. speciosa	Western catalpa	50'	4–8
Cercis spp.	Redbud	20'	5–9
Fraxinus americana 'Empire'	Empire ash	50'	3–9
F. mandschurica 'Mancana'	Mancana ash	45'	3
F. nigra 'Fall Gold'	Fall gold ash	50'	2–5
F. pennsylvanica (all cultivars)	Green ash	50–60'	4
Gleditsia triacanthos inermis (all cultivars)	Thornless honey locust	35–70'	4
Koelreuteria paniculata	Golden raintree	30–40'	5
Malus spp.	Apples and Crabapples	12–25'	Varies
Prunus x blireiana 'Newport'	Newport plum	12–24'	4–5
P. cerasus	Montmorency cherry	15–25'	3
P. padus	European bird cherry	40'	4–7
Sophora japonica	Japanese pagoda tree	50'	4–7
Sorbus aucuparia	European mountain ash	45'	3–7
Tilia cordata	Littleleaf linden	75'	3–8
Tilia spp.	Linden	45'	3–7

High-water plants (need regular watering or moist soil)

BOTANICAL NAME	COMMON NAME	HEIGHT	ZONE
Acer negundo*	Box-elder	50'	2–9
A. rubrum	Red maple	45–50'	3–7
A. saccharinum	Silver maple	50–65'	3–9
Betula fontinalis*	Rocky Mountain birch	40–50'	4–6
Carpinus betulus 'Fastigiata'	Columnar hornbeam	35'	4–7
Populus alba spp.	Silver poplar	45–75'	3–9
P. angustifolia* (forms a colony)	Narrowleaf cottonwood	50'	3
P. deltoides spp.	Cottonless cottonwood	75'	3–9
P. sargentii*	Plains poplar, Cottonwood	90'	4
P. tremula 'Erecta'	Upright European poplar	60'	2–5
P. tremuloides*	Quaking aspen	35–50'	2
Quercus rubra	Northern red oak	40'	4–8
Salix amygdaloides*	Peachleaf willow	35–50'	3
S. matsudana	Navajo globe willow	35'	3

Above and below: The tall, narrow, irregularly shaped Western catalpa (Catalpa speciosa) puts forth an outstanding show of fragrant white flowers in late June, followed by long, thin seedpods. Despite its lush appearance, the catalpa can tolerate quite dry soils.

Evergreen Trees

XXX-rated plants

(Plants established for at least a year need to be watered up to ½" every two weeks during the growing season, above and beyond natural precipitation.)

BOTANICAL NAME	COMMON NAME	HEIGHT	ZONE
Juniperus deppeana	Alligator bark juniper	25–50'	5–9
J. monosperma*	Oneseed juniper	20–50'	5–9
J. osteosperma*	Utah juniper	10–20'	5
J. scopulorum*	Rocky Mountain juniper	10–20'	3–8
Pinus aristata*	Bristlecone pine	30'	4–7
P. edulis*	Colorado piñon pine	15–40'	4
P. monophylla	Singleleaf piñon pine	10–25'	4
P. ponderosa*	Ponderosa pine	60–150'	4
P. strobiformis*	Southwestern white pine	60'	5–7

XX-rated plants

(need ½" applied water every week during growing season)

BOTANICAL NAME	COMMON NAME	HEIGHT	ZONE
Juniperus spp.	Juniper	30–75'	Varies
Picea pungens*	Blue spruce, Colorado spruce	75–100'	3–7
Pinus flexilis*	Limber pine	75'	4–7
P. jeffreyi	Jeffrey pine	120'	5
P. nigra	Austrian pine	60'	4–8
P. sylvestris	Scotch pine	90'	3–8

X-rated plants

(need 1" applied water every week during growing season)

BOTANICAL NAME	COMMON NAME	HEIGHT	ZONE
Abies concolor*	Concolor fir, White fir	70'	3–7
A. lasiocarpa*	Corkbark fir, Subalpine fir	80'	5
Picea engelmannii*	Engelmann spruce	60'	2–5
Pinus contorta latifolia*	Lodgepole pine	20–100'	2
Pseudotsuga menziesii*	Douglas fir	60–130'	4–6

Above: Tough yet beautiful, crabapple trees (Malus spp.) are perfect for a dry climate.
Below: Eastern mountain ash (Sorbus aucuparia) can fit into a Xeriscape's moderate zone of water use.

When placed in a location protected from drying winds, Eastern redbud (Cercis canadensis) does quite well in Colorado.

ABOVE: *Boston ivy or Japanese creeper* (Parthenocissus tricuspidata) *needs no support for its wild behavior.*
OPPOSITE: *Scarlet trumpet honeysuckle* (Lonicera sempervirens) *requires a support to climb.*

VINES

Vines are great for Xeriscape. Here's what they can do for you:

- Cool a wall they grow on in the summer by as much as 20 degrees, without blocking winter sun and heat.
- Provide quick shade and vertical elements when grown on trellises and arbors, whereas trees would take decades to do the same.

- Add a welcome note of lushness to the landscape through bright green foliage, beautiful flowers, and, sometimes, brilliant fall color.
- Double as groundcover—especially Hall's honeysuckle, Virginia creeper, and some of the wild clematis vines—anchoring soil and providing the green expanse in deep shade where the sun doesn't shine and grass doesn't thrive.
- Mask eyesores such as an unattractive view, a chain-link fence, or a stark concrete wall, making them appear more appealing.

Because most of the growing energy of vines goes into making foliage rather than supporting themselves, they can quickly fill a vertical space without taking up much ground space (as little as 1 square foot). Is that exciting, or what?

A simple frame with wide spaces can be built and anchored about a foot away from a south- or west-facing window. A vine growing up this contraption will absorb heat in the summer that would normally reflect into the room while still letting in plenty of light.

BASICS FOR GROWING VINES

- Vines need support and well-drained, well-prepared soil in the planting hole. Plant them 3–6 inches away from the wall or support; they do better with air circulation.
- Use a 3-inch layer of mulch over the roots to keep them cool in summer.
- The best location is where roots can be kept cool (by shade or mulching), but their leaves can drape over into the sunshine. If the base of the plant must be in the sun, use mulch or place a large rock next to it.
- Water vines well when young and keep weak or dead wood pruned out.
- Large, vigorous species need moderate to severe pruning nearly every season to avoid the vines taking over trees and damaging shutters and wooden structures. Grapevines need pruning in order to bear the best crop of fruit.

Remember the old saying about vines: "The first year they sleep, the second year they creep, and the third year they leap." Be prepared—or locate the vines where they will have the room they need to grow, without fear of overtaking your world.

Vines

XXX-rated plants

(Plants established for at least a year need to be watered up to ½" every two weeks during the growing season, above and beyond natural precipitation.)

BOTANICAL NAME	COMMON NAME	HEIGHT	ZONE
Clematis ligusticifolia	Western virgin's bower	20'	3
Parthenocissus quinquefolia	Virginia creeper	35'	3
P. q. engelmannii	Engelmann ivy	20–35'	3
P. tricuspidata	Boston ivy, Japanese creeper	20–30'	3
Polygonum aubertii	Silver lace vine	20'	4–7

XX-rated plants

(need ½" applied water every week during growing season)

BOTANICAL NAME	COMMON NAME	HEIGHT	ZONE
Campsis radicans	Trumpet creeper	30'	4
Clematis paniculata	Sweet autumn clematis	20'	4
C. tangutica	Golden clematis	9'	5
Ipomoea spp.	Morning glory	Varies	Annual
Lonicera japonica 'Halliana'	Hall's honeysuckle	20–30'	4
L. sempervirens	Scarlet trumpet honeysuckle	10–12'	4
Mauryanda antirrhiniflora	Snapdragon vine	6'	Annual
Parthenocissus inserta	Woodbine	35'	3
Vitis spp.	Grape	Varies	Varies
Wisteria macrostachya	Wisteria	15–30'	5

Below: Sweet autumn clematis (Clematis paniculata or C. maximowicziana).
Top Right: Jackman clematis (Clematis x jackmanii).
Bottom Right: Golden clematis or yellow lantern clematis (Clematis tangutica).

X-rated plants

(need 1" applied water every week during growing season)

BOTANICAL NAME	COMMON NAME	HEIGHT	ZONE
Akebia quinata	Fiveleaf akebia	30–40'	4
Ampelopsis brevipendunculata	Blueberry climber	25'	4
Aristolochia durior	Dutchman's pipe	30'	4
Celastrus spp.	Bittersweet	20–36'	Varies
Clematis x jackmanii	Jackman clematis	12'	3–8
Cobaea scandens	Cup-and-saucer vine	40'	Annual
Euonymus fortunei var. radicans	Common wintercreeper	20'	5–9
Hedera helix	English ivy	90'	5
H. h. 'Baltica'	Baltic English ivy	90'	5
Polygonum baldschuanicum	Bukhara fleeceflower	20–30'	4

Vegetable gardens are a good choice for Xeriscape, for the simple reason that they are not usually hooked up to the "pour it on" lawn sprinkler system. Hand watering or drip systems are more appropriate. Some crops are harmed by overhead watering because the wet leaves can attract undesirable insects or lead to disease.

"Edible landscaping" has been championed by California author Rosalind Creasy in more than 20 books, starting in 1982 with *The Complete Book of Edible Landscaping* (Sierra Club Books). Citing the decorative nature of many garden crops, especially leafy vegetables, she recommends including them in containers, flowerbeds, and massed beds. By the same token, some traditional garden flowers such as nasturtiums (*Tropaeolum majus*), cottage pinks (*Dianthus caryophyllus*), and daylilies (*Hemerocallis* spp.) are edible and drought-tolerant, too.

In any vegetable garden where the soil is poor, improve it as much as possible the first year, and continue doing so every year. Unlike some plants that flower more in poor soil, and herbs that generate more of their aromatic oils in poor soil, vegetables are *very clear* about needing rich soil if you want lots of produce. Don't hold back; put in as much organic soil amendment as the law will allow.

Author Mel Bartholomew's "square foot gardening" is a conservation-minded method because it saves many resources, including your time as well as water. In *Square Foot Gardening*

(Rodale Press, 1981), he says that the traditional method of dropping hundreds of seeds out in a long, straight row is more suited to big-time agriculture than weekend home gardeners.

Instead, he advocates setting the seeds out at their ultimate spacing, giving each a little well of sand to start in so there is less chance of damping off (tiny seedling being destroyed by soil-born fungus). The beds are misted daily, or more often if needed, until the seeds sprout, then mulched to conserve moisture.

Then they are watered weekly or semi-weekly, according to their needs, with Bartholomew's favorite precision watering can: an empty 2-cup cottage cheese container. They each get a container full of water at their appointed time, whether once a week or twice, and this doesn't take too long because you are working with a limited number of plants.

I recently learned by looking at (naturally!) www.squarefootgardening.com that Bartholomew was an engineer who retired early and developed this system. Since 1981, he's written three more books on square foot gardening, all still in print and available on the website, along with videos from a series on PBS, a free, downloadable pamphlet on the method, a teachers' guide, and other items. The original book, the website says, is the country's best-selling gardening book, with over a million copies sold. No one has improved on this system for conservation of resources, so I say stick with what works—after all, it came from an engineer.

Vegetable Watering

If you really want to fine-tune your vegetable watering, take this chart into consideration. It turns out the various crops don't all need consistent soil moisture throughout their season. They will produce what you want as long as you keep the soil moist during their "critical moisture period."

CROP	CRITICAL MOISTURE PERIOD
Asparagus	Crown set and transplanting
Beans (dry and green)	Flowering
Beets	Root expansion
Broccoli	Head development
Brussels sprouts	Sprout formation
Cabbage	Head development
Carrots	Seed germination, root expansion
Cantaloupes	Flowering, fruit development
Cauliflower	Head development
Celery	Continuous
Corn	Silking
Cucumbers	Flowering, fruiting
Eggplants	Flowering, fruiting
Greens (turnip, kale, etc.)	Continuous
Leeks	Continuous
Lettuce	Head expansion
Okra	Flowering
Parsnips, rutabagas	Root expansion
Peas	Flowering, pod swelling
Peppers	Transplanting, up to ½" fruit
Potatoes (Irish)	After flowering
Potatoes (Sweet)	First and last 40 days
Pumpkins	Fruiting
Radishes	Continuous
Rhubarb	Leaf emergence
Squash (winter and summer)	Fruit development
Tomatoes	Fruit development
Turnips	Root expansion
Watermelons	Fruit development

HERBS

Many herbs are very drought-tolerant. Often native to the Mediterranean coast, they thrive in conditions of poor soil, good drainage, and usually full sun. If overwatered or overfertilized they will produce little oil, but sometimes-lavish growth.

Well-drained soil is essential for most herbs, so if this isn't what you have in the yard, consider raised bed or container gardening. Most herbs need about a foot of well-drained soil.

Some herbs can be used as landscape plants. Rosemary is an old favorite that is welcome as a small shrub in most gardens (in mine, certainly). It's usually not hardy in Colorado, so grow it in a container to bring inside in winter.

Herbs can also be mixed decoratively through the garden, or used to form a design of their own, if you're extra patient and/or artistic.

The following is a list of herbs that will grow in or need moist soil to thrive: (Sorry, but XXX-, XX-, and X-rated info is not available on herbs. You'll have to wing it.)

Angelica	Mints
Basil	Sweet bay
Chervil	Sweet marjoram
Comfrey	Summer savory
French sorrel	Watercress
Leeks	Wintercress
Lovage	

"What's wintercress? I never heard of it," you say. Neither had I. It's called "yellow rocket" sometimes, and is considered a noxious weed in some places. Great! Let's get some!

These herbs will tolerate dry soil:

Aloe vera	Garlic
Anise	Hyssop
Borage	Lavender
Caraway	Parsley
Chamomile	Rosemary
Chicory	Sage
Chives	Shallots
Coltsfoot	Tarragon
Coriander	Thyme
Cumin	Top onion
Dill	Winter savory
Fennel	Wormwood
Fenugreek	

Like wintercress, top onion was another new one on me. I've been told it's used in pickling and is also called Egyptian onion.

ABOVE: *Serbian bellflower* (Campanula poscharskyana) *is a great choice for rock gardens in partial shade.*
OPPOSITE: *Starring in this garden designed by Jerry Nelson, sweet woodruff* (Galium ordoratum) *is a favorite Xeriscape beauty for dry shade.*

SHADE GARDENS

Most drought-tolerant plants are sun-lovers. And I don't know about you, but I tend to think of dry, shady areas as a bit of the dead zone—bare earth with a few dried-up leaves that blew in from somewhere else. But in fact, there are numerous good Xeriscape plant choices for dry shade. You won't find as many options for screaming-bright flowers, but you will find cheerfully colored foliage, even multi-colored plants with combinations of cream, green, and pink leaves that succeed in lighting up the dark spaces.

Dry shade is a good place to build a subtle, restful palette of textures and colors. Then you won't get fretful wishing you had 16 options each for your orange and purple color scheme. Woodland wildflowers grow well in the shade, and a little judicious pruning to let in more light can help turn a full-shade area into a more flexible, dappled-shade environment. Building a beautiful shade garden is a nice challenge. Have fun with it.

Dry-Shade Plants (pages 176–179)

NOTE: Most of the plants listed here prefer filtered shade or part-day shade. The hardcore plants that will take full shade are noted with an asterisk (*). The ability of shade to reduce the watering needs of plants reduces the distinctions between X-ratings of these plants, but if you're really interested, many of them occur in the previous lists, sorted out. And, I did mention it's largely a guess, right?

Deciduous Trees

BOTANICAL NAME	COMMON NAME	HEIGHT	ZONE
Acer ginnala	Ginnala maple	20'	2
Aesculus x carnea 'Ft. McNair'	Ft. McNair horsechestnut	50'	4–8
Carpinus betulus	European hornbeam	35'	4–7
Celtis occidentalis	Common hackberry	65'	3
Crataegus ambigua	Russian hawthorn	15'	4–6
Robinia pseudoacacia 'Purple Robe'	Purple Robe common locust	50'	3
Quercus bicolor	Swamp white oak	50'	4–8

Smooth sumac (Rhus glabra) *in flower. Its red fall color is outstanding.*

Deciduous Shrubs

BOTANICAL NAME	COMMON NAME	HEIGHT	ZONE
Acer ginnala compacta spp.	Compact amur maple	8'	2
A. glabrum	Rocky Mountain maple	18'	4
Caragana arborescens	Siberian peashrub	10–15'	2–7
C. microphylla arborescens	Littleleaf peashrub	6'	2
Chaenomeles speciosa	Flowering quince	6–10'	5
Colutea arborescens	Common bladder senna	8'	6
Cotoneaster divaricatus	Shrub cotoneaster	6'	5
C. multiflorus	Flowering cotoneaster	5–6'	5
Euonymus alatus	Winged euonymus, Burning bush	6'	4
Fendlera rupicola	Cliff fendlerbush	5'	5
Jamesia americana	Waxflower, Mountain mockorange	6'	4–8
Kerria japonica	Japanese kerria	6–8'	5–8
Kolkwitzia amabilis	Beautybush	10'	4
Ligustrum amurense	Amur privet	8'	4
L. regelianum	Regel privet	4–5'	4
Lonicera korolkowii	Blueleaf honeysuckle	10'	4–7

BOTANICAL NAME	COMMON NAME	HEIGHT	ZONE
L. k. var. *floribunda* 'Blue Velvet'	Blue velvet honeysuckle	10'	3
L. tatarica	Tatarian honeysuckle	12'	4
Philadelphus microphyllus	Littleleaf mockorange	6'	6
Physocarpus monogynus	Mountain ninebark	6'	5
P. opulifolius	Common ninebark	4–7'	2–7
Potentilla fruticosa	Bush cinquefoil	2–4'	2–9
Ptelea trifoliata	Wafer ash	10–15'	5
Rhamnus cathartica	Common buckthorn	20'	3
R. frangula	Alder buckthorn	10–18'	3–9
Rhus glabra	Smooth sumac	10'	3–9
R. trilobata	Three-leaf sumac	3–6'	5
R. typhina	Staghorn sumac	10'	3–9
R. t. 'Laciniata'	Cutleaf sumac	8'	3–9
Ribes aureum	Golden currant	6'	2–7
R. cereum	Wax currant	4–5'	2–7
Rosa hugonis	Father Hugo rose	6–8'	5
R. glauca	Redleaf rose	10–30'	3
Rubus deliciosus	Boulder raspberry, Thimbleberry	5'	4
R. parviflorus	Western thimbleberry	3'	4
Shepherdia argentea	Silver buffaloberry	6–12'	2
Sorbaria sorbifolia	Ural false spirea	6'	2–8
Spiraea nipponica 'Snowmound'	Snowmound spirea	4–6'	4
S. vanhouttei	Vanhoutte spirea	6'	4
*Symphoricarpos albus**	Snowberry	3–6'	3
*S. occidentalis**	Western snowberry	3'	3
S. orbiculatus	Indian currant coralberry	3–6'	2
S. x *chenaultii* 'Hancock'	Hancock coralberry	2–3'	4–7
Syringa persica	Persian lilac	5–6'	4–8
Viburnum lantana	Wayfaring-tree viburnum	10'	4–7
V. lentago	Nannyberry viburnum	15'	2–9
V. l. 'Mohican'	Mohican viburnum	6'	4–7

Evergreen Trees

BOTANICAL NAME	COMMON NAME	HEIGHT	ZONE
Picea pungens	Blue spruce, Colorado spruce	75–100'	3–7
Pinus nigra	Austrian pine	60'	4–8
P. ponderosa	Ponderosa pine	60–150'	4

Evergreen Shrubs

BOTANICAL NAME	COMMON NAME	HEIGHT	ZONE
Cotoneaster apiculatus	Cranberry cotoneaster	3'	5
C. horizontalis	Small-leaved cotoneaster, Rockspray cotoneaster	1–3'	5
Juniperus chinensis 'Pfitzerana,' 'Pfitzerana Glauca,' 'Pfitzerana Compacta'	Pfitzer, Blue pfitzer, and Compact pfitzer junipers	4–8'	4
J. depressa 'Effusa'	Effusa or common juniper	2'	4

Ponderosa pine (Pinus ponderosa).

BOTANICAL NAME	COMMON NAME	HEIGHT	ZONE
J. horizontalis 'Bar Harbor,' 'Blue Chip,' 'Hughes,' 'Prince of Wales,' 'Wiltonii,' 'Youngstown'	Bar Harbor, Blue chip, Hughes, Prince of Wales, Blue rug, and Andorra junipers	6–18"	4
Mahonia aquifolium	Oregon grapeholly	6'	5–9
M. a. 'Compacta'	Compact Oregon grapeholly	3'	5–9

Groundcovers

BOTANICAL NAME	COMMON NAME	HEIGHT	ZONE
*Aegopodium podagraria** 'Variegatum' (very aggressive)	Variegated bishop's goutweed	6–12"	4
*Ajuga reptans**	Bugleweed	8–10"	4
*Arctostaphylos uva-ursi**	Kinnickinnick, Bearberry	4–6"	2
Cerastium tomentosum	Snow-in-summer	6–8"	4

Groundcovers (continued)

BOTANICAL NAME	COMMON NAME	HEIGHT	ZONE
Duchesnea indica (spreads a lot!)	Mock strawberry	4"	5
Euonymus fortunei*	Wintercreeper	6–18"	5
Festuca ovina var. glauca	Blue fescue	4–10"	4–9
Fragaria chiloensis	Wild strawberry	6–10"	5
Galium odoratum*	Sweet woodruff	8–10"	4–8
Gazania linearis 'Colorado Gold'	Hardy gazania	8–12"	5
Iris pumila	Dwarf bearded iris	4–8"	4
Juniperus communis var. saxatilis	Mountain common creeper	1'	2–9
Lamium maculatum	Dead nettle	8–12"	4
Mahonia repens	Creeping mahonia	6–12"	4
Polygonatum commutatum	Great Solomon's seal	7"	3–8
Potentilla verna var. nana	Creeping potentilla	2–6"	3
Sedum spp.	Stonecrop	3–18"	Varies
Sepervivum arachnoideum	Hen-and-chicks, Cobweb houseleek	4"	3
Thymus pseudolanuginosus	Woolly thyme	1–2"	3
T. serpyllum citoides	Lemon thyme	2–4"	3
Veronica liwanensis	Turkish veronica	1–2"	3
Vinca minor*	Periwinkle, Myrtle	3–6"	5
Waldsteinia ternata*	Barren strawberry	4–6"	6

Perennials

BOTANICAL NAME	COMMON NAME	HEIGHT	ZONE
Alchemilla mollis	Lady's mantle	12–18"	3–8
Anemone sylvestris	Snowdrop anemone	6–18"	4
Aquilegia spp.	Columbine	18–24"	Varies
Bergenia cordifolia*	Pigsqueak	12–16"	2
Brunnera macrophylla*	Siberian forget-me-not	12–18"	3–8
Campanula spp.	Bellflower	6–12"	4
Centranthus ruber	Red valerian, Jupiter's beard	1–3'	4
Chrysanthemum maximum	Shasta daisy	1–2'	4
Coreopsis rosea	Pink coreopsis	18–24"	4
C. verticillata spp.	Threadleaf coreopsis	18–30"	4
Corydalis lutea	Yellow corydalis	1'	5
Crambe cordifolia	Giant kale	4–5'	6–9
Echinacea purpurea	Purple coneflower	2–3'	4
Gaura lindheimeri	Whirling butterflies	2–4'	4
Hemerocallis spp.	Daylily	2–3'	3
Heuchera sanguinea*	Coral bells	6–12"	4
Hosta spp.*	Plantain lily	1–2'	4
Iberis sempervirens	Evergreen candytuft	1'	4
Iris germanica	Bearded iris	5–30"	4
Liatris spicata	Blazing star	2–5'	3
Linum perenne	Blue flax	1–2'	4

Red coral bells (Heuchera sanguinea) *are versatile under a newly planted tree. It enjoys the sunshine when the tree is young and will be equally at home as the tree matures and shades the understory.*

The low-maintenance Vanhoutte spirea (Spiraea vanhoutte) does well in full sun and also in partial shade. For a beautiful shrub, leave it unshorn.

BOTANICAL NAME	COMMON NAME	HEIGHT	ZONE
Nepeta faassenii	Catmint	1–2'	3
Oenothera fruticosa youngii	Sundrops primrose	6–24"	4
O. missouriensis	Missouri evening primrose	12"	4
Penstemon spp.	Penstemon	Varies	Varies
Physostegia virginiana	Obedient plant, False dragonhead	2–3'	4
Tradescantia virginiana	Common spiderwort	18–26"	4

Annuals

BOTANICAL NAME	COMMON NAME	HEIGHT
Abronia umbellata	Sand verbena	6–24'
Centaurium erythraea	Centaury	20"
Cleome hasslerana	Spiderflower	3–5'
Collinsia grandiflora	Blue lips	8–15"
Consolida ambigua	Rocket larkspur	1–2'
Cosmos bipinnatus	Cosmos	1–3'
Digitalis purpurea spp. (biennial)	Foxglove	3–4'
Dyssodia tenuiloba	Dahlberg daisy	8–12"
Erysimum perofskianum	Afghan erysimum	16"
Eschscholzia californica	California poppy	8–12"
Gaillardia pulchella	Blanket flower, Indian blanket	1–2'
Helianthus annuus 'Italian White'	Italian White sunflower	10'
Lantana camara	Lantana	4–6'
Nemophila maculata	Five spot	1'
N. menziesii	Baby blue-eyes	1'
Nierembergia hippomanica	Cupflower	6–8"
Oenothera deltoides	Desert evening primrose	2–10"
Phacelia campanularia	California bluebell	18–30"
Salvia sclarea	Clary sage	3'
Tropaeolum majus 'Alaska'	Nasturtium	6–12"

Vines

BOTANICAL NAME	COMMON NAME	HEIGHT	ZONE
Campsis radicans	Trumpet creeper	30'	4
Clematis ligusticifolia	Western virgin's bower	20'	3
Lonicera heckrottii	Goldflame honeysuckle	10–20'	4
L. japonica 'Halliana'	Hall's honeysuckle	20–30'	4
Parthenocissus inserta	Woodbine	35'	3
*P. quinquefolia**	Virginia creeper	35'	3
P. q. 'Engelmannii'*	Engelmann ivy	20–35'	3
Tropaeolum majus	Indian cress	8–12'	Annual

Fern

BOTANICAL NAME	COMMON NAME	HEIGHT	ZONE
*Dennstaedtia punctilobula**	Hay-scented fern	1'	3–8

CHAPTER 10

IRRIGATION

*You don't need high tech to
achieve irrigation efficiency,
just a little common sense.*

ABOVE: *Bulbs take advantage of natural spring irrigation.*
OPPOSITE: *When footsteps show in the lawn, it means
your grass is starting to wilt.*

Irrigation is the 5o-cent word used to describe watering your landscape. For commercial landscapes such as golf courses or public parks, irrigation can be complex and almost sci-fi sophisticated. In some instances, weather stations broadcast wind velocity, temperature, humidity, precipitation, and the strength of solar radiation to a central irrigation control station. That station then broadcasts information to satellite controllers to open or close irrigation valves depending on the amount of evaporation from the soil and transpiration (water lost by leaves to the atmosphere).

Luckily, the average homeowner doesn't have to deal with anything nearly this complex. You don't need high tech to achieve irrigation efficiency, just a little common sense.

Efficiency just means getting the job done right without waste. You only need to do two things to achieve irrigation efficiency. *The first is to not water more than the plant needs. And the other is to not water anything but your plants.* There are a number of techniques and tools to help you with this—and that's what this chapter is all about.

WHAT YOUR PLANTS NEED

Rather than watering on a schedule, make sure your landscape really needs water. There are a couple of elementary ways to do this.

LOOKING FOR WILT

One of the best ways to tell if your lawn needs water is to check for wilt. Lawn wilt is recognized when you walk on it and you can see your footprints: The grass leaf blades don't spring back into an upright position when stepped on. The turf will also take on a blue cast that indicates the soil is dry.

The best time to do this is in the evening or early morning. During the middle of a hot day, some plants will wilt just from the heat, but will return to normal firmness as the evening cools. If there isn't enough moisture in the soil, then they will remain wilted.

PROBING

Another way to determine if your plants need water is to probe into the soil with a hand tool such as a trowel or screwdriver. If it comes out with mud clinging to the blade, there is no need to water. If the opposite happens or you can't penetrate the soil, it is time to water. You might consider purchasing a soil coring device that will pull a plug of soil about a foot or so long, making it easy to see how far water has penetrated. These inexpensive devices are available through most garden catalogs.

Probing is the key to making sure you are watering the soil to the necessary depth. It's always important to saturate the soil throughout the root zone. It is a natural tendency for

a dry clay soil to resist water penetration; therefore, it takes a lengthy period of water application to make that penetration.

Inexperienced gardeners commonly assume enough water has been applied once the surface has been soaked for a few minutes. If watering like this continues, only the upper inch or so of soil gets wet, the complete root zone will be denied water, and the plant will succumb. The other consequence is that only the upper roots will survive, resulting in a shallow-rooted plant that requires repeated and frequent water applications. It is best, for the health of the plant, to water thoroughly and infrequently, rather than lightly and frequently.

The only way to make sure water has penetrated the whole root zone is to employ the probing technique using a trowel, screwdriver, or coring tool. Not only is it important for newly planted annuals, perennials, shrubs, and trees, it holds true for the entire life of the plant.

The root zone for most plants is typically 6–12 inches deep. Even mature tree roots seldom stray much below 12 inches, although they can spread horizontally two to three times the height of the tree.

in the future. You will be watering for the needs of the plant, and if you have measured carefully, water will not have extended beyond the root zone. Water seeping below the root zone means wasted water.

WATERING JUST THE PLANTS

Now that you know how to give your plants the water that they need, the next step is to ensure you're not watering anything besides the plants. I'm talking about drenching sidewalks and the air and cars and all the other ways we waste water while irrigating.

CONTROLLING RUNOFF

The control of runoff water makes a big difference in the amount of water saved. One of the ways to control runoff is to take steps that will allow water to penetrate the soil where the plants are. Plants in the low to moderate water zones appreciate good drainage away from the roots once the soil has been saturated. This means these plants do best planted on a slope. A slope means there will be some surface runoff, which can be controlled in a planting bed by making a soil basin around each plant.

CYCLING

Runoff is a common problem with lawns that slope away from the house toward the sidewalk. To help prevent runoff, particularly on clay soils where it is difficult for water to penetrate, irrigate in two or more cycles. For example, if you have determined that the sprinklers need to run for a total of 15 minutes, divide the time into two parts. Water for seven minutes during one cycle. Wait awhile, say a half hour, then start over and water for another seven or eight minutes. There will be less runoff and more water will soak into the soil.

OLLAS

Surface runoff also can be controlled by placing plastic pop bottles or pottery urns around your garden. According to Curtis Smith of New Mexico State University Cooperative Extension, it was a common practice in the early days of the southwestern United States for gardeners to bury unglazed pottery urns, called *ollas* (pronounced oh-yahs), in the garden. They were filled with water, which slowly seeped through the pottery walls into the soil, keeping a ready supply of water for the surrounding plants. Each olla was capped to keep evaporation to a minimum. If

Choosing plants that need little irrigation minimizes runoff. On this slope, basket-of-gold (Aurinia saxatilis) *serves that purpose.*

When first watering a new lawn or planting bed, water for a set period of time. At the end of that time, use your probe to check water infiltration. If it has not reached the required depth, add a little more watering time and check in another location. After doing this exercise three or four times, you will eventually see that the water has reached the full extent of the root zone. The accumulated time it took to saturate the root is the amount of time to run the irrigation cycle the top portion of the olla is glazed, that portion can be left above ground to add structural interest. Ollas are a perfect solution to the problem of surface water runoff.

The modern version of an olla is the use of quart-sized plastic bottles with the bottoms cut off. Drill a 1/32-inch hole in the cap, invert the bottle and bury the neck of the bottle in the soil up the shoulder. Fill the bottle from the severed end and allow the water to seep into the soil through the perforated cap. Several such bottles can be placed throughout the garden to facilitate watering. The bottles are as effective as the ollas, but the ollas look a lot better.

Soaker hoses make a great temporary irrigation system for watering trees during a drought.

SOAKER HOSES

Soaker hoses are another way of enhancing water infiltration and minimizing surface runoff. Soaker hoses look very much like a regular garden hose. They come in 50-foot lengths and are typically black in color. The difference is that they weep water from the hose walls. They can be laid in a serpentine pattern through a garden bed or in concentric circles around a tree or shrub. The water seeps out of the walls and slowly allows moisture to penetrate the soil. The water is not as subject to evaporation by the wind or the sun.

Soaker hoses won't carry water uphill, so they work best on level ground. When there is a slight slope, the connection to the water source needs to be uphill. Ideally, place the hose back and forth across the slope with the inlet side at the top of the slope.

With many different irrigation devices such as the soaker hose on the market these days, it becomes a little confusing for first-time gardeners to choose the right implement for the job. I know a fastidious young woman who bought her first home with a yard. She was quite excited about the prospect of caring for her landscape and keeping up its appearance. So one of her first purchases was to buy a garden hose. She chose one to match the black trim on her white house because she knew it would be visible from the street and would look nice coiled up out front. Her first task with the hose was to hand water a dry spot in her front lawn. She connected a spray head to the hose, turned on the water, and stood waiting for the water to come through. After a reasonable amount of time, no water appeared. She turned around to discover that all the water was weeping through the sides of the hose. She had just purchased her first water-conservation tool.

TIMERS

A hose end timer is a great asset for those of us who get carried away doing something else while watering the lawn. You can set a stove or tabletop timer, but you might not always be in earshot when it goes off. You also might forget to set such a timer. The hose end timer, on the other hand, will turn off the water at the prescribed

A hose timer is an excellent tool to prevent overwatering, in case you forget to turn off your manual sprinkler.

time and you won't be able to turn on the water without setting the timer. The simplest devices are spring-loaded and may be set for durations of five minutes to a couple of hours. They cost very little. More complicated timers can be set to turn on any day during the week, at any time, for two or three cycles, and for periods of time from one minute to several hours. Either type of hose end timer will ultimately save water.

SPRINKLERS

At the other end of the hose, there are sprinklers that can be more water-efficient than others. It doesn't matter the brand or whether they are plastic or metal. It is the kind of spray that makes the difference in water conservation. A sprinkler that sprays out relatively large droplets and sprays close to the ground is best for water-conservation purposes. It is easier to control where the water is being distributed than it is with a sprinkler that sprays high in the air or sprays fine droplets. The larger droplets close to the ground are not as likely to be carried away by the wind and will not evaporate quickly.

Hand-watering efficiently directs water to just the plants that need it.

Drip irrigation is ideal for infrequently watered plants such as prairie wine cups (Callirhoe involucrata).

BY HAND

Watering by hand can be one of the most water-conserving activities you can do in the garden. It is particularly valuable when trying to get new plants or seeds started among other established plants. It is useful for shrubs and perennials that are out of any watering zone and need an extra drink during long dry spells. It comes in handy, too, when higher-water-demanding plants are mixed in with lower-water-demanding plants, although it would be better to have them separated. Of course, potted annuals will need daily watering by hand if they have not been set up on a drip irrigation system. With a spray wand attached to your garden hose or a watering can, you can direct water right where you need it, and avoid overwatering other plants. The converse to all of this is that it is the least efficient as far as your time goes.

AUTOMATIC IRRIGATION

Automatic irrigation systems have evolved to help landscape owners to be more efficient with their time. However, they haven't necessarily been designed to water efficiently. To start with, the clock or controller that automatically opens the valves for the sprinkler system can be a detriment to conservation. A common practice is to turn on the controller early in the spring and let it run on a schedule, be it daily, every other day, every third day, and so on. This is convenience at it zenith.

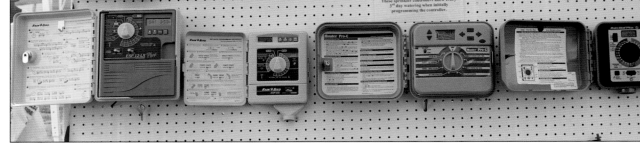

These sprinkler controllers allow every 3rd day watering when initially programming the controller.

ABOVE: *A wide selection of controllers is available to make automatic irrigation easy, but don't get over-whelmed: You only need one!*
RIGHT: *There's no need to irrigate landscapes such as Sandra and Mike West's in the spring, which naturally brings adequate moisture.*

However, watering on a schedule of any kind can mean watering 30 to 50 percent more than is necessary. There are several factors that can turn a schedule into a water waste mode. Sprinklers running during a rainstorm or right after certainly don't make any sense, and they can be spraying water far and wide during a windstorm. Also, if it has been cloudy and windless since the last irrigation cycle, the soil may not have dried out enough to warrant another application of water.

CONTROLLERS

Early irrigation controllers didn't have the flexibility of modern controllers. You could set the irrigation cycle to run any day during a seven-day time period and each zone could be set for a specific length of time. That was about it. They didn't lend themselves to conserving water. Today, however, controllers can be a big help toward saving water, if the owner bothers to do some tweaking from time to time.

A modern controller can be very reasonably priced, making it affordable to change out that old controller. Even at a low price, controllers now have many features that can make them water-conservation devices instead of just conveniences to keep the lawn soaked. Here are a few features to look for when making your purchase:

- Two or more separate programs so you can irrigate your high-water Kentucky bluegrass on one schedule while watering your moderate- and low-water zones on another schedule or two.

- Multiple start times per program allow the irrigation cycle to start over again once the first or even the second cycle has been completed. It is a mechanism for cycling your irrigation system, as mentioned earlier in the chapter. On heavy clay soils, it is best to break up an irrigation time into segments to facilitate water penetration and minimize runoff.

- A rain sensor with a sprinkler bypass switch on it is a good way to conserve water after it has just rained. A rain sensor is fastened to the eave of your house and is connected to the controller by two wires. When the rain sensor becomes saturated with precipitation, it allows the controller to bypass the next watering cycle although the clock keeps running. When the rain sensor dries out, the bypass is closed and the watering cycle will be turned on the next scheduled day. Rain sensors are very reasonably priced and easy to install.

- Interval watering days and individual watering days give your controller plenty of flexibility to irrigate when your landscape needs it and not just according to a set schedule. The controller can be set to water every other day, every third day or twice a week, once a month, and so on. It is a feature that is valuable during a drought when your water utility sets the schedule for you. However, programming on individual days that you choose is ideal for water conservation. For example, a good practice for watering your lawn is to "train" the roots to stretch as deeply as possible for water. One way is to extend the interval between irrigations by one day. If the soil has been well amended, the interval can eventually be as long as 10 days and still the lawn will remain green.

- A water budget from 20 to 200 percent is based on how much irrigation your landscape typically needs at any time during the irrigation season. Let's say you have discovered, by probing the soil during the spring, that you need to run your sprinklers for 15 minutes per application. That is your base water budget for the season, or 100 percent. However, as the season progresses, you'll find that 15 minutes isn't long enough to keep the lawn as green as you would like. It is hot, windy, and there has been no natural precipitation for a while. So increase your water budget up to, for example, 125 percent. Your sprinkler will then automatically run for 19 minutes. As the season progresses into the fall when the temperatures are cool and there is extra moisture, you may want to set your water budget for less than 100 percent. Adjusting your controller each month to fit the weather conditions has proven to be an effective way to save water. Often controllers are set to apply enough water to keep the grass green during the hottest month of July. All the other months need much less water. Each month leading up to July and away from July needs appreciably less water. So changing the water budget is essential for water savings.

- A backup battery keeps your clock on schedule during electrical blackouts. The sprinklers won't turn on, but the clock will maintain the schedule you have set and will be ready to go when the electricity comes back. This is particularly valuable during a drought when tickets can be imposed by the water utility for watering on the wrong day. Remember to replace the battery once a year.

- Precise station timing in one-minute intervals gives you the ability to apply just the amount of water that is required. Again, this feature can also keep you out of trouble when your water department is carefully timing the length of your watering cycle during a drought.

Automatic Irrigation System Terms

Spray head: A head refers to a sprinkler that usually pops up from the lawn or flowerbed and sprays water over it.

Spray nozzle: Some brands of spray heads have plastic inserts with openings of a certain size referred to as the nozzle. Selection of the nozzle size depends on the amount of pressure available to the spray head. The nozzle must be matched to the pressure to ensure a proper spray pattern.

Impulse head.

Valve manifold: A series of valves in a usually green plastic box at the edge of the lawn. Each valve receives its signal from the controller via underground wires to open or close. Each valve controls the amount of water each zone will receive.

Zone: Refers to a break-up of the landscape into sectors that are irrigated separately. The difference depends on the mini-environments (or microclimates!) in the landscape and the types of plants planted there.

Take your pick of soil moisture sensors.

CONTROLLER ACCESSORIES

Certain accessories for your controller can make it even more water-efficient. There are rain sensors, which have been mentioned previously, soil moisture sensors, and humidistats. The soil moisture sensor and humidistat are attached to the controller in as straightforward a manner as the rain sensor. The difference is in their placement and what they are sensing.

The soil moisture sensor does what its name implies. It is placed in the soil in a location that perhaps has a half-day of sun exposure and the other half in the shade. Therefore, it will be sensing the moisture in the soil that isn't in either extreme of all-day sun or shade. When the soil is moist where the sensor is placed, the controller will not turn on the irrigation cycle. When the soil is dry, the controller will activate the sprinklers to turn on during the set schedule.

ABOVE: *A humidistat monitors atmospheric conditions to control irrigation.*
RIGHT: *Either the fence or the rotary head wasn't very well placed in this landscape.*

The humidistat is placed on the west or east side of the house where there is not all-day shade or sun. It senses the amount of humidity in the air. If it has recently rained or it is cloudy and moisture is hanging in the atmosphere, the humidistat will do the same thing as the rain sensor and soil moisture sensor. The controller will not turn on the irrigation valves.

The sensors are the most valuable when there are regular rain showers. They are not of much value during a drought, when there is no natural precipitation or moisture to sense.

Early morning irrigation minimizes the loss of water to wind and evaporation.

AUDITING THE SYSTEM

One of the many duties of a professional landscape manager is to make an audit of the irrigation system. On a more simple scale, a homeowner can do the same thing. It is just a matter of turning on each zone and checking to see if it is operating as efficiently as it can. Here is what to look for:

- Blocked spray heads could involve many situations, but the most common is vegetation that has grown up in front of the sprinkler head or some alteration to the landscape after the sprinkler system was installed. The remedy is to move the obstruction, raise the head so it sprays over the obstruction, or add another head to make complete coverage.

- Mixed heads means there are pop-up sprinkler heads and rotary or impulse sprinkler heads in an irrigation zone. Pop-ups apply water three times as quickly as the rotary or impulse heads. If a zone is operated to get adequate soil saturation from the rotary/impulse heads, the pop-ups are then running three times longer than need be. If the zone is programmed for the amount of water the pop-ups can apply, then the rotary/impulse heads are not watering enough. The obvious remedy is to either make the zone all pop-ups or all rotary/impulse heads.

- Damaged, missing, tilted, plugged, or sunken heads are easily identified as one turns on each zone by hand and inspects each head as it operates. The remedy is to make the repairs as soon as the audit is complete. It is a good idea to keep spare heads, fittings, hoses, and clamps on hand to make repairs quickly and resourcefully.

- Low pressure or high pressure can be a source of incomplete coverage. Pressure problems normally are not with the supply from the main in the street. Well-run water utilities work very hard to be sure there is adequate pressure to your connection in the street, although checking with your water provider may be a starting point. If the pressure is good at the street, but not good anywhere on your property, then it is a problem from the street connection to the house. If pressure is OK in the house, but not in the irrigation system, then take a closer look at the irrigation system.

Low pressure means that the spray from each head will not be adequate to overlap the spray from the surrounding heads, leaving dry areas in the lawn or flowerbeds. Ideally, the spray from one head should hit the neighboring heads. There are a couple of design reasons why the spray might not go that far. If the buried hose to remote areas of the system is not the right size to carry the volume of water to properly operate the heads, water pressure will be reduced. Also, if there are too many heads on a zone, water pressure will be lacking. The remedy is to replace the hose with the right size and to reduce the number of heads in the problematic zone. Such a remedy is doable if a person does some research on irrigation design, is mechanically inclined, and doesn't have anything else to do in life. On the other hand, it might be worthwhile to hire a professional irrigation specialist.

High pressure for overhead spray heads is a problem when it comes to control of the spray pattern. Too much pressure causes very small droplets to be discharged from the spray nozzles. They get carried by the wind to places not intended to be watered, and evaporate quickly, reducing efficiency. Each sprinkler head is designed to work within a certain pressure range, which is usually specified on the package or accompanying literature. If the head is operated within the proper pressure range, the droplets will be large and less influenced by the wind and heat from the sun.

Drip and microspray irrigation systems are designed to operate on very low pressures. High pressures cause too much water to be emitted, defeating their advantages of applying water over a long period of time. Long, slow applications allow for thorough soil penetration and minimal runoff. The remedy is to reduce the pressure by adding a pressure-reducing valve to the line leading to the valve manifold, or you can use pressure-compensating emitters.

• Zone overlap means that an irrigation zone does not match the vegetative zone or exposure zone. Sometimes an irrigation system is designed with heads on one zone in both the shady north side of the house and on a west-facing slope. If the west slope is watered adequately the north side exposure will be overwatered. The same thing can happen when an irrigation system is designed to water both the lawn and the rock garden on the same zone. The remedy in each situation is to break up the overlap into two separate zones, one for the north side and one for the west-facing slope. The lawn should always be a separate zone from the xeric planting beds.

• The middle of the day is the wrong time of day to water. Overhead spraying in the middle of the day means there is more chance of evaporation. Evaporation occurs as the droplets from the sprinkler fly through the air. It also occurs after the droplets hit the ground and immediately start to evaporate from the soil and leaf surfaces. Each incidence of midday watering doesn't probably amount to a lot of water loss, but carried out over a season of watering, it can add up. The remedy is to water early in the morning up to about 9 a.m. There is much less evaporation at that time, plus the wind usually is not blowing, which contributes to evaporation. Watering at night is also a preferred time. In the western United States the air is dry, so watering at night does not cause fungi and diseases to develop.

• Having the run time too long or too short can be a problem. If the run time is too long, it causes runoff or percolation of water below the root zone. If the run time is too short, it causes the root system to be too shallow or inadequately watered, which can lead to the death of the plant. The remedy for an inappropriate run time is to perform the soil probe test with a screwdriver or trowel, as covered earlier in this chapter.

No matter how we irrigate, be it by dragging a hose or the use of an automatic system, we don't have to water as much as we think we do. One man I knew had a flow meter on his hose. Before the drought of 2002, he was irrigating his extensive lawn with 3,600 gallons of water per application. During the drought, his irrigation time was restricted, and he discovered, much to his delight, that the lawn only needed 2,300 gallons and looked just as good as it did before the drought. My advice to him was and is to continue cutting back to see if it will still look good with even less water. It probably will.

CHAPTER 11

MULCHING

Mulching, the sixth Xeriscape principle, is a very good thing—if done properly and in moderation.

ABOVE: *Mulching can be a design feature as well as a water-saving method.*
OPPOSITE: *Virtually all plants except those adapted to severe desert conditions can benefit from mulching.*

When I was teenager in windy Wyoming, I had a little garden. I planted vegetable and flower seeds, and then I waited impatiently for them to sprout and grow large enough so I could start spreading on the only mulch I knew about then: a steadily increasing layer of grass clippings.

It took almost no time at all for me to tire of carefully watering the seeds every day to keep them moist while not disturbing the soil. When I finally got to mulch it was such a relief! After the clippings started piling up, I could set the running hose down on top of them somewhere and happily watch the water snake around under the clippings without disturbing the soil. Plus, I got to do the whole procedure way less often than before, and that made me happy, too.

Imagine my excitement to learn many years later that scientific research confirms what I had learned in my tender gardening years. That is, mulching, the sixth Xeriscape principle, is a very good thing—if done properly and in moderation. In fact, with a few cautions, there's almost nothing bad to say about mulching.

MULCH BENEFITS

Interestingly enough, the best mulch for water conservation might not be the one that looks the best, is the most expensive, or reduces heat alone. Mulch should do the following:

- Limit reflectivity. Bare sand or clay soil develops a very light, reflective surface during the hot summer months that bounces the heat and light of the sun back onto plants, adjacent surfaces, and buildings. Mulch provides a darker and more fragmented surface that cuts down on the reflectivity and keeps the area around plant stems and leaves cooler, so less water is evaporated from the soil and plants.

- Curtail heat. The soil surface stays cooler under mulch than when bare, so less water is evaporated. Mulch also helps retain moisture around the root zone by protecting roots from extremes of heat and cold. Winter protection is a big part of the function of mulch. It regulates the temperature of the soil around the roots, preventing freeze damage, frost heave that could damage new root systems, and too-early emergence of spring bulbs.

- Hold and build soil. By insulating against freezing and thawing, mulch prevents cracks from forming in the soil surface. By retaining moisture in the root zone, it encourages root growth that stabilizes the soil. Organic mulch eventually breaks down and improves the quality and water-holding capacity of the soil near the surface, though this is a slow process, depending on the size of the mulch particles.

CHAPTER 11: **MULCHING**

- Prevent weeds. By blocking out sunlight, mulch helps prevent some (but by no means all!) weed seeds from germinating and competing with landscape plants for available soil moisture. In gardens, it's safer to mulch to control weeds than to cultivate (break off or dig them out with a hoe) because the roots of the garden plants are left undisturbed.

- Keep water in the root zone. Because mulch reduces evaporation and transpiration, water is retained in the upper layers of the soil where most annuals, perennials, and groundcovers draw their moisture.

- Control erosion. Mulch softens the impact of falling rainwater and slows it down so it can soak into the soil before running off. It also prevents soil from being disturbed or washed away from around plants.

- Reduce maintenance. Periodic weeding and occasional replacement are all that are needed for the maintenance of mulch areas.

- Serve as a design feature. Mulches fulfill many functions in a Xeriscape. In addition to all their water-conserving qualities, they separate water-use zones when used under shrub and tree plantings. As discussed in the Appropriate Plant Selection chapters, there are many reasons to separate tree and shrub plantings from turf, and mulch provides a non-water-using soil covering for those areas. Mulch can be used as attractive groundcoverings for utility areas or other places where turf would be non-functional, or difficult to irrigate.

ABOVE: *Rock mulch serves the same purposes as organic mulch: cooling the soil and reducing evaporation.*
OPPOSITE: *Two colors of rock mulch join wood mulch to form an integral part of this formal Xeriscape design at Denver's Centennial Garden.*

Reducing Soil Temperature

In the spring of 1988, an experiment at the University of California, Irvine, compared moisture savings and soil temperature reduction under several mulching materials: peat moss, costing 30 cents/square foot for each 2-inch layer; commercial compost, at 18 cents/square foot for each 2-inch layer; and shredded fir bark, costing 6 cents/square foot for each 2-inch layer.

The materials were compared at depths of 1, 2, and 4 inches. Those that did best in preventing moisture loss proved to be the fir bark at 2 and 4 inches. The soil beneath all three mulch types proved to be 10 degrees cooler 1 inch below the soil surface than the unmulched controls.

In another experiment, a 3-inch layer of mulch reduced soil temperature as much as 10 degrees as far down as 8 inches below the surface. Unmulched soil reached temperatures as high as 100–108 degrees Fahrenheit in the top few inches, high enough to kill roots.

Reducing soil temperature is one way mulching conserves moisture. It also reduces exposure to wind, which can pull moisture up and out of the soil through evaporation. One study showed that a 2-inch layer of leaf litter reduced evaporation 45 to 65 percent, depending on the type of leaf. (Pine needles did the best.)

Of course, entire landscapes covered with mulch are unattractive and boring, but when combined with water-conserving vegetation and a well-designed hardscape, mulch can be both effective and attractive, adding diversity and texture.

You can also use mulch to accent turf. Many organic materials such as shredded bark, compost, and leaf mold are dark brown and provide a background color for flowers and other plants. In general, organic mulches lend a naturalistic, informal note, while inorganic mulches such as gravel are often used for more formal designs. Make sure to match the texture of the mulch with the size of the plants, e.g., coarse mulch with shrubs, finer-textured mulch in perennial beds.

ABOVE: *Mulch created from recycled tree trimmings doubles as a pathway through this garden.*
BELOW: *Use a fuzzy weed-barrier fabric under mulch on a slope to help keep it in place.*

If you like a clean, consistent look in your landscape, mulches are your baby. Just remember what I said about how landscapes look more professional when the number of different materials is limited. Match the mulch to the purpose and plant size, but don't get too carried away with different sizes, colors, textures, and types. More than one color of rock mulch is especially disturbing.

- Provide waterless groundcover. Whether turf or groundcover, all plants covering the soil are growing and using water out of the soil, while mulches don't. Mulch lets most, though not all, water percolate through slowly, making it available for nearby plants.

Are mulches starting to sound just too good to be true? Well, OK, there are a few potential problems.

MULCH CHALLENGES

POSING A FIRE HAZARD

Especially with dried pine needles, straw, and evergreen boughs, mulch can pose a fire hazard. Locate mulch beds with flammable mulches away from wooden walls and fences.

CREATING A NITROGEN DEFICIENCY

Extremely fresh (not aged) organic mulching materials such as sawdust, grass clippings, straw, nut and grain hulls, manure, and chipper waste may draw nitrogen out of the soil as the material breaks down, causing a temporary deficiency in the soil. (Yellowing of the lowest plant leaves is a sign of this.)

This problem can be prevented by adding nitrogen to the mulch. According to the Colorado State University Cooperative Extension Service publication on mulches, for each 100 square feet of mulched area, add 2 pounds of a complete fertilizer, such as 10-6-4, or ¼ pound of ammonium sulfate. Never use a "weed-and-feed" type of fertilizer in mulched areas or you will kill or maim whatever you have planted there.

Bacteria do break down organic matter and utilize soil nitrogen in the process, but bacteria do not travel far—we're talking millimeters, here—and thus, cannot "steal" soil nitrogen from very deep in the soil. If nitrogen deficiency is happening, especially when a weed barrier is used, then something else is wrong—possibly the oxygen/carbon dioxide concentrate in the root zone beneath the mulch is off kilter, and the mulch is too deep.

ADDING SALT

Partially composted mulches such as mushroom compost and manure can have a high level of salts that may damage plants. Apply them in the fall so winter rains and snowmelt can dilute the salt concentration. Naturally, if your soil test indicates a high-salt soil, you should skip using these mulches altogether.

CREATING RODENT AND PEST PROBLEMS

Some organic mulches encourage insect pests such as slugs, snails, sowbugs, and earwigs by creating a dark, moist environment. Rodents may tunnel under a thick layer of mulch, especially straw, leaves, and corncobs. When these mulches are used, they should not be placed closer than 6 inches from the base of woody plants. When mulch is placed too close, some rodents living in the mulch will chew the bark of the plant, girdling and killing it. (This happens in non-mulched areas, too, so don't be too hard on yourself if it does!)

BEING INCORRECTLY APPLIED

Too thick a layer of mulch may reduce the penetration of oxygen and water into the soil, which can kill shallow-rooted plants. All mulch reduces oxygen and increases carbon dioxide concentrations to some extent.

Also, for desert-adapted plants any mulch may be too much! These tough guys are adapted to life without mulch. For one thing, any leaf litter from their tiny leaves usually just blows away. They're used to fast-draining (sandy) soil, which allows their big root systems to take advantage of every drop of moisture that gets within range. It works both ways, though. They can't cope with too little evaporation, so if you're trying to grow them in a slow-draining clay soil, a thick mulch may cause roots to rot. Colorado horticultural expert and garden writer Lauren Springer advises no organic mulch on desert plants, as it may enrich the soil too much.

Too little mulch can also be a problem. If weed control is a primary consideration, realize that sunlight has been shown to penetrate as much as 4 inches into bark or similar-density mulching materials. To prevent sunlight from encouraging weeds to grow, use the upper limit recommended for mulch depth given in the charts that appear later in this chapter, or use a slightly thinner layer over a weed-barrier fabric.

BLOWING AWAY

Large chunky bark mulch and tiny-textured wood mulch are the most susceptible to blowing away in the wind. Mulches with strips of bark or different-sized particles tend to knit together better to withstand wind. Cedar mulch is said to be the best for this. Chipper debris from tree-trimming, often available free from city forestry departments, features a useful variety of particle sizes, which works well against the wind. Here's a case where cheapest may be best, and it's much less painful to the pocketbook if it does blow away!

A combination of fuzzy weed-barrier fabric, designed to keep mulch on slopes, and rock mulch makes a good armor for very windy areas. (In Wyoming, all bets are off—even rock mulch has been known to take off!)

HOW TO MULCH

The recommended depth for most organic mulches is 2–4 inches. Mulching too thin can lead to weed problems, but don't overmulch either, or you may be depriving your plant of water. A rule of thumb is to apply a 1- to 2-inch layer for a mulch with mostly ½-inch particles, and thicker layers for larger particles. Apply rock mulches in a thinner layer, 1–2 inches or the thickness of the rock if large. Rock mulches are usually combined with weed-barrier fabric to ward off the weeds for a few years anyway. Keep it thin, especially with fabric/mulch combos over dry-adapted plants—or you might just end up with plant skeletons.

A cubic yard of mulch (27 cubic feet) covers:

- 80 square feet when 4 inches deep
- 100 square feet when 3 inches deep
- 160 square feet when 2 inches deep
- 325 square feet when 1 inch deep

It takes 3 cubic yards to cover 1,000 square feet 1 inch thick, and 2 cubic feet to cover 8 square feet 3 inches deep. Organic mulches will all break down eventually, in a year or less, or over several years depending on the mulch and the climate, so they need to be periodically replenished.

When to Mulch

When you apply your mulch depends on what purpose it is serving:

USE	TIME TO MULCH
For water conservation	In late spring, after soil has absorbed spring moisture, and before summer heat dries it out
Enhance landscape appearance	Anytime
When landscape construction is completed	Posthaste—don't wait for the planets to line up right
Control weeds	Anytime
Protect fall transplants and keep soil above freezing longer so roots can develop	After transplanting
Reduce plant heaving due to freezing and thawing late or prevent early emergence of spring bulbs	After ground is frozen—late fall or early winter, usually after second or third freeze of the fall

A fine-textured mulch does its job quietly in this landscape, not competing with the striking hardscape.

In the process of breaking down, organic mulching materials enrich the soil. If a primary aim is to improve the soil, choose an organic mulch. Earthworms will assist by incorporating some of the mulching material into the top layer of the soil.

ORGANIC MULCHES

The most appropriate mulch for each plant is its own leaf and twig litter; pine trees do best with pine needle mulch, and deciduous trees and shrubs utilize nutrients from their own leaves. You can take a cue from nature by not raking up the dead leaves from all the shrubs and trees but letting them become mulch themselves.

This is especially beneficial during winter when leaf layers provide some insulation for the roots. If you can't bear not to be spic-and-span, at least wait until spring to do the cleaning, then compost the leaves. This rule doesn't apply to lawn areas— leaf layers left on turfgrass equals dead grass.

Organic Mulch Recommendations

(pages 201–204)

MATERIAL	RECOMMENDED DEPTH
Shredded bark, cedar mulch, aspen mulch	3–4"

Advantages: The best choice for windy sites. Binds the soil, lets water in, and holds it in the soil well. Pieces tend to knit together, making the mulch sturdier and less prone to wash away than chunk bark or wood chips. Slow to break down because of the lignin (plant carbohydrate that decomposes slowly) in it. Comes in many textures and colors, including some colors sprayed on with dyes.

Disadvantages: Expensive. May compact over time. Can be unsightly and ineffective if applied in too thin a layer, and slime mold can develop on aspen mulch (ick). Dispel it with a water/bleach solution.

MATERIAL	RECOMMENDED DEPTH
Pole peelings	3–4"

These are thin strips of wood manufactured from the trunks of pine and spruce trees rather than the bark.

Advantages: About half the price of other commercial wood mulches, since they utilize the whole tree. Available in most locations.

Disadvantages: Turns from the nice woody tan/brown color to gray very quickly, within 6 months.

MATERIAL	RECOMMENDED DEPTH
Wood chips	3–4"

Advantages: Lets water in effectively. Keeps moisture in the mulch layer, but allows a little to evaporate. Cools the soil. Reduces weeds. Improves the water-holding capacity of the soil after breakdown. Many sizes are available but the largest and smallest should be avoided in unprotected or windy locations.

Disadvantages: Breaks down and disintegrates in a year or two, depending on wood species. Small sizes break down quickly and will require more frequent addition of nitrogen to replenish what they initially take from the soil as they decay.

MATERIAL	RECOMMENDED DEPTH
Chunk bark	4–6"

Advantages: Coarse texture. Large size lets more water in but doesn't hold it in as well as finer-textured materials. Can be long-lasting. Recent research has shown it to have superior weed control capability compared to shredded bark. (Bird netting can be put over it to keep it in place, but use this as a last resort, as birds and small game critters can get trapped in it.)

Disadvantages: May blow around in windy areas or wash away on slopes. Fairly expensive. Not always available, except regionally. Breaks down slowly, so doesn't add to soil structure and nutrients. The bigger the chunks, the faster they blow or float away.

MATERIAL	RECOMMENDED DEPTH
Chipper debris	3–4"

This mixture of shredded bark, wood chips, and leaves is available from tree-trimming operations, often free for asking and hauling from city or private tree crews. (Look in the White or Blue Pages for your municipal arborist or parks department, or in the Yellow Pages for private companies.) Some cities are recycling Christmas trees in this way.

Advantages: Inexpensive. Lets water in effectively. Adds humus as the debris breaks down and is incorporated.

Disadvantages: Mixture of materials may lead to uneven appearance. May create nitrogen deficiency in soil, if incorporated as it breaks down. In spring add half of the nitrogen fertilizer dose recommended on p. 197.

I use chipper debris and find it gives a very rustic appearance, which is usually OK for the effect I want at the edges of the landscape. However, very small or delicate plants are hard to spot against the mottled surface. Mulch around small plants with higher-quality, more even-looking material, or start with a layer of the cheap stuff, then top dress with the good-looking pricey mulch material.

MATERIAL	RECOMMENDED DEPTH
Sawdust, wood shavings, recycled shingles	1–3"

Advantages: Available and comparatively inexpensive in many areas. Decomposes quickly, adding humus to the soil. Free of most weed seeds and diseases.

Disadvantages: Increases soil acidity. This may be favorable for some plants, but toxic to others. Appearance not uniform. Breaks down rapidly, except for shingles. Blows in the wind when dry. Nitrogen must be added to the soil or to the sawdust (see p. 197) to avoid nitrogen depletion. Smolders in a fire and is hard to extinguish.

LEFT AND OPPOSITE PAGE: *Mulching is one of the more satisfying tasks in landscaping. It's quick, easy, and puts the finishing touch on the scene.*

Organic Mulch Recommendations (continued)

MATERIAL	RECOMMENDED DEPTH
Pine needles	2–3"

Advantages: Easily applied and gives favorable appearance. Available and cheap in many areas. Loose, light, but helps bind soil. Lets in a lot of water compared to wood mulches, and holds little itself. Increases soil acidity when it decomposes, which helps acid-loving plants such as pines, kinnickinnick, and blueberries. Best for winter protection of fall transplants.

Disadvantages: Not always available in quantities. Can be a fire hazard. Lasts a short time. Not kid-friendly (too prickly—which can be to your advantage if you're trying to discourage foot traffic!).

Evergreen boughs	2–4"

Advantages: Available and comparatively inexpensive in many areas. Easy to handle; quickly applied and easily removed.

Disadvantages: Fire hazard when dry. Should not be applied adjacent to buildings. Makes great homes for mice and other small rodents.

Lawn clippings	1" at a time

Advantages: Experts say it's better to leave the clippings on the lawn unless they've become matted. Dry out the clippings in thin layers on plastic or pavement for a day to prevent the anaerobic decomposition of fresh grass, which can lead to slime, smell, and flies. Readily available. Lets some water in, holds little, and inhibits evaporation. Best used in small areas. One caution: Don't put weed- and-feed treated grass clippings on your vegetable garden or wildflower plantings. The "weed" part of "weed and seed" is weed poison, and you don't want traces of it in your foodstuffs. Similarly, such clippings can also kill or damage wildflowers.

Disadvantages: May contain weed and grass seeds that will contaminate planting beds with undesirables. Heats up and creates offensive odor if not dried first. Correct for nitrogen deficiency as directed on p. 197.

Sphagnum peat moss	1–3"

Advantages: Improves physical conditions of most soils when incorporated. Source of fertility that is slowly available to plants. Greatly increases the water-holding capacity of the soil. Holds water in the soil very effectively, and holds a great deal of water itself. Easy to handle and adds to the appearance of the soil. Often increases the soil acidity, which is generally advantageous.

Disadvantages: Not always available and often rather expensive. Impervious to water when dry. May blow in windy sites. May not let water in when it is wet. Cannot easily be used on slopes because it erodes; best used in small confined areas. Breaks down rapidly.

NOTE: Sphagnum peat is found in boggy areas of Canada and the northern U.S., and regenerates quickly with the moisture it gets, in sharp contrast with...

MATERIAL	RECOMMENDED DEPTH
Bog or sedge peats	

Don't use this, ever. This category includes mountain peat in Colorado, which is mined from 10,000-year-old meadows, never to be replaced in our lifetimes, or anyone else's either. Use sphagnum peat instead.

Straw from wheat, oats, barley, or rye	4–6"

(not hay—it has too many weed seeds)

Advantages: Generally available and comparatively inexpensive. Decomposes slowly, adding humus to the soil. Easily lets water in, cools the soil, and holds some water in the soil, though not as well as some other mulches. Good for temporary cover, gardens, and grass seeding.

Disadvantages: Often rather unsightly. May blow and scatter. Will mat down and can get moldy. Harbors insects, diseases, weed seeds, and rodents. Some danger from fire when dry, so should not be applied next to buildings. Needs addition of nitrogen (see p. 197). Anchor with wire mesh.

Leaves/leaf mold	2–4"

Advantages: Lets some water in and keeps it in. Holds the soil. Readily available at little or no cost, but should be partially rotted before being applied. Improves the water-holding capacity of the soil. One of the best mulching materials for trees, woody perennials, and wildflowers in a naturalized setting. Shredded leaves are more compact and easier to use.

Disadvantages: Leaves, when used exclusively, frequently pack too heavily when applied over tender herbaceous perennials and may be injurious to them. Harbor insects, diseases, weed seeds, and rodents. Nitrogen needs to be added (see p. 197). Matting may lead to runoff of water. Can be a fire hazard. Dries and blows. Unshredded leaves are difficult to handle.

Fallen leaves: an easy way to create leaf mold.

Mulching is especially important in a new garden with lots of space between plants. It maximizes water retention and minimizes weed growth.

Partially decomposed compost   2–4"
Advantages: Can be made from garden and kitchen waste. Readily available. Costs little other than labor and storage. An excellent means of adding organic matter into the soil upon incorporation and improving water-holding capacity. Is average at letting water in. Holds some water itself, but is excellent at holding it in the soil. Before spreading, sift to remove all large, uncomposted pieces. Looks very "serious gardener-y," or eco-wise.
Disadvantages: Needs to be stored and aged on or near the site. Is unsightly and bulky during storage. Takes time to collect and compost. May have weed seeds. Doesn't stop weeds from growing. Better just used as a top dressing on full beds, and in small areas. Can really attract vermin if only partially decomposed.

Strawy manure   2–4"
Advantages: Acts as a low-level fertilizer and improves the water-holding capacity of the soil. Will be incorporated into the soil and have to be renewed each year. A good soil builder, adds humus, and contains available plant food.
Disadvantages: Source of supply may be limited. May contain high levels of salt. Harbors insects, disease, and weed seeds. Unsightly, objectionable to apply, and may "burn" plants because of high ammonia content unless heat-treated or aged. Decomposes rapidly; should be replenished frequently. Why are we even talking about this as a mulch? Use it for soil amending.

Ground or crushed corncobs   2–3"
Advantages: If available, cost is comparatively low. Cobs should be finely ground. Decomposes very slowly. Easily applied, and gives favorable appearance. Greatly increases water-holding capacity of the soil.
Disadvantages: Attracts rodents, especially when first applied. Soil nitrogen is less available, so supplementing may be needed (see p. 197). May retain too much moisture at surface or compact if kept wet.

Spent hops   2–3"
Advantages: May be available for the hauling at a local brewery. Easy to handle, and effective in letting water into the soil and holding little themselves. Can be low-level fertilizers, adding humus to the soil. Decomposes slowly. Greatly increases the water-holding capacity of the soil. Nice color. Non-flammable.
Disadvantages: Available in limited areas. Disagreeable odor until dried, unless you're a beer fan. Nitrogen is less available, so supplementing may be needed (see p. 197).

Organic Mulch Recommendations (continued)

MATERIAL	RECOMMENDED DEPTH
Cocoa bean hulls	2–3"

Advantages: Attractive dark brown color. Long-lasting.
Disadvantages: Very expensive. Molds may form on surface, or the material may compact and form a crusty surface. Blows away really fast.

Newspaper	1" or less

Advantages: Available and cheap. Easily applied. Lay the paper down six to eight sheets thick and immediately weight down with a light covering of soil or sand to keep it in place. Keeps some water in, controls erosion, and can be incorporated into the soil as it weathers. May be used in small areas as a temporary mulch.
Disadvantages: Decomposes rather rapidly. Lets little water in. Unsightly and may dry out and blow away if not covered.

Shredded paper	1–2"

My cousin, amateur gardener Ann Mayer, works on her garden on winter evenings by shredding all the credit card applications she gets in the mail, to use as a mulch in her vegetable garden next summer. She says it works quite well, and you don't even have to have a good credit rating. (You could use shredded office paper, too, if you don't get any of those applications.)
Advantages: Free to inexpensive — all you need is a shredder and lots of waste paper. Lets water in readily and mats down with watering, staying in place. Decomposes quickly, which can be an advantage or not, though it does add organic matter to the soil. Till it in at the end of the season.
Disadvantages: May blow around if it dries out too much.

Snow	2"–6'

Advantages: Sometimes called "the poor man's mulch," an excellent insulator against cold and drying winds. Nature's best mulching material. Keeps plants in dormancy during midwinter warm spells. Can also provide instant sculpture when rolled into snowpersons.
Disadvantages: Sometimes objectionable, depending on the circumstances. Unavailable without cooperation of weather. Can't be bought, borrowed, or even stolen, without a lot of hassle. Can be used, when compacted into spheroids, as ammunition!

INORGANIC MULCHES

Inorganic mulches consist generally of several types of rock, or woven or spun fabric. Weed-barrier fabrics are usually covered with some other mulching material for a more attractive appearance. *Sheet plastic should not be used; it's worthless for mulching.* What we really think of when it comes to inorganic mulches is rock, whether crushed stone, river rock, or gravel.

It would be tempting to try to oversimplify the amount of energy (as in fossil fuel) it takes to bring rock mulch to your yard. The price is an indication of how much energy is expended, but it's not quite that easy. It undoubtedly takes lots of energy to mine, possibly crush, and transport rock products; it also takes energy to grind up wood products or other organic mulches and transport them. In addition, rock mulches last for several years, while organic amendments must be renewed periodically, every year in many cases. Between the two options it's hard to say which takes more energy.

However, there is one cost involved in using rock mulches that is inescapable: the fact that every rock used is being irrevocably moved from one environment to another, with no chance for regeneration. With river rock, for instance, you should realize that natural areas such as stream beds, shorelines, and mountains are being plundered to make decorative landscapes.

Rock mulches, though they can be very striking and decorative, are not perfect. They are long-lasting but hard to clean. They'll block weeds if installed thickly enough, but they act as a heat sink, bouncing tremendous amounts of heat and light back to adjacent plants, people, and homes. Even if weed-barrier fabric has been used, after a few years dirt accumulates in the rock layer itself, and weeds start to grow.

On the other hand, rock mulches are a better choice for alpine wildflowers. These plants are adapted to very poor soil and little moisture, and may actually die if mulched with a more moisture-retentive bark-type mulch. A thin layer of pea gravel makes a good mulch for desert plants, as it keeps soil cool underneath, and somewhat mimics the "desert pavement" environment from which many of these plants hail.

Inorganic Mulch Recommendations

(pages 205–207)

MATERIAL	RECOMMENDED DEPTH
Plastic film	3–10 mm

Advantages: None, unless you're using it temporarily to kill grass or a specific fungal infection, or you want nothing to grow. As Mackenzie Helton, Denver landscape contractor and lecturer, says, "It's the dead zone underneath plastic; no worms or anything!"

Disadvantages: No water comes in unless holes are punched for the alleged plants. Then weeds come through those holes as well as the ones punched by the mulch, especially rock mulch. Must be covered or masked with other materials. Heat that develops under the plastic can injure plant roots. Lack of air and oxygen exchange is very hard on nearby plants, too. Doesn't work well on slopes because whatever material is used to cover it slides off. Labor-intensive to install. Causes rapid runoff of moisture. Increases danger of creating "zero-scape" or "uglyscape."

Are you convinced yet? If you're wondering why I'm carrying on about this, it's because, when I said to Helton, in my naiveté, "Surely, no one is using plastic for that anymore!" he reported having seen some of it being installed as we spoke, in the year 2003, right in the City and County of Denver!

Woven fabrics	3–10 mm

Advantages: Used to exclude weeds. Often combined with organic mulches for a more natural appearance. One type has a nap to it on one or both sides. The fuzzy side helps wick moisture into the soil. The nap snags and helps hold wood mulch in place, either on flat, on sloped, or in windy areas. Helton extends the fabric underneath the edging he uses, allowing it to come up on the other side, and be trimmed off at ground level after the edging is anchored in place. This really gives the system the edge on fighting off grass invasion of the planting area.

Disadvantages: Expensive. Labor-intensive to install. Pins needed every 3–4 feet to keep the fabric in place. Be sure to overlap the edges of adjacent pieces of fabric 3–4 inches, putting the upper side on top, so mulch doesn't get trapped under the fold while answering the call of gravity. Must have a UV-blocker to keep from breaking down quickly, and some are much better than others.

"Mountain pavement"	2–3"

A half-and-half combination recommended by Helton for a very natural look. He says it mimics the look of the open ground in the mountains. Half of the mixture is "squeegee" or "scree," a material used in road-building that is about half the size of pea gravel; the other half is crusher fines—the chips and dust from flagstone. Helton advises to have the supplier deliver them

Rocks serve as a large-scale mulch. They're particularly useful in retaining moisture (and soil!) on this slope.

together (not separated). That way they'll be partly mixed in transit. You can mix them a little more when you're wheelbarrowing them around, but they're pretty well mixed by then.

Advantages: Well-behaved and versatile. Helton says it "only tracks in for a day or two, and is a very good surface for the dog run or pathway." (Squeegee alone is also good for dog areas.) Use a 2-inch layer if mulching for a garden, and a little thicker layer for controlling weeds in a pathway.

Disadvantages: Not as easy to remove if you decide to change to something different. Well, what rock mulch isn't? At least this one could be used as a base for a brick path.

Inorganic Mulch Recommendations (continued)

MATERIAL	RECOMMENDED DEPTH
Pea gravel	One pebble–3"

This is author Lauren Springer's favorite mulch for low-water gardens, especially those featuring desert-adapted flowers.

Advantages: She says it lets water in easily, keeps soil from eroding, keeps the soil and root temperatures cool, and doesn't interfere with plants reseeding themselves. "I spread it out just one layer thick," she says, "and crowd plants together so there aren't as many weeds." She gets the benefit of a clean-looking finished site for a couple of years, then the plants cover the mulch. Meanwhile, the fine-textured size of the mulch shows off the plants, and only competes minimally with their growth.

Disadvantages: "If you're the type who likes to mess around in the garden, rearranging plants frequently," explains Springer, "you have to figure out if you mind moving the pea gravel aside each time." If you're using a thicker layer for a service area or play area for kids, it's awkward to walk on. This might be good for kids — it slows them down just a bit — and you can add some aggregate stepping stones for a sophisticated-looking pathway.

A thin layer of pea gravel is an ideal mulch for desert plants.

Crushed stone   1–3"

Advantages: Lets all moisture into the soil, keeps none itself, and keeps moisture in the root zone. Many colors available.

Disadvantages: Expensive. Can be very reflective if too white. Will not prevent growth of some weedy grasses unless combined with weed-barrier fabric. Acts as a heat sink. Extremely difficult to remove.

Lava rock   2–3"

Advantages: Holds some water in the pores of the rock, but allows much of the water into the soil. Lightest and most porous of the inorganic mulches. Available in a variety of colors. Tends to cool off faster than crushed rock or gravel.

Disadvantages: Breaks down under people traffic (poor circulation planning), but does not integrate into the soil to improve its water-holding capacity. Only regionally available. Will not prevent growth of some weedy grasses without being combined with plastic or weed-barrier fabric.

Decomposed granite   2–3"

Advantages: Long-lasting. Lets water in and holds it in the soil. Holds some water itself. Very dense mulch that excludes weeds. Many colors possible. Often used as an informal pathway.

Disadvantages: Only regionally available. Disintegrates over several years.

The long strips of shredded wood mulch knit together to resist movement by wind and water.

Gravel, river rock   1–3"

Advantages: Lets water in very well, holds none itself, and keeps water in the soil. Lasts a long time, comes in a variety of sizes and colors, and doesn't break down. If large enough it will limit traffic over the area, and this may be a good thing!

Disadvantages: Expensive. Must be mined, as are all inorganic materials, from natural areas. Can be pushed down into the soil. Doesn't integrate with the soil to help water-holding capacity of the soil. Unsightly if used in large areas. Tends to slide or be washed down slopes. Hard to keep clean under pines and other fine-leaved trees. Will not prevent growth of some weedy grasses unless combined with weed-barrier fabric.

CHAPTER 12

MAINTENANCE

*The general rule of thumb is,
the more water a plant needs,
the more maintenance it needs.*

Maintenance is the seventh and final principle of Xeriscape. If you've carefully planned and designed your landscape around the first six principles, this one should be a snap.

Remember, the general rule of thumb is, the more water a plant needs, the more maintenance it needs. Because this is Xeriscape, the high-maintenance "movie star" plants have been replaced (or only used sparingly) and what you're faced with is a much more reasonable group of botanical organisms better suited to their natural surroundings and only needing a little attention to stay beautiful. It's like beginning a race with a huge head start.

ROUTINE MAINTENANCE

It was once said that garden maintenance is like your laundry: It is always there, and it will pile up if it isn't tended to regularly. So some of the same tasks are going to always be part of your Xeriscape gardening routine.

This Xeriscape slope was planted all at once, however, the left side has been maintained while the right side has fallen into neglect.

ABOVE AND OPPOSITE: *Regular maintenance ensures that your Xeriscape will stay neat and attractive.*

WEEDING

One of those routine tasks is going to be weeding. There is just no way around it. It will be more of a chore early on, when the Xeriscape is just getting established, and less so as it matures, but it will be with you from the first day in the garden to the last. Weeds come in two forms: the noxious ones that are carried in by the wind, animals, or humans, and the ones that are seedlings from the ones you have planted. A weed can be any plant that you don't want. If you are brand-new to gardening, it will take a growing season or so to get the hang of which plants are the ones you want and the ones you don't. In that time, you will have seen the ones you question grow to maturity. When they do, you can decide then on their acceptableness in your Xeriscape. In the future, you will be able to identify the unacceptable ones early and get rid of them.

One of the most obvious ways to determine if a plant is a weed is to ask yourself if you planted it. If you placed an ID tag from the original pot next to a representative of the plant

when you planted it, this will be easier. When the garden begins to fill with maturing plants and weeds, you can more accurately identify which is which.

When it comes to weed removal, it is worthwhile to pay heed to the old saying, "A stitch in time saves nine." The sooner you nip weeds in the bud, no pun intended, the easier it will be. The advantage to small-weed removal is that the roots will be small and when pulled or dug out, the chance of removing the whole root is better. Even bits of roots left in the soil can produce another pesky weed. Many weed species at maturity have deep roots that can be broken off when pulled out. Smaller weeds are also more vulnerable to chemicals like glyphosate or "2, 4-D" that might be sprayed on them. The more leaf surface that is covered with the chemical, the better the chance of making a complete kill. When more leaves have formed, there are more surfaces to cover, which lessens the likelihood of getting them all. Besides, a large dead plant looks obvious in a garden. Small ones are less conspicuous.

I recommend wandering through the garden every week in the quest for weeds. In a week they don't get too big, and if you have been diligent in this practice it won't take long to pull or pry them out. Choose a morning for the coolness and choose a time when the soil is moist. They will come out much more easily.

Personally, I like to take a gallon sprayer containing glyphosate and spot-treat the little dickens, being careful not to get the spray on any desirable green leaves or stems. Glyphosate is only effective on green growing plants. It

Eradicating weeds when they are still small saves a lot of work later on.

becomes inert when it contacts soil, and is consumed by soil organisms in a short time. You must, however, be sure that you don't get spray into any runoff stream from your landscape. It will still be active in the flow and can come in contact with plants downstream in your garden and beyond. It could cause some liability problems.

Deadheading blossoms from time to time helps keep the garden tidy.

DEADHEADING

Flowers are beautiful, but they don't last forever. As a result, your second maintenance chore is born. Dead flower heads can mess up the appearance of a flowerbed. They can also spread seeds where you don't want them and essentially become undesirable plants like weeds. Perennials in the composite or daisy family have this self-sowing problem, and spent flowers should be removed immediately after they begin to fade. This is called deadheading. A number of plants produce multitudes of seeds, such as catmint, and need the same treatment.

In other cases, it is advantageous to deadhead to encourage re-blooms later in the season. Dianthus or pinks, sundrops, flax, and salvias, to name a few, benefit from this practice. Whatever the reason for deadheading, it is always one of the tasks that befall a Xeriscape owner. But it can be a pleasant task, especially when working with fragrant lavenders, hyssops, and mint.

ABOVE: *Appropriate plant choice can affect maintenance. The showy spent flower heads of silver-edge horehound* (Marrubium rotundifolia) *remain decorative through the winter—no deadheading required!*
BELOW: *Periodic pruning helps shape a tree and allows light to filter into the garden.*

Somewhat more extreme is the task of cutting some plants back to the ground right after they have gone dormant. Doing so tidies up the garden considerably. Perennials that become tall and leggy during the season's growth, such as Russian sage, hyssop, or hollyhock, will keep the garden from looking cluttered and unfocused if whacked off close to the ground.

On the other hand, there are those perennials that provide winter interest that can wait until spring to be cut in a similar fashion. Plants such as ornamental grasses, bluemist spirea, and gayfeather either hold attractive seed heads or have an appealing structure.

The spring cutting and removal of dead stems allows new fresh growth to emerge without intermixing with old growth. It gives the landscape a tended appearance, most appreciated in many covenant-controlled communities.

Sucker Removal

A simple but often overlooked landscape characteristic is the appearance of suckers or shoots from the base of a tree or shrub. A number of plants labeled as trees are actually shrubs in nature, so their tendency is to grow multiple stems from the base of the tree trunk. In some cases, it might be worthwhile to allow the tree

TOP: *Proper plant selection would have eliminated the need to chop these junipers so severely. Small plants in small spaces require little or no pruning.*

ABOVE AND BELOW: *Trimming a shrub in an inappropriate manner, as seen above, robs the viewer of the opportunity to see its graceful form. Astonishingly, both these shrubs are the same species of forsythia.*

to revert and become a shrub, but most of us appreciate the tree shape. So this means we will constantly need to be cutting the suckers or shoots back down to the ground. This is a never-ending duty if the "tree" is going to look maintained. Doing it regularly and often enough so the shoots can be cut with hand pruners, rather than waiting until it takes a set of loppers to do the job, will simplify the routine. Some of the trees with this tendency are ones in the plum family such as the Shubert chokecherry or the Newport plum. Also, crabapple trees can be a nuisance. Of course, we could avoid this chore if we just didn't buy them, but then we'd miss some very attractive plants for our landscape.

PRUNING

Inevitably, woody plants in a Xeriscape are going to reach a point where it is necessary to prune. There are three reasons why. One is that overhanging branches begin to interfere with other activities in the garden such as lawnmowing or walking on the sidewalk. If the Xeriscape is well planned, and enough space has been provided for the plant to grow, pruning shouldn't be much of a chore. An occasional branch may have to be cut from time to time for control.

The second reason is that deciduous trees can become thick with branches, or canes in the case of deciduous shrubs. The trees become unsightly. In the mix, some branches crisscross each other,

which can cause the bark to rub off as they sway together in the wind. Pruning can open the tree, allowing more sunlight to filter through to the ground and increase the foliage production in the middle of the tree, if that is what you want. It also helps to maintain a pleasing structure. Shrubs can be opened up and "renewed" by removing old canes at their bases. As with trees, more light is admitted to the center for more foliage development; light reaches the under-story of plants; flower production increases with a predominance of younger canes; and the shape of the shrub can be enhanced. In some cases, if pruning has been put off too long, it may be beneficial to cut the whole plant back to the ground and allow new shoots to form a new shrub.

Third, when branches or canes die for what-ever reason, it is beneficial to cut them out for the sake of appearance, and in some cases for safety reasons if the branch is large.

There are many guide booklets, videos, and classes on proper pruning techniques. It is worthwhile for Xeriscape owners to learn how to prune appropriately if they want to have healthy, attractive woody plants. Pruning that must be achieved higher than you are able to reach from the ground is best done by a bonded professional.

Shearing is not for the Xeriscape owner. Shearing means "trimming" the outer fringe or branch tips of the whole plant. If hedge trimmers

TOP: *Regular maintenance of your irrigation system prevents scenes such as this in your landscape.*
ABOVE: *Naturalistic landscaping, where appropriate, eliminates many types of traditional maintenance chores.*

Although these trees were both planted 15 years ago, one was maintained through proper pruning while the other was left to grow unattended. The attractive maintained tree now stands healthy and strong, whereas the dense and lopsided unmaintained tree poses a threat to both life and limb. Illustrations courtesy of The National Arbor Day Foundation.

have to be taken to a shrub to keep it within bounds, or to conform to what the owner thinks it should look like, it is probably the wrong plant for that location. During planning, the right sized or shaped plant should be chosen and thus shearing can be avoided altogether. As mentioned before, limited pruning is all that needs to be done to control a wayward branch or two.

IRRIGATION SYSTEM MAINTENANCE

Automatic systems are very convenient. It is com-forting to know that they are on duty respond-ing to the clock settings you have set. You can go about your daily life without giving it much thought. However, it is not *all* automatic. Maintenance is still required.

Once a week it will pay to turn the system on by hand and run it through each zone during daylight hours so you can see what is happening. At the same time walk through the whole landscape and look for indications of dry spots. This weekly inspection might reveal heads that are leaking or even zones that may not be working. Heads could have been turned or tilted and are spraying the sidewalk and street, or you might have inadvertently run the lawnmower wheel over a sprinkler head and broken it.

Areas with drip irrigation will require you to take a trowel and dig into the soil in different locations within each zone to see if the soil is moist. If it's not as moist as you think it should be, perhaps a valve isn't opening or more time may be needed per zone. Catching these glitches early will make a significant difference in water usage and plant vitality.

Occasionally, an irrigation zone will not turn off. Water can run until you make the discovery. With that in mind, it is worthwhile to have the system working while you are home from work and during your waking hours. The cause for this misfortune is usually a fleck of dirt in the control valve under the diaphragm. Isolate the control valve with the manual valve. Then remove four screws or more from the cover— there is the diaphragm. Remove it. Rinse it with water and flush the valve cavity with a splash of water from the hose. Replace the diaphragm and reverse the procedure. It is a simple task that can be accomplished by us everyday folks. We can make the repair without having to wait for or pay a professional, and save having to replace plants that died from the lack of water.

Sprinkler head maintenance is a critical factor in overall water savings when operating an automatic irrigation system. An often-neglected task is that of being sure that the heads are even with the soil surface or grade.

On older model irrigation systems and even some new ones, the sprinkler head might be connected to the supply line via a short piece of PVC pipe threaded at both ends called a nipple. The connection is very ridged. If the top of the sprinkler is slightly above grade, someone stepping on it or running over it with a lawnmower wheel can snap it off. So if you are still dealing with a system that was put in during the '80s or earlier, it is important to be sure the heads are flush with the soil surface. It is simply a matter of attaching the proper length nipple. Heads below grade cannot water the area they are intended to water because the spray pattern is interrupted by the grass blades or soil around

Through regular cultural practices such as aeration and not *overwatering, you can avoid many diseases and pests making themselves at home in your lawn.*

ABOVE AND BELOW: *Although deer and rabbits find some landscape plants less tasty than others, you might simply have to learn to accept the hungry visitors.*

the head. Retrofitting with a longer nipple is appropriate.

Modern irrigation systems have sprinkler heads that are connected to the supply line via a swing pipe. A swing pipe is a piece of flexible tubing with connection fittings at both ends. This arrangement doesn't seem to be as susceptible to breakage as the old nipple connections, but the heads themselves can be broken if they stick up too high above grade. Also, heads can be set too low sometimes when installed. The fix is even simpler than in the past. Dig up the head and the swing pipe, and raise or lower the whole arrangement to the appropriate level.

DISEASE AND PEST MANAGEMENT

There are reams of information available from county extension offices, bookstores, and garden centers on how to identify and deal with the wide variety of diseases and insects that can attack your garden, Xeriscape or otherwise. So I won't go into details here, but just provide an overview. It is generally recommended that an integrated pest management plan (IPM) be implemented. It isn't as complicated as it sounds. It is a practical method of getting the most out of your Xeriscape with minimum damage to the environment and harm to the gardener.

Simply put, IPM consists of four steps. One is to observe what is going on in your garden by making regular visits looking for trouble spots, or, on the other hand, to find positives such as beneficial insects. The next is to identify your discoveries and decide what course of action to take, if any. The best resource is your county extension office. Third, monitor the situation to see if it is getting better or worse. If it is getting worse, then the fourth step will need to take place, and that is to manage the problem rather than eradicate it.

Some management techniques can include cultural practices such as using disease-resistant plants or transplanting to a location where the plant may get favorable light. Management of a pest or disease can also include mechanical removal, such as spraying an insect off with a strong spray of water from the garden hose or picking off caterpillars by hand. Biological methods may be the introduction of ladybugs to feed on aphids or the planting of small-throated flowers that attract lacewings and hover flies whose larvae also feed on aphids. As a last resort, chemicals may have to be used.

Xeriscapes attract wildlife. In the forms of bees, birds, and butterflies, it is great. However, Xeriscapes also attract larger critters such as deer and rabbits, which are cute until they nibble all the tulips to the ground. Then even the most liberal of gardeners will see red. When Xeriscapes are close to an open space or undeveloped land, the problem will be persistent, and there doesn't seem to be an easy answer. Eight-foot-tall fencing helps, but doesn't improve the appearance of most landscapes. Besides, deer seem to clear even tall fences with little trouble and rabbits can go underneath just as easily. Sour-tasting chemicals applied to plant leaves work, but each bit of new growth requires a new application. It is a never-ending task that is difficult to keep up with. The use of plants not attractive to deer and rabbits is another alternative—although no plant is immune if creatures are hungry enough.

Rabbits can be live trapped, but there are rules set by the fish and game department that must be adhered to. It is best to consult with them before starting your trapping program. Once trapping begins, I have found that it is difficult to keep up with the multiplying ability of rabbits. You can relocate a rabbit or two one week, and a week later another one takes its place. They either appear out of thin air or someone else is trapping them elsewhere and dumping them off in your neighborhood.

What it boils down to is this: There is no truly foolproof way to eliminate deer and rabbits. You can discourage them, but you can't exclude them entirely.

The other critters that can ruin a Xeriscape are your own pets. Cats in the garden are generally pretty benign, although there are exceptions.

Generally, cacti are fairly pet-resistant!

I remember once seeing four kittens chasing each other through a bearded iris bed. At one point all four were able to climb one very stout stalk before it and the kittens came crashing to the ground. Needless to say, the tall stately plants in their spring prime were no longer much of a show.

The real problem seems to be with dogs and Xeriscape. I'm often asked if there is any way to keep a garden or a lawn while owning a large dog or two. The answer is no, if the dogs are young and run freely in the back yard. Mature trees and cacti might survive, but most annuals, groundcovers, and lawns cannot endure daily large-dog traffic, particularly where they run along a fence trying to make contact with the dog on the other side. It is a choice between having the dogs and having a landscape. Trying to mend what the dogs wear out is futile. The only realistic alternatives are to have a dog run with occasional supervised release into the yard, or isolating parts of the landscape with an "invisible fence."

COMPOSTING

As you maintain your garden, you will accumulate unwanted vegetation. Grass clippings (if you don't use a mulching lawnmower), weeds, deadheads, plant stems that have been cut back, and autumn leaves are some of the vegetation that will be on hand from time to time. There is no sense in sending it to the landfill when your garden needs it. The answer to all this waste is to compost it.

Composting is a way to facilitate the breakdown of vegetative matter into an unrecognizable organic material that no longer emanates an odor. The resultant compost can be turned back into the soil on a regular basis. Organic material continues to break down over time in the soil to a point that it is no longer effective as an amendment. As a consequence, it is a valuable maintenance practice to recycle yard waste into compost and then back into the soil. It is cyclic.

The simplest recipe for composting is to mix finely ground green vegetative matter with a smaller portion of brown vegetative matter, also finely ground. The ratio is about ⅔ green to ⅓ brown. Both materials are kept in a pile or in any kind of container that will hold at least 12 cubic feet. After that it's just a matter of turning the contents efficiently. Turning with a shovel or fork every week or two keeps the right kind of microbes working to break down the organic matter. The other key is to keep the pile moist. It should not be any wetter than a wrung-out sponge. After about six weeks the compost should be ready to be added to the soil. Adding nitrogen speeds the process.

PLANNING FOR EASE OF MAINTENANCE

If you've been reading from the start of this book, you know that maintenance is the seventh and final principle of xeriscaping—but it doesn't happen just at the end. Ease of maintenance begins in the planning and design stage of Xeriscape construction. Much future work can be eliminated or reduced at this stage. Consider in each phase of Xeriscape development how it is going to effect chores in the future. Here are some examples that have been covered previously, but are useful to summarize again:

- Slope away from the house to keep water from causing foundation problems later.

- Plan for good drainage in some locations and water retention in others so you can accommodate appropriate growing conditions for plants.

- Provide bermed planting beds or grading for good drainage for plants that come from arid climates (low-water-zone plants). Grade to accommodate moderate- or high-water plants by directing runoff, either natural or irrigation, to those zones; roof drain water can be piped or ditched to places where extra water is needed. Swales can be carved into the Xeriscape to collect runoff from the lawn or from your overwatering neighbor.

- Use decorative boulders, stepping stones, cobble, and flagstone as points of interest, surfaces for walking, ornamentation, dry streambeds and walls, and as giant water-retentive forms of mulch. Note that the use of rock in this way is a far cry from the yard paved in rock to "reduce maintenance." Make all portions of flowerbeds accessible so that maintenance is easier. Placing stepping stones through a wide bed allows you to walk in amongst the plants to give them attention.

- Terrace steep slopes to hold water in place from irrigation or from natural precipitation. This allows water to soak into the soil, and

Compost heaps provide a depository for garden wastes generated during maintenance chores.

can turn a dry hillside or slope from being only able to support the most xeric of plants to one where even higher-water plants can thrive. A terraced slope is easier to maintain, too: The irrigation chore is reduced and the mowing routine is eliminated (when turf is replaced). No more negotiating the slope contour with a lawnmower!

SOIL AMENDMENT

With a properly amended soil, maintenance chores are reduced. Once grading is complete, but before decorative rocks are put into place, soil amendment, as described in the Soil Improvement chapter, should be accomplished. Less water need be applied to keep plants alive. The use of commercial fertilizers can be reduced or eliminated. This is particularly important in the establishment of a lawn, whether of cool-season or warm-season grass types. A soil amended according to the plants' natural needs means plants under less stress and therefore more inclined to be insect- and disease-resistant.

Most Xeriscape plants enjoy a well-drained soil, but too much of a good thing can be detrimental. In a sandy soil with little or no organics, the water will drain too quickly, leaving the root zone dry. Organics will help hold water in place. In clay soils the opposite can occur: Water is retained too easily and doesn't drain away. It will "drown" the roots, leading to the death of the plant. The addition of organics in this case will help to open up the clay, allowing air into the soil.

IRRIGATION

If an irrigation system is used, install it after soil prep to make that step less complicated. See the Irrigation chapter for planning for maintenance of irrigation systems.

Redirect rain or snow runoff as a way to reduce the irrigation chore. There is no reason roof runoff in your yard has to be limited to the 5 feet away from the foundation as home builders recommend. That is just a minimum to keep the foundation and basement floor from moving in expansive clay soils. The water can be piped or ditched (called water harvesting) to other parts of the landscape to provide extra water to high-water zones. As long as it is allowed to soak into the soil and not stored, you will not be awry of western water law. At any length, it means that it is one area in the landscape that won't dry out shortly after precipitation has ceased. The task of your watering will be minimized and treated water from the spigot won't be wasted.

Over-irrigation means more maintenance. A landscape overwatered becomes overgrown. Overgrown plants need trimming and pruning to keep them in check. Weeds appreciate high water applications, so weeding becomes more burdensome. Excess water can lead to development of certain fungi and mildews that can affect the health and appearance of vegetation. Excess water in clay soils can deny air to the roots of plants, causing stress, which can bring on disease and insect attacks. So don't water too much! It is as simple as that. See the Irrigation chapter for more detail.

PLANTING

Planting considerations can help you avoid maintenance headaches at a later date. Step one is to remove the container in which the nursery has nurtured the plant BEFORE you plant it in the ground. While this seems fairly obvious, there are documented cases where plant and container have both been stuck in a hole. Step two is to help the roots that have been confined and compressed in the container to spread out once planted. This can be done by making four slices the length of the root ball where it was confined by the container. When a perennial, small shrub, or tree is removed from the container and just plopped into a hole in the soil with no accommodation for root spread, the roots will likely remain confined, never able to reach the water and nutrients that should be

Compost creates a ready supply of soil amendment.

available to a naturally seeded plant. Eventually, the plant will live in poor health, requiring extra attention, or be mistakenly overwatered because of a misunderstanding of the true problem. Poor root development can mean premature death, too, which means more work and money for the gardener in replacing it.

Just a word of warning: Don't assume that when you have hired professionals to plant for you, that they will open up the confined roots from a container. This is particularly true with balled and burlapped trees. If you are not watching, or even if you are watching and they think you don't know any better, it is much more efficient in the eyes of some unscrupulous contractors to leave the wire cage in place around the root ball. No matter what the excuse, the wire must be removed or there will be a stunted tree in your future or one that dies early.

A friend recently modified his landscape around an ash tree that was planted by others 10 years earlier. While stripping sod to permit

A simple but well-maintained Xeriscape like this one is preferable to an elaborate design that you don't have time to keep up with. Photo by Connie Ellefson.

the tree to be out of the turf area and in a planting bed, he discovered a fully intact wire basket just under the sod. It wasn't even rusted to a great extent.

Step three is to properly prepare the soil (see the Soil Improvement chapter). Even if the roots are loosened from the soil ball that has developed in the container or sliced to encourage root growth, the roots may not spread to their full potential unless the soil has been properly loosened.

The rule of thumb is to amend the soil in an area or volume equivalent to 2½ to 3 times the root ball formed by the container and to the depth of the root ball. Amendment can mean replacing about ⅓ of the site soil with compost and mixing it with the rest of the site soil. Because you have taken extra steps in the beginning, you will be giving the plant its best chance of survival and a trouble-free existence.

The next maintenance consideration to take into account when planting is placement. We have

all seen junipers growing up underneath the eaves of houses or an elm with the middle cut out of it by the power company because it enveloped overhead power lines. When we see such lack of forethought, we think we'd never be guilty of it. However, there must be something inherent in us to not see the big picture. It can happen when we plant annuals so closely that the end result is a cake of vegetation with diminished flower production.

It can happen again when we place the cute gallon-size Pfitzer juniper under the picture window, or better yet when we plant two or three of them there. It happens to us all. In the case of juniper, the most notorious of misplaced plants, it means we must buy a good electric hedge-trimmer with our plant purchase because we'll need to use it early and often to keep it within the space in which we have designated it to live.

Too many plants with too little space can be remedied in the planning stage. A drawing with the planned plants proportionally situated according to mature spread and height will bring us

back to reality. Most garden catalogs describe the mature height and width of the plants they sell. The same is true of garden centers. Plant tags list both dimensions.

Paying close attention to this one factor can vastly reduce future chores. Let's again use junipers as an example. Junipers are outstanding when it comes to the small amount of water it takes to keep them attractive, so they are an excellent selection for a Xeriscape. However, not all junipers are the same. A local wholesale catalog lists 35 varieties, and I'm sure that is only a small sampling of what is available. When there is a space 6 feet wide and 6 feet long under a window that is 3 feet from the ground, it isn't wise to choose for that location a blue Pfitzer juniper destined to be 12 feet tall and 10 feet wide. Several others exist that fit the bill perfectly at only 18 inches high and 4–6 feet in diameter. Oh, and how good they look when allowed to grow unmolested by a hedge trimmer!

ABOVE: *Give desert plants a good home and they will respond enthusiastically.*
RIGHT: *One way to reduce the maintenance chore of replacing expired plants is to pick species adaptable to changing conditions, such as the airy coral bells (Heuchera x 'Coral Cloud'), which are equally at home in sun or shade.*

Another planting consideration is to ensure the plant you are placing in the landscape likes the amount of light it is going to receive. If a plant that grows in nature in a shady environment is placed in the blazing sun in your landscape, there is going to be a replacement chore and expense in the future. Again, plant catalogs and nurseries usually state the conditions under which the plant grows. That is good information to heed to prevent disappointment later. In some cases it might be wise to choose a plant that likes either sun or shade. An example would be coral bells. Planted next to a small tree in a new landscape, coral bells do fine exposed to ample light and heat. As the tree grows and begins to cast more shade, coral bells are equally at home. If a sun-loving plant such as the bearded iris is placed there to begin with, it will have to be replaced with a shade-loving plant as time passes.

Keeping the number of plant varieties down to a few means not only a visually satisfying landscape, but also less maintenance. A simple

planting plan can be less confusing to the viewer. It will look more organized and will maintain continuity of theme or goals. It will also be easier to define irrigation zones.

For example, a landscape architect I know bought a condominium with a ready-made Xeriscape. The plant selection was wonderful. There were two ponderosa pines, two mugo pines, three crabapples, three hackberry trees, three different plum trees, five gambel oaks, four golden currant shrubs, two fernbushes, four rabbitbrushes, 12 shrub roses, two roses of Sharon, one Apache plume, and 70 species of perennials—all in the space of 750 square feet. Rather than being a landscape, it was the beginning of the first known Xeriscape jungle. The architect said the plants in this landscape would have required more than 4,000 square feet to minimize horticultural conflicts and nearly 7,500 square feet to be aesthetically pleasing when mature.

The landscape would have been better served to have had two or three trees framing the condo, a few select shrubs for foundation planting, a small buffalograss lawn, and swaths of three to five kinds of long-blooming perennials bordering the walk leading to the front door. Logically, the less complicated the plantings are, the less work to keep everything separated, pruned, weeded, deadheaded, and so on.

FINAL THOUGHTS ON MAINTENANCE

Don't look at maintenance as a chore, but let it be the method by which you keep compliments coming your way. The casual visitor to your landscape will look around and be wowed by your yard's display of color, form, textures, design, and points of interest and realize it was all accomplished through the creativity of man or woman! In contrast, he or she may subconsciously think that the automatic sprinkler system keeps it green and the lawn service maintains the lawn level while the rest is left up to nature to take care of. That is the ultimate compliment. In the meantime you can feel self-satisfied that you've planned for a minimum of upkeep, while being diligent about attending to the routine tasks that are required. If it doesn't look like it needs maintenance, you've done your job.

Bartholomew, Mel. *Square Foot Gardening.* Emmaus, Penn.: Rodale Press, 1981.

Chatto, Beth. *Beth Chatto's Gravel Garden: Drought-Resistant Planting Through the Year.* London: Frances Lincoln, 2000.

———. *The Dry Garden.* Sagaponack, N.Y.: Sagapress, 1996.

Colorado WaterWise Council. *Evidence of Care: Xeriscape Maintenance Journal 2002.* Vol. 1. Littleton, Colo.: Colorado WaterWise Council, 2002.

———. *Evidence of Care: Xeriscape Maintenance Journal.* Vol. 2. Littleton, Colo.: Colorado WaterWise Council, 2003.

Creasy, Rosalind. *The Complete Book of Edible Landscaping.* San Francisco: Sierra Club Books, 1982.

Ellefson, Connie Lockhart, Thomas L. Stephens, and Doug Welsh. *Xeriscape Gardening: Water Conservation for the American Landscape.* New York: Macmillan; Toronto: Maxwell Macmillan Canada; New York: Maxwell Macmillan International, 1992.

Fairchild, D. H., and J. E. Klett. "Woody Landscape Plants for the High Plains." Fort Collins, Colo.: Colorado State University Technical Bulletin LTB93-1, June 1993.

Feucht, James R., and Jack D. Butler. *Landscape Management: Planting and Maintenance of Trees, Shrubs and Turfgrasses.* New York: Van Nostrand Reinhold Company, 1988.

James, Theodore. *Flowering Bulbs Indoors and Out.* New York: Macmillan; Toronto: Maxwell Macmillan Canada; New York: Maxwell Macmillan International, 1991.

Keesen, Larry. *The Complete Irrigation Workbook: Design, Installation, Maintenance, and Water Management.* Cleveland, Ohio: Franzak & Foster, 1995.

Knopf, Jim. *Waterwise Landscaping with Trees, Shrubs, and Vines: A Xeriscape Guide for the Rocky Mountain Region, California, and the Desert Southwest.* Boulder, Colo.: Chamisa Books, 1999.

———. *The Xeriscape Flower Gardener: A Waterwise Guide for the Rocky Mountain Region.* Boulder, Colo.: Johnson Books, 1991.

Nold, Robert. *Penstemons.* Portland, Ore.: Timber Press, 1999.

Phillips, Judith. *Natural by Design.* Santa Fe: Museum of New Mexico Press, 1995.

———. *Plants for Natural Gardens.* Santa Fe: Museum of New Mexico Press, 1995.

Schultz, Warren. *The Chemical-Free Lawn: The Newest Varieties and Techniques to Grow Lush, Hardy Grass.* Emmaus, Penn.: Rodale Press, 1989.

——— and Marilyn Rogers, eds. *Ortho's All About Lawns.* San Ramon, Calif.: Ortho Books, 1999.

Springer, Lauren. *The Undaunted Garden: Planting for Weather-Resilient Beauty.* Golden, Colo.: Fulcrum Publishing, 1994.

Sunset Books and Sunset Magazine. *Sunset Western Garden Book.* 6th ed. Menlo Park, Calif.: Sunset Publishing, 1995.

Tannehill, Celia, and James E. Klett. "Best Perennials for the Rocky Mountains and High Plains." Fort Collins, Colo.: Department of Horticulture and Landscape Architecture, Colorado State University, Bulletin 573A, 2002.

Wasowski, Sally, and Andy Wasowski. *Requiem for a Lawnmower: Gardening in a Warmer, Drier World.* 2nd ed. Lanham, Md.: Rowman & Littlefield, 2004.

Wasowski, Sally. *Gardening with Prairie Plants: How to Create Beautiful Native Landscapes.* Minneapolis: University of Minnesota Press, 2002.

Weinstein, Gayle. *Xeriscape Handbook: A How-To Guide to Natural, Resource-Wise Gardening.* Golden, Colo.: Fulcrum Publishing, 1999.

Winger, David, ed. *Xeriscape Color Guide: 100 Water-Wise Plants for Gardens and Landscapes.* Denver, Colo.: Denver Water; Golden, Colo.: Fulcrum Publishing, 1998.

———. *Xeriscape Plant Guide.* Denver Water and American Water Works Association. Golden, Colo.: Fulcrum Publishing, 1996.

Woodward, Joan. *Waterstained Landscapes: Seeing and Shaping Regionally Distinctive Places.* Baltimore: Johns Hopkins University Press, 2000.

City of Boulder Open Space and Mountain Parks
www.ci.boulder.co.us/openspace/

Colorado ET
www.coloradoet.org

Colorado Native Plant Society:
http://carbon.cudenver.edu/~shill/conps.html

Colorado Springs Utilities: Xeriscape
www.csu.org/xeri

Colorado State University Cooperative Extension
www.ext.colostate.edu/

Colorado State University Cooperative Extension Resource Center
www.cerc.colostate.edu/factsheet.html

Colorado State University Soil, Water, and Plant Testing Laboratory
www.colostate.edu

Denver Water: WaterSaver
www.watersaver.org

Denver Water: Xeriscape Information
www.denverwater.org/xeriscapeinfo/xeriscapeframe.html

Lady Bird Johnson Wildflower Center
www.wildflower.org

National Wildlife Federation
www.nwf.org/backyardwildlifehabitat

Organic Gardening Magazine
www.organicgardening.com

Square Foot Gardening
www.squarefootgardening.com

University of Colorado Museum of Natural History
http://cumuseum.colorado.edu

NOTE: Citations followed by the letter "p" denote photos.